I0343686

Muslims, Jews and Pagans

Gorgias Islamic Studies

9

Gorgias Islamic Studies spans a wide range of subject areas, seeking to understand Islam as a complete cultural and religious unity. This series draws together political, socio-cultural, textual, and historical approaches from across disciplines. Containing monographs, edited collections of essays, and primary source texts in translation, this series seeks to present a comprehensive, critical, and constructive picture of this centuries- and continent-spanning religion.

Muslims, Jews and Pagans

Studies on Early Islamic Medina

Michael Lecker

Gorgias Press
2017

Gorgias Press LLC, 954 River Road, Piscataway, NJ, 08854, USA

www.gorgiaspress.com

Copyright © 2017 by Gorgias Press LLC

First published in 1995.

All rights reserved under International and Pan-American Copyright Conventions. No part of this publication may be reproduced, stored in a retrieval system or transmitted in any form or by any means, electronic, mechanical, photocopying, recording, scanning or otherwise without the prior written permission of Gorgias Press LLC.

2017

ISBN 978-1-4632-0664-2

Printed in the United States of America

TABLE OF CONTENTS

Map: The markets of Medina (Yathrib) on the eve of Islam IV
Foreword V
Preface VII
Introduction IX
1. The ʿĀliya: orchards and fortresses 1
2. The Aws Allāh clans 19
3. Qubāʾ: Muslims, Jews and Pagans 50
4. The Ḍirār Mosque (9 A.H.) 74
Concluding remarks 147
Appendices 150
A Mujammiʿ b. Jāriya and the Ḍirār Mosque 150
B The image problem of Abū Qays b. al-Aslat 154
C Abū Qays nearly embraces Islam 156
Bibliography 165
Index 171
Corrigenda to the 1995 edition 181

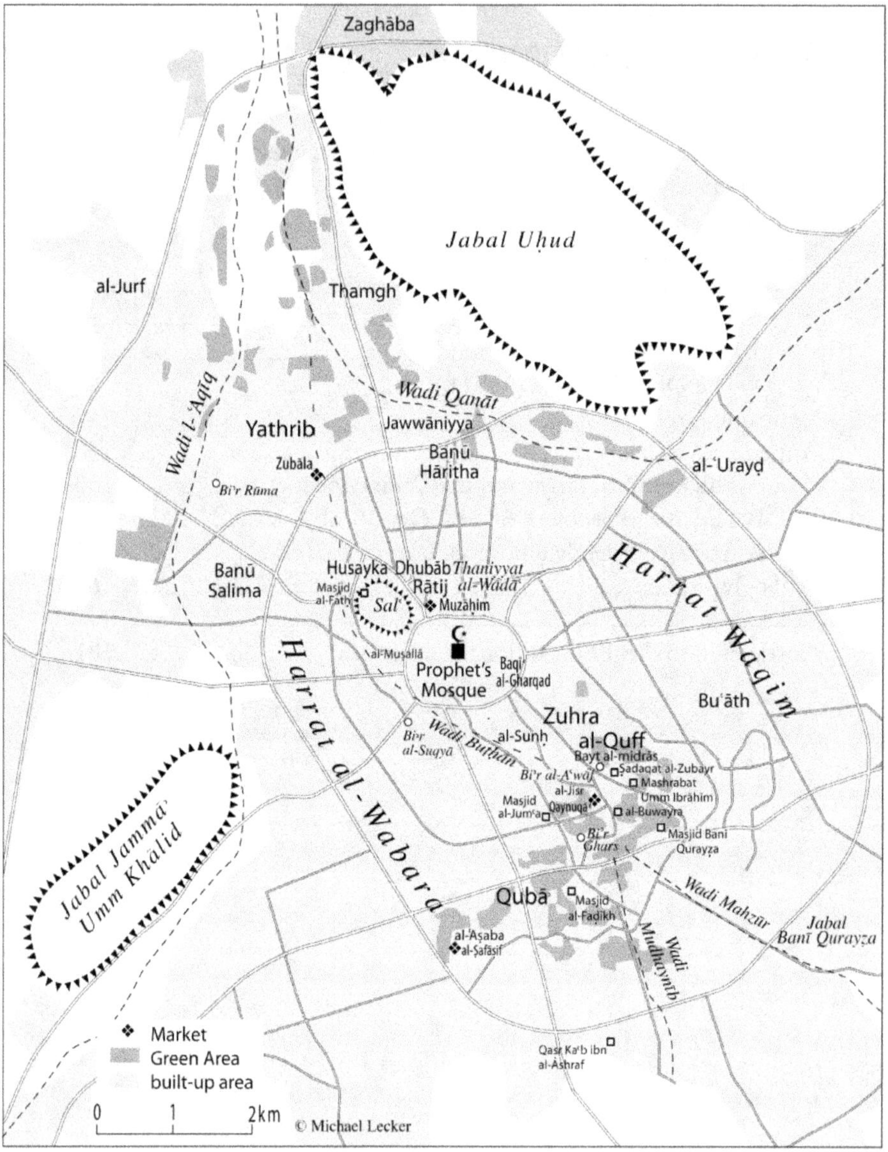

The markets of Medina (Yathrib) on the eve of Islam

FOREWORD

In the late 1970s, I was a PhD student at the Hebrew University of Jerusalem and my thesis supervisor was Professor M.J. Kister.[1] When I arrived to receive his first instructions, they were simple: "Start reading." It was a good piece of advice. He meant, of course, the primary sources – for the secondary literature did not matter much.

How times have changed; thanks to technological advances in recent decades, a laptop computer, *al-Maktaba al-Shāmila* and an Internet connection are all that a researcher must equip himself with in order to conduct original research in the field of Islamic studies. One only has to ascertain what one is looking for and to then ask a corresponding question that has a chance of being answered. Thereafter, the relevant pages in the primary sources must be consulted prior to publication, because the digital texts are not without error. Moreover, they often omit the footnotes found in the printed book. Even then, in many cases this can now be carried out without the printed book, as a growing number of primary sources can be easily downloaded from the Internet in the form of PDF files. This ease of access is good news for scholars who are far from a research library. Not such good news, though, for publishers in the Arab world!

With regards to the study of the Prophet Muḥammad's life and time, research on a specific tribe during the transition period from the Jāhiliyya to Islam, based on genealogical and geographical evidence, is still a practicable PhD project. Sadly, my own attempt in this vain, a monograph on the Banū Sulaym tribe published in the 1980s, had little impact. Nevertheless, anyone who undertakes a similar project will soon discover that solid pieces of information concerning individuals, tribes, places and other important areas, regardless of the "noise" that surrounds them, if arranged accord-

[1] For more information about Professor M.J. Kister and his works, see: www.kister.huji.ac.il.

ing to clear guidelines, allow us to draw a reliable picture of an Arabian tribe during that period. The time required for such a project is a fraction of that required before digital text repositories and the Internet were born.

The claim that the Qur'ān is the best source for Muḥammad's life is absurd. In this regard, Ibn Isḥāq's *sīra* remains a fundamental source. Yet its employment is fraught with difficulties. In order to best utilise it, we must understand much about its context. For example, when and how it emerged, the interests and loyalties of its creators and the background of the differences and contradictions it contains. Much work still remains to be done, guided by an open mind, a critical eye and command of Classical Arabic. A good starting point is the assumption that we do not know exactly what was going on in Mecca and Medina at that time, particularly the crucial last decade of Muḥammad's life.

A promising course for getting beyond the internal limitations of the *sīra* literature remains the study of Medina's geographical history, with the improvement of its map as a side product. The rather basic map attached to the 1995 edition is replaced here by a more accurate one. While the market town named Zuhra received its proper place, there are still lacunae where other pre- and early Islamic place names, known from the literature, should be added. The more accurate the map, the better our understanding of Muḥammad's struggle for the Medina oasis. The reprint of this book will perhaps encourage further studies along this course.

The book has been out of print for many years. I wish to thank Adam Walker for his initiative to publish the reprint. I also congratulate the Gorgias' able technical team for the successful reproduction of the original book.

Michael Lecker
Jerusalem

PREFACE

This study is an analysis of the evidence on Upper Medina (al-ʿĀliya in Arabic) and its inhabitants on the eve of the Islamic era and during the early days of Islam.The conclusions reached in it should be considered part of the preparatory work which I believe ought to precede the writing of a comprehensive narrative life of the Prophet Muḥammad. Because of the present state of our knowledge of the Prophet's history and the immense difficulty of interpreting the Arabic sources in their proper context, the extant biographies of Muḥammad are quite inadequate and often include uncritical and arbitrary statements.

The book is dedicated with deep gratitude to Prof. M.J. Kister on the occasion of his 80th birthday.

I am also indebted to Prof. Michael Cook for his encouragement and careful reading of the full draft, and to Prof. Uri Rubin for commenting on the first chapter. Prof. Frank Stewart read the first three chapters and made many suggestions, much improving the final product.

In addition, my thanks are due to the Mutual Fund of the Hebrew University for providing me with a research grant; also to Mr. Shmuel Shemesh of the Hebrew University and to Mr. Abe Alper of the Friends of the Hebrew University (New York) for their help. I wish to thank the Turkish Government and the Sülymaniye Library, and in particular its director, Mr. Muammer Ülker, for permission to work there. I am also grateful to Prof. William Brinner and Prof. Dr. Wolfgang Röllig for their help in Berkeley and Tübingen, respectively. The librarians at the Oriental Reading Room of the National and University Library at Givat Ram, Jerusalem, made my work there both pleasant and efficient. I am indebted to Ms. Roza I.M. El-Eini for polishing my English style and to Mr. D. Lensky for producing the camera-ready copy. The preparation of this book for publication was supported by a grant from Yad Avi Ha-Yishuv. I thank them all warmly.

A note on conventions: I have used the name Medina even when referring to the pre-Islamic period (during which it was called Yathrib). The word "Banū" ("the sons of") preceding the name of a tribe is either contracted to "B." or omitted.

INTRODUCTION

Scholars of Islam have in recent years grown accustomed to a constant flow of Arabic texts which were hitherto only available in manuscript form.[1] For example, Ibn al-Kalbī's *Jamharat al-nasab*, which until lately had been available solely in manuscript form, appeared almost simultaneously in three different editions (one being incomplete).[2] Of great importance is the recent publication of a facsimile of Ibn ʿAsākir's *Ta'rīkh madīnat Dimashq* and of the extant parts of Ibn al-ʿAdīm's *Bughyat al-ṭalab fī ta'rīkh Ḥalab*. These books preserve many records copied from earlier compilations, now lost, which can no doubt change the form of scholarship in a number of key areas, above all in those of Umayyad history and the history of Palestine under the Muslims.[3] Mention should be made of the recent publication in Cairo of Muqātil b. Sulaymān's *Tafsīr*.[4] Some of Muqātil's unique texts

---

[1] Alas, some editions of Arabic texts are "printed manuscripts" rather than scientific editions; G. Makdisī, "Hanbalite Islam", in M.L. Swartz (trans. and ed.), *Studies on Islam*, New York-Oxford 1981, 216–74, at 218. It is of course immeasurably better to have a bad edition than no edition at all.

[2] Ed. Nājī Ḥasan, Beirut 1407/1986; ed Maḥmūd al-ʿAẓm, Damascus 1406/1986. The third (*Jamharat al-nasab wa-mukhtaṣar al-jamhara wa-ḥawāshīhi*, ed. ʿAbd al-Sattār Aḥmad Farrāj, I, Kuwayt 1403/1983), was not completed due to the premature death of the editor. In R. Firestone, *Journeys in Holy Lands: The Evolution of the Abraham-Ishmael Legends in Islamic Exegesis*, New York 1990, 179, n. 1 and 247, the book's title is wrongly quoted as *Ghamarāt an-Nasab* and translated as "The Abundance of Kinship".

[3] For two recent studies which make extensive use of the former source (though from rather different points of departure), see S. Leder, "Materialien zum Ta'rīḫ des Haiṯam ibn ʿAdī bei Abū Sulaimān Ibn Zabr ar-Rabaʿī", in *ZDMG* 144 (1994), 14–27; M. Lecker, "The *Futūḥ al-Shām* of ʿAbdallāh b. Muḥammad b. Rabīʿa al-Qudāmī", in *BSOAS* 57 (1994), 356–60. Cf. the convincing case for Ibn ʿAsākir presented by G. Conrad, "Zur Bedeutung des Tārīḫ Madīnat Dimašq als historische Quelle", in W. Diem and A. Falaturi (eds.), *XXIV. Deutscher Orientalistentag*, Köln 1988, Stuttgart 1990 (*ZDMG Supplement VIII*), 271–82.

[4] Ed. ʿAbdallāh Maḥmūd Shiḥāta, al-Hay'a al-Miṣriyya al-ʿĀmma li-l-Kitāb, 1980–87. The edition was quickly withdrawn from the shelves of Cairo

are used further on in this monograph. Finally, ʿUmar b. Shabba's *Ta'rīkh al-Madīna al-munawwara* only recently became available.[5] In short, thanks to this new wave of publications we are now better equipped than ever before to study the early Islamic period.

The fresh crop of texts includes much which is unknown to us on the life of the Prophet Muḥammad, as indeed on many other aspects of early Islamic history.[6]

Besides the reconstruction and interpretation of texts, this monograph includes aspects of historical-geography, prosopography and several observations concerning the literary properties of the historical tradition. The results take us some way towards a better understanding of Medina and its society on the eve of the Hijra and during the early Islamic period.

At the heart of the monograph's four chapters is the constant of the elevated area south of Medina, which in the early Islamic period was called al-ʿĀliya or al-ʿAwālī.[7] Focusing on the area

---

bookstores; cf. Versteegh, "Grammar and exegesis", 206, n. 1; *idem, Arabic Grammar and Qur'ānic Exegesis in Early Islam*, Leiden 1993, ix, 130.

[5]Edited by Fahīm Shaltūt (Mecca 1399/1979) from a (partial) unique MS in a private library in Medina; see Fahīm Shaltūt, "Ta'rīkh al-Madīna al-munawwara ta'līf ʿUmar b. Shabba al-Numayrī", in Abdelgadir M. Abdadlla, Sami Al-Sakkar and Richard T. Mortel (eds.), *Studies in the History of Arabia, Proceedings of the First International Symposium on Studies in the History of Arabia*, Riyāḍ 1399/1979, II, 3–8; Ḥamad al-Jāsir, "Mu'allafāt fī ta'rīkh al-Madīna", no. 3, 328 f (where al-Jāsir draws attention to the curious fact that Rushdī Malḥas described the MS and correctly identified its author as early as in February 1934 in an article which appeared in the newspaper *Umm al-Qurā*). For the quality of the edition see the many corrections to the edited text made by al-Jāsir in various issues of his journal, *Majallat al-ʿArab*. The book was made available commercially only recently and until then it was distributed on a private basis. (I take this opportunity to thank Dr. Lawrence Conrad for providing me with a copy of Ibn Shabba's book when supply was still scarce.)

[6]In a foreword to a new English edition of his *Muḥammad* (translated by Anne Carter, New York 1980, ix), M. Rodinson writes: "My book does not propose to bring out new facts about the subject. None have been discovered for a long time, and it is unlikely that any will be". Rodinson's pessimism is totally unwarranted.

[7]Not to be confused with western Najd which is also called ʿĀliya; see Lecker, *The Banū Sulaym*, 1, 89, 90n. Cf. F.M. Donner, *The Early Islamic Conquests*, Princeton 1981, 310, n. 140.

rather than on events and reading the texts in conjunction with the map of Medina helps clarify a number of obscure points. The major events in the life of the Prophet, such as the Hijra and the main battles, always remain in the background. Yet, it should be emphasized that this is by no means a history; rather, it is an introductory study investigating in depth certain aspects of the Prophet's Medinan period and the Islamic literature dealing with it.

Some assumptions underlying my work

A few assumptions, which to some extent overlap, underlie my work on the Prophet Muḥammad in this monograph and elsewhere.[8]

THE IMPORTANCE OF NON-*sīra* SOURCES

On the whole, the *sīra* (i.e., *sīra* compilations and *sīra* material in other sources) is unsatisfactory as the sole source of information on the Prophet and his time. While its outline of major events may perhaps remain unchallenged in the future, other sources must be consulted. To demonstrate the importance of non-*sīra* material we may refer to the events leading up to the Ḥudaybiyya Treaty between the Prophet and the Quraysh (end of 6 A.H.): it is only in a later legal work that we find a precious report on a treaty between the Jews of Khaybar and the Meccans which was abrogated by the Ḥudaybiyya Treaty. In order to secure himself from a Meccan attack from behind during his imminent charge on Khaybar, the Prophet was willing to grant the Meccans important concessions in return for a truce. This truce contradicted the Khaybar–Mecca Treaty and in effect abolished it. The report helps make the whole affair, and the Prophet's concessions in

[8] They are often relevant, I believe, to other chapters of early Islamic historiography as well. Classification of the early historical material along chronological lines (*Sīra, Ridda, Futūḥ, Rāshidūn*, Umayyads) may serve a practical purpose, but is often superficial and unhelpful; the first two Islamic centuries are best studied as a whole. In addition, classification according to "genres" (History, *Adab*, Qur'ān exegesis) often obscures the simple fact that different "genres" use identical material which they draw from the huge repository of Islamic tradition.

particular, intelligible to us as Khaybar was conquered shortly afterwards.[9]

THE IMPORTANCE OF KNOWLEDGE ABOUT MEDINA

Our best source is certainly Samhūdī (d. 911/1506), the most important historian of Medina.[10] Much of the evidence in the present monograph comes from Samhūdī who quotes extensively from Muḥammad b. al-Ḥasan, known as Ibn Zabāla,[11] ʿUmar b. Shabba[12] and other historians who wrote about Medina. Samhūdī is an outstanding scholar; he not only quotes his predecessors, but often also adds his own illuminating observations and critical remarks. Occasionally we lament that Samhūdī, who is, incidentally, always careful to separate his predecessors' words from his own, does not have more extensive extracts from their works;[13] but then, we have to bear in mind that his book,

[9] M. Lecker, "The Ḥudaybiyya-treaty and the expedition against Khaybar", in *JSAI* 5 (1984), 1–11. Cf. Watt, "The expedition of al-Ḥudaybiya reconsidered", in *Hamdard Islamicus* 8 (1985), 3–6, where the writer undertakes the peculiar task of defending the Prophet against an accusation made by a young Muslim scholar that "whatever the motivation, the Prophet's action at al-Ḥudaybiyya fell short of the standards of honor, valor, and adherence to principles that one would expect from a Prophet of God imbued with a divine mission". Watt comments on this: "With all this I strongly disagree. In the actions of the Prophet there was nothing dishonourable or cowardly and no neglect of principles". The tension between the Prophet as an ideal figure and the Prophet as the leader of a political entity is obvious; credit should be given to Muḥammad Ḥamīdullāh who, many years ago, drew attention to the report which reveals the crux of the matter; see Lecker, *op. cit.*

[10] On whom see Wüstenfeld, *Medina*, 3–6; *GAL*, II, 173 f; *GAL S*, II, 223 f; Ḥamad al-Jāsir, "al-Samhūdī ashhar mu'arrikhī al-Madīna", in *al-ʿArab* 7, iii (1972), 161–87.

[11] On whom see *GAS*, I, 343 f (he died towards the end of the second century A.H.). See also F. Rosenthal, *A History of Muslim Historiography*², Leiden 1968, 475: Sakhāwī describes Ibn Zabāla's book as "a big volume". Sakhāwī died in Medina in 902/1497 (*GAL S*, II, 31). See also J. Sauvaget, *Le mosquée omeyyade de Médine*, Paris 1947, 26. Ibn Zabāla also wrote a *Kitāb al-shuʿarā*; see *GAS*, II, 93.

[12] Above, x.

[13] Most unfortunate is his decision not to include in his book information from Ibn Zabāla on fortresses belonging to the Jews whose locations were no longer known in his own time: *wa-qad dhakara Ibn Zabāla asmāʾa kathīrin minhā* (i.e., the fortresses) *ḥadhafnāhu li-ʿadam maʿrifatihi fī zamāninā*;

the *Wafā' al-wafā*, is only an abridgement of the original work which was destroyed during his lifetime by a fire in the Prophet's Mosque.

The geographical evidence is particularly important; the Medinans of the first and second Islamic centuries (and later too), knew a great deal about their town and were intensely interested in its pre-Islamic history.[14] A better knowledge about the still largely unexplored Medinan society and topography is indispensable for a real understanding of the Prophet's Medinan time, and is possible to gain[15] simply because we have abundant information, most of which comes from outside the *sīra*. This "stepping outside the *sīra*" can help us achieve a better vantage point from which to view the historical accounts.[16] In certain vital areas (not in all, of course) stepping outside the *narrative* of the *sīra* leaves us safely within the realm of the very large and generous, though often problematic, historical tradition of Islam. We can sometimes find, as will be seen later, a reliable or even irrefutable testimony on Medinan society in the transition period from Jāhiliyya to Islam. While ethnological studies and the literatures of the conquered people can provide confirmation of certain details,[17] the backbone of future research will remain the Islamic literature, for which there is no real alternative.

Obviously, the history of pre-Islamic Medina is always relevant to the history of the Prophet and it merits serious study before we are caught in the whirlwind of events of the Prophet's

Samh., I, 165:–3.

[14] Ibn Zabāla, for example, quotes *mashyakha min ahl al-Madīna* for the story of the settlement of the Aws and Khazraj in Medina; Samh., I, 178:1.

[15] For the opposite view see the review by G. Hawting of Lecker, *The Banū Sulaym*, in *BSOAS* 54 (1991), 359 f. Future studies by specialists (i.e., scholars interested in tribes *and* in the geography of medieval and modern Saudi Arabia) will further enlighten us concerning the preservation of place-names from the early Islamic period down to our time.

[16] Contrast this approach with P. Crone's more radical approach of stepping outside the Islamic sources altogether for the study of Islam's origins; *Slaves on Horses*, 15 f.

[17] Crone, *Slaves on Horses*, 16.

time.[18] There is a clear sense of continuity often reflected in the genealogical literature.[19]

THE IMPORTANCE OF GEOGRAPHICAL AND GENEALOGICAL EVIDENCE

The sources abound in records of fortresses, clan quarters, markets, orchards, fields and irrigation systems. These are vital for the study of the Prophet's biography and are far more useful and reliable as a historical source than, say, dialogues or speeches. The genealogical information makes it possible to identify clans that played no role or were insignificant in events during the Prophet's time. The science of genealogy provides us with the necessary and convenient framework within which the history of Medina should be studied.[20]

This monograph and further detailed research on the geographical-history of Medina and its inhabitants will put us on firmer ground when we approach the narrative of the *sīra*. Naturally, such research demands a jigsaw-puzzle approach to the sources; in other words, collecting small pieces of information and organizing them so as to form a picture. The collection of dispersed data is rather time-consuming and there is the danger of losing sight of the forest for the trees. But this approach pays off. One often finds unexpected links between seemingly unrelated and remote

---

[18] That J. Wellhausen was well aware of the importance of pre-Islamic Medina is evident from his *Medina vor dem Islam* (*Skizzen und Vorarbeiten* IV).

[19] For example, the Battle of Buʿāth a few years before the Hijra is in the background of the unique story of al-Zabīr b. Bāṭā al-Quraẓī: he was able to escape the fate of his fellow tribesmen, the Qurayẓa, and save his family and property because he spared a man of the Khazraj in Buʿāth. The son of Mukhallad b. al-Ṣāmit al-Sāʿidī who was killed in Buʿāth was the governor of Egypt at the time of Muʿāwiya; Ibn Ḥazm, *Ansāb*, 366. One of the battles, known collectively as the *ayyām al-anṣār*, viz., the War of Ḥāṭib, was caused by Ḥāṭib b. al-Ḥārith whose two sons were killed in the Battle of Uḥud; Ibn Qudāma, *Istibṣār*, 303.

[20] Goldziher's sharp and no doubt justified criticism of the genealogists, and of Ibn al-Kalbī in particular (*Muslim Studies*, I, 172 f), is more relevant to the ancient history of the Arabs than it is to the generations immediately preceding the advent of Islam. At any rate, his harsh verdict should not discourage us from using and studying tribal genealogies and this was certainly not his intention. For Medina the richness of the evidence assures us that the picture we have of its tribal genealogies is basically sound.

facts. A sense of real life is frequently created as the individuals, clans and places come to form a single whole.

THE EXISTENCE OF ILLUMINATING INDIVIDUAL REPORTS

On reading the vast and often repetitive historical tradition of Islam one may not be alert to the possibility of finding something *really* new or significant; yet there are records, sometimes quite small and hardly recognizable in the mass of material, of outstanding importance, like hidden pearls.[21]

LACUNAE IN THE EVIDENCE

That there are large lacunae in our evidence was realized many years ago by Th. Nöldeke. He remarked that we have to take into consideration that not every letter of the Prophet and not every expedition are reported. There were, he said, negotiations with tribes of which we know nothing. Only this, he continued, can account for the fact that many tribes that had fought against the Prophet became his allies shortly afterwards, for example, the Fazāra.[22]

---

[21] The identification of such reports is a prominent feature in M.J. Kister's work. See for example Samhūdī's report on the Prophet's market in Kister's "The market of the Prophet", in *JESHO* 8 (1965), 272–76 and Muqātil b. Sulaymān's report on the negotiations between the Prophet and the Thaqīf in his "Some reports concerning al-Ṭā'if", in *JSAI* 1 (1979), 1–18. Also Muṣ'ab al-Zubayrī's report on the background to the attack on the Muslims at Bi'r Ma'ūna in his "The expedition of Bi'r Ma'ūna", in G. Maqdisi (ed.), *Arabic and Islamic Studies in Honor of H.A.R. Gibb*, Leiden 1965, 337–57, at 352. Curiously, Ḥamad al-Jāsir, independently of Kister, recognized the significance of the last-mentioned report; see Lecker, *The Banū Sulaym*, 137, n. 147. Some studies by the present writer (e.g., "Muḥammad at Medina") are similarly based on reports of outstanding importance. Cf. Crone's pessimistic remarks about "the point of diminishing returns" which one reaches in going through the huge corpus of Islamic tradition; *Slaves on Horses*, 11. A text of outstanding historical importance is studied by A. Noth, "Eine Standortbestimmung der Expansion (*Futūḥ*) unter den ersten Kalifen (Analyse von Ṭabarī I, 2854–2856)", in *Asiatische Studien* 43 (1989), 120–36, who (at 120) gives further examples of such texts.

[22] Nöldeke, "Die Tradition über das Leben Muhammeds", 168. Nöldeke, whose article appeared in 1914, could have referred in this context to Wellhausen, *Muhammed in Medina*, Berlin 1882, 182 f = Waq., II, 422), where a truce with 'Uyayna b. Ḥiṣn al-Fazārī is mentioned: *wa-kānat bayna l-nabī (ṣ) wa-bayna 'Uyayna mudda, fa-kāna dhālika ḥīnu nqiḍā'ihā.* See also Watt, *Medina*, 92; U. Rubin, "*Barā'a*: a study of some Quranic passages", in *JSAI* 5

Finally, rather than covering a large area at the expense of depth, I have preferred to take "soundings". At the present stage of research, to extract from the sources what they *can* offer, the correct questions must often be asked from a practical point of view, i.e., those questions likely to receive answers. The sources are quite unpredictable. The seemingly complex questions of: "What were the names of the fortresses in Qubā' and to whom did they belong?" are answered in generous detail (below, Chs. 3 and 4). However, the replies to apparently simple queries such as: "How long did the Prophet stay in Qubā' after the Hijra and with whom did he stay?" leave one totally perplexed.

(1984), 13–32, at 16, n. 21. For a proposed treaty between the Muslims and the leaders of the Ghaṭafān, 'Uyayna and al-Ḥārith b. 'Awf, during the Battle of the Ditch, see Ḥamīdullāh, *Wathā'iq*, 74, no. 8; Waq., II, 477 f. Cf. the negotiations with the Sulaym in Lecker, *The Banū Sulaym*, 239 f.

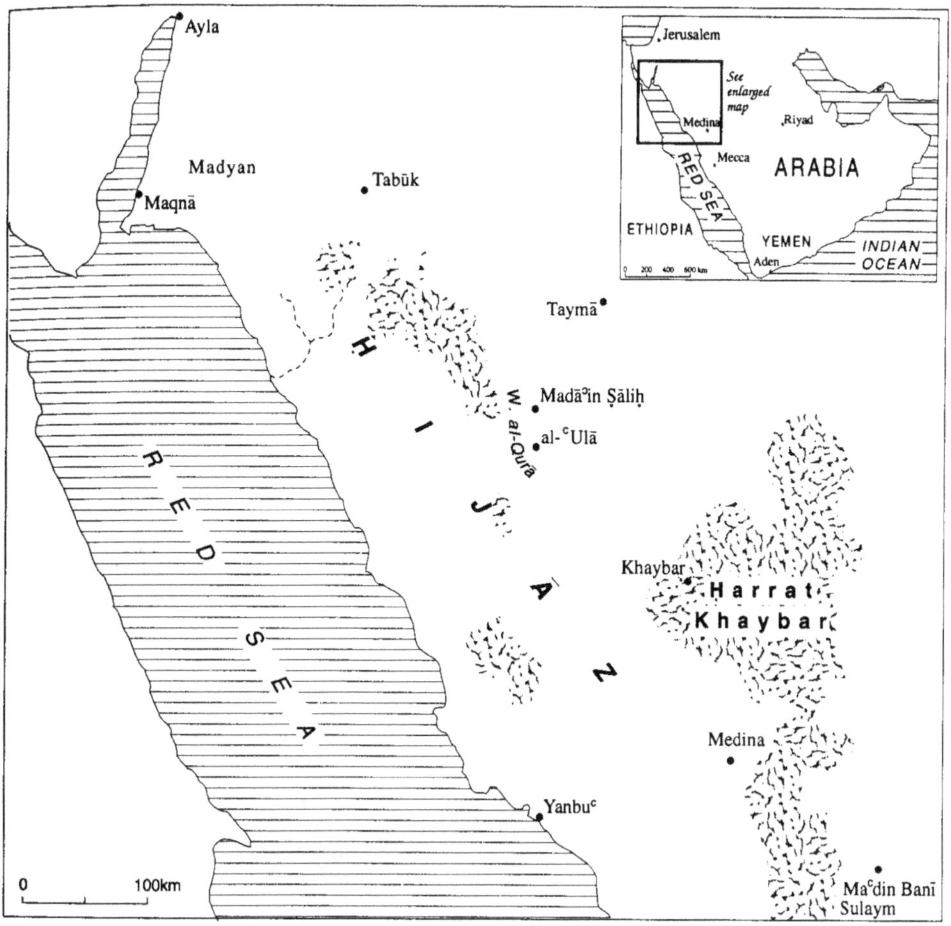

Map 1: North-Western Arabia

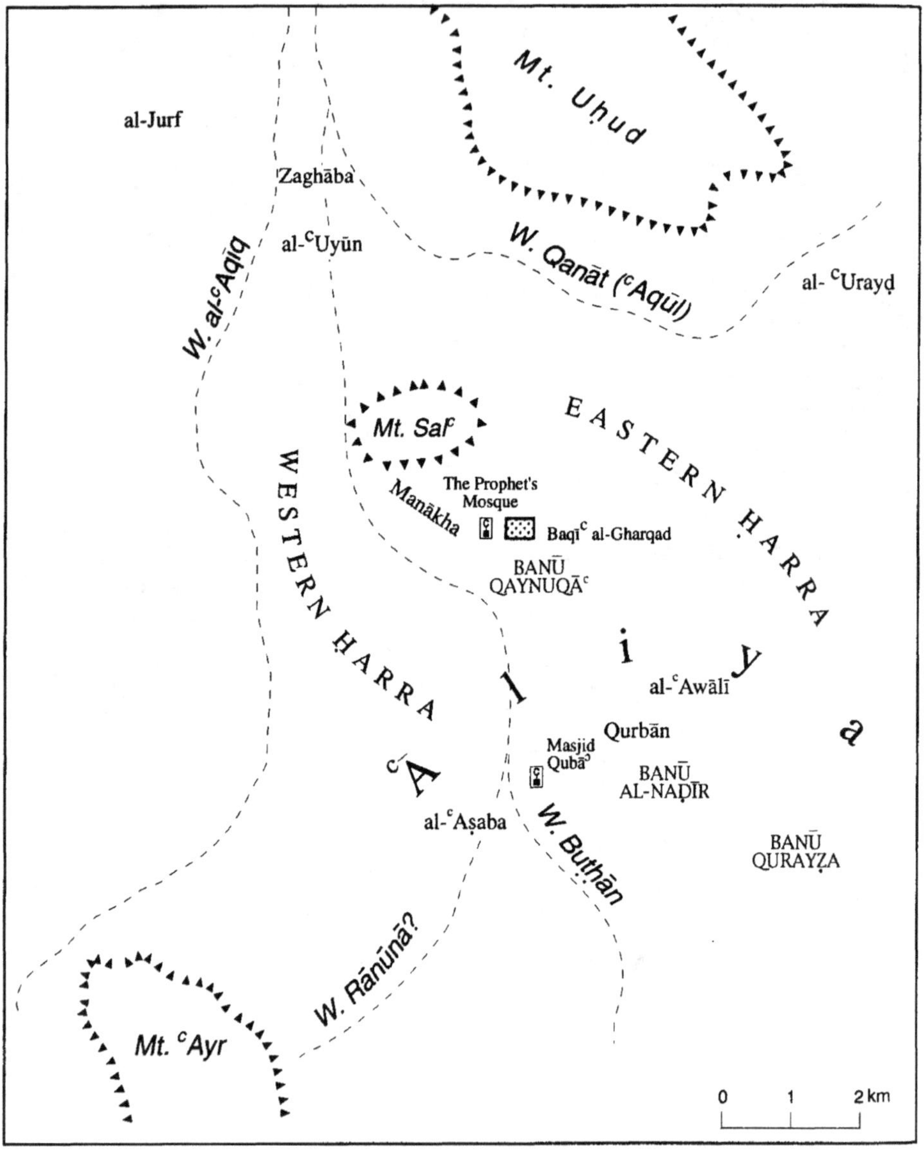

Map 2: Medina and its surroundings

CHAPTER ONE

THE ʿĀLIYA: ORCHARDS AND FORTRESSES

To begin with, we have to acquaint ourselves with the area of the study. Upper Medina was called in Arabic al-ʿĀliya or, in its plural form, al-ʿAwālī,[1] and Lower Medina was called Sāfila. Upper Medina is the area south of Medina starting a mile or a little more from the Mosque of the Prophet.[2] The differences in altitude are small: most of the built-up area of modern Medina lies at a height of 600 to 605m, rising to about 620m in the south and falling to 598m in the north.[3]

The ʿĀliya area now includes from west to east the villages of Qubāʾ, Qurbān and ʿAwālī.[4] Qurbān and ʿAwālī are modern place-names (although, as mentioned, ʿAwālī is attested to as the name of the whole area and not just part of it). In terms of agricultural potential, little has changed since pre-Islamic times.

---

[1] Also *ʿuluww*, which is far less common; see *Masālik al-abṣār*, 123; also *Sīra Shāmiyya*, III, 378 (the Prophet's stay in *ʿuluww al-Madīna*, [more specifically,] in Qubāʾ). Qays b. al-Khaṭīm calls the area *al-ẓawāhir*; *Dīwān*, 205, n. 1.

[2] See s.v. ʿĀliya in Samh., II, 1260–62; *Khulāṣat al-wafā*, 580; *Maghānim*, s.v. al-ʿĀliya, 243–45 and s.v. al-ʿAwālī, 286–87.

[3] Makki, *Medina*, 4. On climatic differences between Upper and Lower Medina see *op. cit.*, 32. I shall henceforth refer to Upper and Lower Medina by their Arabic names, ʿĀliya and Sāfila, respectively.

[4] The Qubāʾ and ʿAwālī villages are separated by Qurbān; "Waṣf al-Madīna", 19, 31. Philby, *A Pilgrim in Arabia*, 76 writes (not very accurately) that the Qurayẓa tribe, "whose name ... survives to this day in the Harrat al Quraiza, appears to have occupied the southern extremity of the district, where the ruins of its villages may be seen at ʿAwali, Qurban and Quba". He further remarks (p. 77): "The thirteen centuries that have passed over the scene since those days have been sufficient to obliterate all superficial trace of the Jewish occupation; and the Arabs of to-day do not encourage enthusiasm for the study of the Jewish stratum of Madina history. It will be long before ever the spade sets to work to reveal those buried mysteries, and the visitor to Sidi Hamza seldom realizes that he is almost within a stone's throw of the old Jewish capital" (i.e., Yathrib in north-western Medina, the site which is described by Philby on p. 76).

The area has heavy soil containing clay. The soil also has some salt but is easy to reclaim. In the valleys where there are pieces of volcanic lava, as in the Qubāʾ area from the south of the Mosque of Qubāʾ to the Buṭḥān Valley, the land is fertile and suitable for farming as it contains clay and silt and is fine-grained.[5] The ʿĀliya offers excellent opportunities for cultivation. That this was true in pre-Islamic times[6] is shown by the (apocryphal) pledge made by ʿAmr b. al-Nuʿmān al-Bayāḍī on the eve of the Battle of Buʿāth to his clan, the Bayāḍa (a subdivision of the Khazraj) in which he said:

> ʿĀmir [the ancestor of the brother-clans B. Bayāḍa and B. Zurayq] made you stay in a poor place [i.e., in the Sāfila of Medina], between salt-land and desert. By God, I shall not have intercourse with a woman [literally: I shall not wash my head] until I make you settle in the quarters of the Qurayẓa and Naḍīr, where sweet water and excellent palm-trees are to be found.[7]

ʿAmr's words reflect the underprivileged status of the Khazraj with regard to the agricultural potential of their lands. (Ironically, even the successes of the Prophet against the Jews did not gain the Khazraj a foothold in the ʿĀliya: the Prophet and the

---

[5] Makki, *Medina*, 16, 17. The upper section of Buṭḥān is nowadays called Umm ʿAshara, its middle section Qurbān and its lowest section, after it enters Medina, Abū Jīda; ʿĀtiq b. Ghayth al-Bilādī, *ʿAlā ṭarīq al-hijra (riḥalāt fī qalb al-Ḥijāz)*, Mecca [1398/1978], 137. The fertility of the Medina region in general is reflected in God's promise, before it was inhabited, to bring to it every kind of fruit (*wa-sāʾiqun ilaykum min kulli l-thamarāt*); *Sīra Shāmiyya*, III, 406. In the modern ʿAwālī village the land is fertile, the texture of the soil being a friable clay loam of volcanic origin. There is an abundant supply of water; Makkī, *Medina*, 135. For a description of the ʿĀliya area see Bilādī, *ʿAlā ṭarīq al-hijra*, 137 f.

[6] As well as at the time of Fīrūzābādī (d. 817/1415); see his enthusiastic description in *Maghānim*, 286.

[7] *Aghānī*, XV, 161–62; Wellhausen, *Skizzen* IV, 33, n. 2. See also Ibn al-Athīr, *al-Kāmil fī l-taʾrīkh*, Beirut 1385/1965–1386/1966, I, 679:–2 (*wa-kānat manāzil Qurayẓa wa-l-Naḍīr khayra l-biqāʿ*). ʿAmr b. al-Nuʿmān led the Khazraj in the Battle of Buʿāth; see *Aghānī*, 162:–4; Ibn al-Kalbī, *Nasab Maʿadd*, I, 422. (The text in Ibn Ḥazm, *Ansāb*, 357 is garbled.)

Muhājirūn received the lands of the Naḍīr and Qurayẓa.[8])

In the 1960s, the modern village of ʿAwālī south-east of Medina still had the largest cultivated area in the Medina region, the second largest was Qubāʾ and the fourth (after al-ʿUyūn area north of Medina which had been developed in the Islamic period) was Qurbān. Combined together, (modern) ʿAwālī, Qubāʾ and Qurbān accounted for over half of the cultivated land in the Medina area.[9] All this demonstrates the above-mentioned important agricultural potential of the ʿĀliya, a situation which remained unchanged from pre-Islamic days to our time.[10]

In the early Islamic period, the ʿĀliya and Sāfila were regarded as two separate areas. This was justified not only by the geographical position, but also by the social and economic peculiarities of the ʿĀliya. For example, the ʿĀliya figures as a separate area in connection with the distribution of the annual stipends by Zayd b. Thābit, at the time of ʿUmar b. al-Khaṭṭāb. This was allegedly done in the following manner: Zayd began with the people of the ʿAwālī, (more specifically) the ʿAbd al-Ashhal (a subdivision of the Nabīt),[11] then went on to the (rest of the) Aws, because of the remoteness of their houses, then the Khazraj. Zayd himself

[8] For a man of the ʿAmr b. ʿAwf boasting, in Qubāʾ, about the good quality of its soil, see al-Zubayr b. Bakkār, *al-Akhbār al-Muwaffaqiyyāt*, ed. Sāmī Makkī al-ʿĀnī, Baghdad 1392/1972, 226. For the praise of the *ʿajwa*-dates grown in the ʿĀliya see Muḥammad b. ʿAbdallāh al-Zarkashī, *Iʿlām al-sājid bi-aḥkām al-masājid*, ed. al-Marāshī, Cairo 1385, 262; M. Lecker, "The bewitching of the Prophet Muḥammad by the Jews: a note à propos ʿAbd al-Malik b. Ḥabīb's *Mukhtaṣar fī l-ṭibb*", in *al-Qanṭara* 13 (1992), 561–69, at 562. Incidentally, there is an indication that garlic was grown in the ʿĀliya: about a man from the ʿĀliya smelling of garlic in the Prophet's Mosque, see *TMD, Tahdh.*, V, 135. For a description of the ʿĀliya a hundred years ago, see "Waṣf al-Madīna", 19.

[9] Compared to other areas in Medina, the land in the ʿAwālī village is less partitioned nowadays and is owned by fewer owners simply because many of its groves are *waqf* lands; Makki, *Medina*, 133–36, esp. Fig. 23 on p. 136. The average size of a farm in Qubāʾ is even slightly bigger.

[10] On the agriculture see also J.L. Burckhardt, *Travels in Arabia*, London 1829, II, 206–16, 231–32; R.F. Burton, *Personal Narrative of a Pilgrimage to al-Madinah and Mecca*[3], London 1924, I, 399–406; Kaḥḥāla, *Jughrāfiyyat*, 180.

[11] In other words, according to this report, their territory was considered part of the ʿAwālī.

was the last to receive his share since his clan, the Mālik b. al-Najjār (of the Khazraj), lived around the Prophet's Mosque.[12] We also hear of the ʿĀliya/Sāfila dichotomy in connection with the Muslim victory at Badr. Two messengers were sent by the Prophet to announce the victory: Zayd b. Ḥāritha went to Medina (viz., to the Sāfila), while ʿAbdallāh b. Rawāḥa went to the ʿĀliya. The latter place is referred to in the report as including Qubāʾ,[13] Khaṭma, Wāʾil, Wāqif, Umayya b. Zayd, Qurayẓa and Naḍīr.[14] Being a place-name and not a tribal name, Qubāʾ is of course the odd one out. The main group inhabiting Qubāʾ was the ʿAmr b. ʿAwf (see below, Ch. 3). Another definition of the ʿĀliya found elsewhere states that it comprised the ʿAmr b. ʿAwf, Khaṭma, Wāʾil and Umayya b. Zayd.[15] We also find ʿAwālī versus *balad* (i.e., the Sāfila) in the following: to stress that the death of the above-mentioned Zayd b. Thābit was a major event, one report tells us that the women of the ʿAwālī came down (viz., to the Sāfila) that day and that the *balad* women also mourned him, not heeding those prohibiting them to do so;[16] the people of the ʿAwālī went down to Abū Hurayra's funeral.[17] Obviously, descending from the ʿĀliya to the Sāfila on the occasion of a funeral was not a common practice, certainly not for women. Zuhrī says that on Friday the Prophet gathered the people of the ʿAwālī in his mosque and that Muslims in the ʿAqīq Valley and other places at a similar distance from the Prophet's Mosque (*wa-naḥw dhālika*) would also go to the Friday-prayer.[18] In question here is the distance travelled to attend the Friday-prayer in the central, *jamāʿa* mosque. Zuhrī, in line with Umayyad policy, wished to establish that even the inhabitants of the relatively remote ʿĀliya

---

[12] Abū Yūsuf, *Kharāj*, Cairo n. d., 49.

[13] Cf. less accurately Wellhausen, *Skizzen* IV, 4, n. 3.

[14] Ibn Saʿd, II, 19. See also below, 125.

[15] Waq., I, 114–15 (... *wa-l-ʿĀliya B. ʿAmr b. ʿAwf wa-Khaṭma wa-Wāʾil, manāziluhum bihā*). See Ibn Saʿd, III, 526: "The ʿĀliya is B. ʿAmr b. ʿAwf, Khaṭma and Wāʾil". It is reported that when the Prophet set out to Badr, he left ʿĀṣim b. ʿAdī, according to one version, in charge of Qubāʾ and the people of the ʿĀliya; see below, 139.

[16] *TMD, Tahdh.*, V, 453:17; *TMD* MS, VI, 577 (s.v. Zayd b. Thābit).

[17] *TMD* MS, XIX, 253:17.

[18] Abū Dāwūd Sulaymān b. al-Ashʿath, *al-Marāsīl*, Cairo 1310/1892, 8.

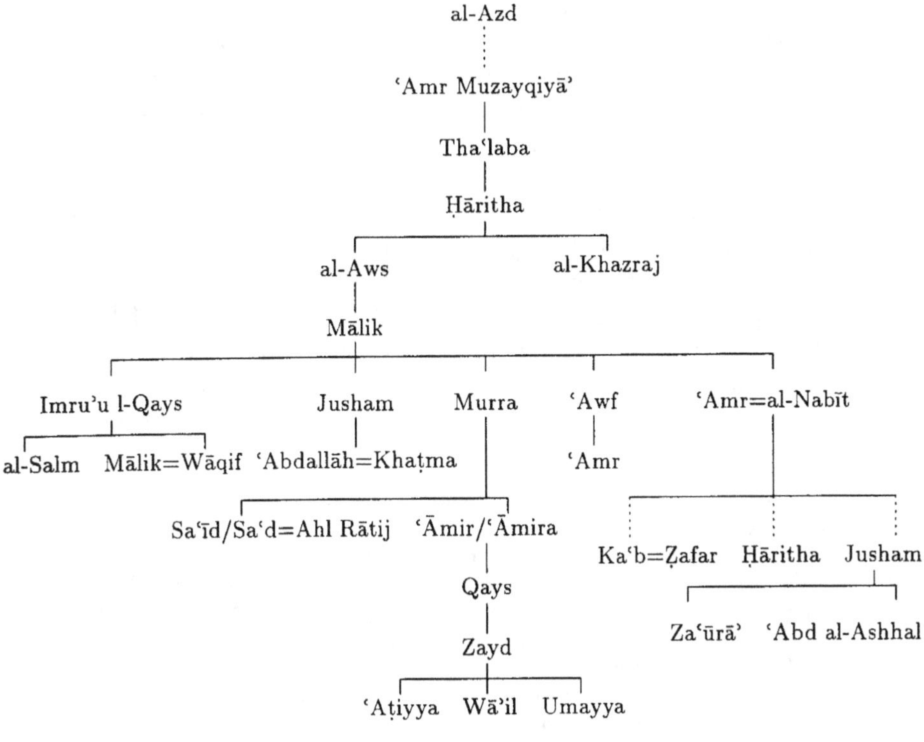
al-Azd
ʿAmr Muzayqiyāʾ
Thaʿlaba
Ḥāritha
al-Aws
al-Khazraj
Mālik
Imruʾu l-Qays
Jusham
Murra
ʿAwf
ʿAmr=al-Nabīt
al-Salm
Mālik=Wāqif
ʿAbdallāh=Khaṭma
ʿAmr
Saʿīd/Saʿd=Ahl Rātij
ʿĀmir/ʿĀmira
Kaʿb=Ẓafar
Ḥāritha
Jusham
Qays
Zaʿūrāʾ
ʿAbd al-Ashhal
Zayd
ʿAṭiyya
Wāʾil
Umayya

The Aws

and ʿAqīq had to attend. The people of the ʿAwālī were not frequent visitors to the Prophet's Mosque. We definitely find them there on a very special occasion, namely the election of ʿUthmān as caliph, when there was great congestion.[19]

The border between the ʿĀliya and the Sāfila was not clearly demarcated. Thus tribal territories located between the ʿĀliya and the Sāfila, such as that of the Jewish B. Qaynuqāʿ or the B. al-Ḥārith b. al-Khazraj, are sometimes defined as parts of the ʿĀliya.[20] Some say that already the place called al-Sunḥ which belonged to the B. al-Ḥārith and was one mile from the Mosque of the Prophet, was in the ʿĀliya.[21] For the historian of Medina, Ibn Zabāla the territory of the Ḥārith was in the ʿĀliya/ʿAwālī; he wrote that the Ḥārith settled in the court named after them *in the ʿAwālī.* (Samhūdī explains: i.e., east of Wadi Buṭḥān and Turbat Ṣuʿayb, in the place "today" called al-Ḥārith, without "Banū".) The Ḥārith built there, Ibn Zabāla continues, a fortress which belonged to the Imru'u l-Qays b. Mālik (al-Agharr b. Thaʿlaba). Then the twin brothers, Zayd and Jusham, separated from the main body of the clan and settled in (what later became known as) al-Sunḥ. They built a fortress called al-Sunḥ, after which the area was called.[22]

[19] Ibn ʿAsākir, *Ta'rīkh madīnat Dimashq* (ʿUthmān b. ʿAffān), ed. Sukayna al-Shihābī, Damascus 1404/1984, 186:11.

[20] See also Lecker, "Idol worship in pre-Islamic Medina (Yathrib)", n. 40.

[21] Indeed, al-Sunḥ was conceived of as being "out-of-town": Abū Bakr's move from al-Sunḥ, where he lived since his Hijra, to the Sāfila, is considered moving *to Medina* (*fa-lammā taḥawwala Abū Bakr ilā l-Madīna*, etc.); see Ibn Saʿd, III, 213. Incidentally, if Abū Bakr lived after the Hijra in al-Sunḥ, we can decide between two versions concerning the identity of his Medinan host: one version mentions Khubayb b. Yisāf, while the other refers to Khārija b. Zayd whose daughter Abū Bakr married. (Abū Bakr stayed among the Ḥārith b. al-Khazraj in al-Sunḥ until the Prophet's death; see Ibn Saʿd, III, 174.) Now Khārija, whose daughter Abū Bakr married, did not live in al-Sunḥ, while Khubayb did; see Ibn Saʿd, III, 524 and 534, respectively. Hence, it can be said that the Khubayb version is supported by external evidence. (At the time of the Hijra, Khubayb was still a pagan; he professed Islam shortly before the Battle of Badr.)

[22] Samh., I, 198. Ibn Saʿd, III, 534 says that the Jusham and Zayd were the owners of the mosque in al-Sunḥ (viz., the fortress was converted into a mosque?) and they in particular were the owners of al-Sunḥ (*wa-hum aṣḥābu l-Sunḥi khāṣṣatan*).

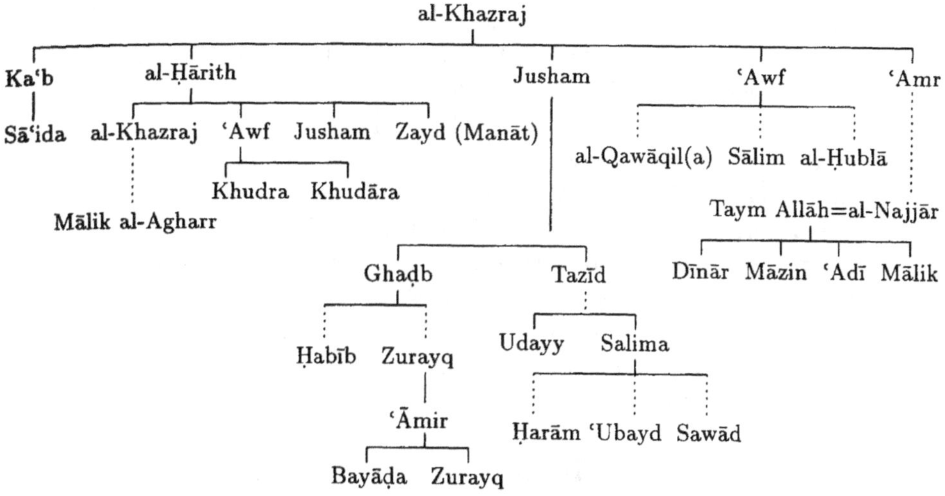
al-Khazraj
Ka'b
Sā'ida
al-Ḥārith
al-Khazraj
Mālik al-Agharr
'Awf
Khudra
Khudāra
Jusham
Zayd (Manāt)
Jusham
Ghaḍb
Ḥabīb
Zurayq
'Āmir
Bayāḍa
Zurayq
Tazīd
Udayy
Salima
Ḥarām
'Ubayd
Sawād
'Awf
al-Qawāqil(a)
Sālim
al-Ḥublā
'Amr
Taym Allāh=al-Najjār
Dīnār
Māzin
'Adī
Mālik

The Khazraj

As we have just seen, there were those who considered the territory of the Ḥārith b. al-Khazraj part of the ʿĀliya. The same is true for the territory of the Jewish B. Qaynuqāʿ. Let us look at some of the evidence concerning the Prophet's Coptic slave-girl Māriya (Umm Ibrāhīm). Ibrāhīm, the son she bore the Prophet, died in infancy. After Māriya, who was brought to the Prophet in 7 A.H., had stayed for some time in the Sāfila, the Prophet transferred her to an orchard he owned in the ʿĀliya; it was (according to this report) one of the orchards of the Naḍīr, who had been expelled from Medina a few years earlier. Māriya stayed on the orchard during the summers and "in the dates season", and the Prophet would visit her there.[23] This orchard is specifically said to have been in the ʿĀliya: the Prophet reportedly put Māriya *in the ʿĀliya*, in the orchard "today" called, Mashrabat Umm Ibrāhīm.[24] The Mashraba can be located approximately. The mosque later built in the Mashraba (presumably after the time of the Prophet) was *north* of "the Mosque of the Qurayẓa" (i.e., the mosque, or "the place of prayer", located in the former territory of the Qurayẓa),[25] near the eastern Ḥarra (or lava-field).[26] So the Mashraba was near the eastern Ḥarra, also known as Ḥarrat Wāqim and Ḥarrat B. Qurayẓa,[27] north of Qurayẓa's territory. Another, slightly different version of the report just quoted is

[23] *TMD, Tahdh.*, I, 311; *TMD* MS, I, 461–62. In the summer the ʿĀliya is cooler and healthier than the Sāfila because it is higher. In the winter, and particularly when it rains, the ʿĀliya has insalubrious pastures and many people are inflicted by fever; see "Waṣf al-Madīna", 32. The reference to the Naḍīr could result from confusion: one expects to find in this context a reference to the Qaynuqāʿ alone (see below).

[24] Ibn Saʿd, VIII, 212. A *mashraba* is either an orchard (Samh., III, 825: *wa-l-mashraba l-bustān*) or "an upper chamber" (*ghurfa, ʿulliyya*); see Lane, *Arabic-English Lexicon*, s.v. Due to the Islamization of the place-name, its former name disappeared. This is a common phenomenon in reports about Medina, though many old place-names were also preserved.

[25] Cf. M. Lecker, "Abū Mālik ʿAbdallāh b. Sām of Kinda, a Jewish convert to Islam", in *Der Islam* (forthcoming).

[26] Ḥamad al-Jāsir, *Muqtaṭafāt min riḥlat al-ʿAyyāshī (māʾ al-mawāʾid)*, Riyāḍ 1404/1984, 136. The Qurayẓa were one day's journey (*marḥala*) from Medina, east of Qubāʾ; Samh., I, 150.

[27] The eastern Ḥarra, unlike the western Ḥarra, includes arable lands; Kaḥḥāla, *Jughrāfiyyat*, 174.

more informative because it includes a pre-Islamic place-name: the Prophet lodged Māriya in the ʿĀliya, (more precisely) *in al-Quff*, in the orchard "today" called Mashrabat Umm Ibrāhīm. Each evening, the report goes on, Māriya and her son, Ibrāhīm, received fresh milk from the Prophet's sheep grazing in al-Quff and his milch-camels grazing in Dhū l-Jadr (in the vicinity of Qubāʾ).[28] The place-name al-Quff helps us link the Mashraba with the former territory of the Qaynuqāʿ: *al-Quff was the village of the Qaynuqāʿ*. They lived in the northern part of the ʿĀliya since their territory was near the end of the bridge of Wadi Buṭḥān on the side of the ʿĀliya.[29] Different, less precise versions associate the Mashraba with the territory of other Jewish tribes. As mentioned, according to one report, Māriya's orchard formerly belonged to the exiled Naḍīr. In another report we are told that Māriya lived in the Prophet's charitable endowment (*ṣadaqa*) in the (former) territory of the Qurayẓa.[30] But the place-name al-Quff clearly supports the association with the former territory of the Qaynuqāʿ.

In short, there was some fluctuation in the boundaries of the ʿĀliya. Hence, the quarters of the Ḥārith b. al-Khazraj and Qaynuqāʿ, located between the ʿĀliya and the Sāfila of Medina, were sometimes thought to be in the ʿĀliya.

The list of tribes inhabiting the ʿĀliya included the Jewish Naḍīr and Qurayẓa and Arab clans belonging to the Aws. There were also some members of the Khazraj, or more precisely of the Zurayq.[31] In addition, there was a large client population of the Balī tribe (see Chs. 3 and 4). The composition of the ʿĀliya clans is crucial to understanding the politics of the Prophet's era. There can be no doubt that when the Prophet arrived at Medina, the Jewish Naḍīr and Qurayẓa were the dominant element in the ʿĀliya and in Medina generally: according to Wāqidī, the Jews,

---

[28] Al-Zubayr b. Bakkār, *al-Muntakhab min kitāb azwāj al-nabī*, ed. Sukayna al-Shihābī, Beirut 1403/1983, 58–59; *Istīʿāb*, I, 54–55 (quoting al-Zubayr b. Bakkār); Lecker, "Muḥammad at Medina", 38, n. 71; *idem*, "Ḥudhayfa b. al-Yamān and ʿAmmār b. Yāsir, Jewish converts to Islam", section 2.

[29] Lecker, "Muḥammad at Medina", 37–38.

[30] Lecker, "Muḥammad at Medina", 35.

[31] They were clients of the ʿAmr b. ʿAwf; see below, 50.

viz., especially the two main tribes of Naḍīr and Qurayẓa, were the owners *par excellence* of fortresses and weapons in Medina and the allies of the Aws and Khazraj.[32]

The special fortifications

The Jews were called "the owners of weapons and fortresses" (*ahl al-ḥalqa wa-l-ḥuṣūn*).[33] These *ḥuṣūn* were different from the common tower-houses of Medina, the *āṭām* or *ājām*. In addition to tower-houses, the Naḍīr and Qurayẓa, as well as some Arab clans living in the ʿĀliya, had fortifications of a kind not found elsewhere in Medina. The details about them come from Samhūdī's description of the courts belonging to the Jewish and Arab ʿĀliya clans (taken from earlier histories of Medina).

First, the weapons. That the Jews owned large numbers of weapons is confirmed by the evidence about the defeat of the main Jewish tribes of the Naḍīr and Qurayẓa, in which the spoils are described in detail. Large numbers of swords, coats of mail, spears and shields were taken as booty from the storehouses of the Qurayẓa. These large quantities, when compared to the number of fighting men from the Qurayẓa executed by the Prophet, prompted Kister to suggest that the Qurayẓa used to sell (or lend) some of those weapons.[34] As to the Naḍīr, their weapons

[32] See M. Lecker, "Wāqidī's account on the status of the Jews of Medina: a study of a combined report".

[33] For example, in a report purporting to relate to the period after the Battle of Badr, in Suyūṭī, *Durr*, VI, 198:3. The Qurashīs instigated the Jews to fight against the Prophet, threatening them of war. They wrote to them, "You are the owners of weapons and fortresses. You ought to fight against our friend ["friend" is used here ironically] or else we will fight against you [literally: we will indeed do such and such deeds] and nothing will interpose between us and the anklets of your women". When their message reached the Jews, the Naḍīr unanimously agreed to a betrayal (i.e., of the Muslims). See also Ḥamīdullāh, *Wathā'iq*, 66, no. 2a–b. Cf. a reference to Qaynuqāʿ, Naḍīr and Qurayẓa as the owners of fortresses (*ḥuṣūn*) in Waq., II, 563 (read: *innī arā amra Muḥammad qad amira*, instead of: … *amina*; cf. Waq., II, 821:11: *la-qad amira amru B. ʿAdī baʿda wa-'llāhi qilla wa-dhilla*; Qurṭubī, *al-Jāmiʿ li-aḥkām al-qur'ān*, X, 233–34).

[34] Kister, "The massacre of the Banū Qurayẓa", 94. For the weapons of the Jews see also F. Altheim and R. Stiehl, *Die Araber in der alten Welt*, vol. V,

were specifically excluded from the movables they were allowed to carry with them when sent into exile.[35]

Second, the *ḥuṣūn*.[36] Samhūdī tells us of the transformation of two *qaṣr*s into *ḥiṣn*s by Muʿāwiya. Muʿāwiya ordered the (re)building of Qaṣr Khall as a *ḥiṣn* (*li-yakūna ḥiṣnan*) for the people of Medina (i.e., for the Umayya living in Medina). Qaṣr Banī Ḥudayla (a subdivision of the Mālik b. al-Najjār) was also constructed by Muʿāwiya *li-yakūna ḥiṣnan*. Aware of the hatred by the Medinans, many of whom must have regarded the

---

i, Berlin 1968, 366. The authors propose that judging by the numbers of weapons taken by Muḥammad as spoils, the Qurayẓa were the richest Jewish tribe but then, they add, Naḍīr's centre of gravity was outside Medina, namely in Khaybar. Cf. Altheim-Stiehl, *Finanzgeschichte der Spätantike*, Frankfurt a.M. 1957, 123f, 130.

[35] Waq., I, 374:1. The quantities of weapons taken from the Naḍīr are considerably smaller than those taken from the Qurayẓa; some said that they managed to hide part of the weapons and take it with them; see *op. cit.*, 377.

[36] A thorough study of Medinan fortifications may change the prevailing assumptions concerning the place of pre-Islamic Arabia in the development of Islamic architecture. The total neglect by Creswell of pre-Islamic Arabia is certainly unwarranted; cf. K.A.C. Creswell, *Early Muslim Architecture*², Oxford 1969, I, 10–11 ("Arabia, at the rise of Islam, does not appear to have possessed anything worthy of the name architecture"). Creswell begins his "Fortification in Islam before A.D. 1250. Aspects of art lecture, Henriette Hertz Trust, British Academy", in *Proceedings of the British Academy* 38 (1952), 89–125, with the following statement: "At the rise of Islam fortification was practically unknown in Arabia and only one town — Ṭā'if — possessed a wall .... According to Masʿūdī, Madīna was not surrounded by a wall until 63 H. (682/3)". Creswell wonders: "When and where did the early Muslims first learn about fortification?" See also R. Ettinghausen and O. Grabar, *The Art and Architecture of Islam: 650–1250*, Penguin Books 1987, 17–18: "Although textual information about pre-Islamic Arabia is not very secure and a serious exploration of the area has barely begun, it is fairly certain, that, at least in the period immediately preceding the Muslim conquest, the Arabs of Arabia had very few indigenous traditions of any significance". G.R.D. King, "Creswell's appreciation of Arabian architecture", in *Muqarnas* 8 (1991) 94–102, at 100a, correctly criticizes Creswell's approach: "... Creswell chose an inappropriate measure of Arabia's architectural skill by stressing the absence of town walls everywhere in the Hijaz but Ta'if. Their absence was a reflection of the lack of political cohesion in pre-Islamic Arabia, rather than a lack of building ability". King mentions *uṭum al-Ḍaḥyān* (99a) and the Mosque of Qubā' (100b). On the former building see also G.R.D. King, "Building methods and materials in western Saudi Arabia", in *Proceedings of the Seminar for Arabian Studies* 19 (1989), 71–78, at 75.

Umayyads as foreign conquerors, Muʿāwiya warned that in an emergency the Umayya would be unable to reach Qaṣr Khall, located in the Ḥarra, some distance from Medina. So, Qaṣr Banī Ḥudayla was built for them in the heart of Medina.[37] Converting a *qaṣr* into a *ḥiṣn* presumably involved improving its fortifications and gate and making it independent in its water supply. Muʿāwiya must have learned his lesson from the siege of the Caliph ʿUthmān.

The terms commonly used in connection with fortifications in Medina are *ḥiṣn* and *uṭum.*[38] However, they are interchanged and used inconsistently. In themselves they cannot be relied upon for discerning separate types of fortifications.

Two different kinds of fortifications can be perceived. First, the ordinary fortress or tower-house, the famous *uṭum.*[39] This was not a purely military building because it was also used as a residence.[40] However, although Aṣmaʿī and others defined the *āṭām* as "houses with flat roofs" (*al-dūr al-musaṭṭaḥatu l-suqūf*),[41] and yet others as "any square house with a flat roof" (*kullu bayt murabbaʿ musaṭṭaḥ*),[42] an *uṭum* in Medina was certainly not an

[37] See Samh., s.vv. Qaṣr Khall; Biʾr Ḥāʾ, 961 f; Kister, "The battle of the Ḥarra", 42, n. 48. The caliph, Sulaymān b. ʿAbd al-Malik, was born in the court (*dār*) of his father, ʿAbd al-Malik in Medina, in (the territory of) the Ḥudayla; Khalīfa, *Taʾrīkh*, I, 426. This court contained the above-mentioned Qaṣr Banī Ḥudayla. (Ḥudayla is often corrupted to Jadīla; for the correct name see Ibn Mākūlā, II, 59.)

[38] *Qaṣr* is rare; Waq., I, 191; Ibn al-Kalbī, *Jamhara*, 636; below, 104n. Cf. L.I. Conrad, "The *quṣūr* of medieval Islam: some implications for the social history of the Near East", in *Abḥāth* 29 (1981), 7–23, at 19.

[39] The poet Aws b. Maghrāʾ (a *mukhaḍram* who died in the time of Muʿāwiya; *Iṣāba*, I, 218; *GAS*, II, 381–82) mentions the *āṭām* of Najrān; in Ṣanʿāʾ there was an *uṭum* called after al-Aḍbaṭ b. Qurayʿ of the Tamīm who reportedly built it following a raid on the people of Ṣanʿāʾ; Yaq., s.v. Uṭum al-Aḍbaṭ; Ibn Qutayba, *al-Shiʿr wa-l-shuʿarāʾ*, ed. Aḥmad Muḥammad Shākir, Cairo 1386/1966, I, 382 (having raided the Ḥārith b. Kaʿb, al-Aḍbaṭ put up [i.e., in Ṣanʿāʾ] an *uṭum*, and the kings built around that *uṭum* the town of Ṣanʿāʾ).

[40] Wellhausen, *Skizzen* IV, 19 wrongly says that the *āṭām* (="feste Häuser") are "für gewöhnlich unbewohnt".

[41] Masʿūdī, *Tanbīh*, 206:18.

[42] *Lisān al-ʿarab*, s.v. *ʾ.ṭ.m.*, 19b. Reference to a man standing on the roof of an *uṭum* is common in the sources; see, e.g., Suyūṭī, *Khaṣāʾiṣ*, I, 64:8.

ordinary house (*manzil*); being stronger or higher, or both, it gave its inhabitants better security and therefore had a military role, as we learn from numerous reports on Medina before Islam and at the time of the Prophet.[43] The Naḍīr, for example, had both *āṭām* and *manāzil* in their territory in the ʿĀliya.[44] They also had special fortifications (see below).

The *āṭām* of Medina, a unique and prominent feature of the Medinan landscape, had a symbolic importance for the people of Medina and were still remembered many years after they had been demolished or fallen into decay. Masʿūdī, for example, reports that the *āṭām* of Medina were pulled down in the days of ʿUthmān b. ʿAffān but their traces remained to his own time.[45] The records of these fondly remembered fortresses are the nucleus around which Ibn Zabāla (fl. in the second half of the second century A.H.) built his chapter on the quarters of the clans. One of the grievances against Caliph ʿUthmān was due to his order to demolish the *āṭām* of Medina. The accusation that the Caliph gave the order seems doubtful. ʿUthmān may have ordered the demolition of some fortresses in order to enlarge the market or make available a tract of land for cultivation, but he would not have had *all* of them pulled down. It is not unlikely that in having some of the fortresses destroyed, ʿUthmān was also motivated by military considerations, and the Anṣār's bitterness (note their overwhelming support for ʿAlī) may not have been based solely on environmental and aesthetic considerations.[46] The *āṭām* were symbols of Anṣārī tribal autonomy and an important component in the prestige of their tribal leaders.

---

[43] Serjeant, "Meccan trade", 483a remarks versus P. Crone that *uṭm* (the form *uṭum* seems to be more common) was not a "turret", as she translates it, but "an ordinary Arab tower house".

[44] Samh., I, 161: *wa-'btanawi l-āṭāma wa-l-manāzila.*

[45] *Tanbīh*, 206.

[46] The Prophet reportedly prohibited the Anṣār from demolishing the *āṭām*; he explained that they were the adornment (*zīna*) of Medina; Suyūṭī, *Ḥujaj mubīna*, 51 (< al-Zubayr b. Bakkār, *Akhbār al-Madīna* < Ibn Zabāla). Cf. R. Veselý, "Die Anṣār im ersten Bürgerkriege (36–40 d. H.)", in *Archív Orientální* 26 (1958), 36–58, at 36–37 = Masʿūdī, *Tanbīh*, 206 (the Anṣār were embittered by ʿUthmān's destruction of the *āṭām*).

Second, the special strongholds of the 'Āliya. In the 'Āliya we find a special type of fortification: a purely military construction, or fortress, which could shelter the whole tribe in time of war. The other fortified houses in Medina, which were of humble dimensions and used also as residences, were found in the Sāfila and in the 'Āliya, but the special strongholds were found only in the 'Āliya.[47] Of the four such fortresses mentioned in the sources, two belonged to the Jewish Naḍīr and Qurayẓa and the other two to Arab clans closely allied with the Jews. These fortresses must have been larger than the residential fortresses and possibly included storerooms and an independent source of water. On the basis of the following data we may assume that the owners of such fortresses were better prepared for sieges than those of residential fortresses.

1. Naḍīr: Two place-names, Fāḍija and Jifāf, are associated with the fortress of the Naḍīr. The Naḍīr as a whole had, we are told, a fortress in the orchard called Fāḍija (the location is presumably given in terms of Islamic Medina). Fāḍija was still known to Samhūdī (d. 911/1505), who defined it as an orchard in the Jifāf area in which an *uṭum* of the Naḍīr belonging to the whole tribe was located (*Fāḍija: māl bi-l-'Āliya ma'rūf al-yawm, bi-nāḥiyati Jifāf, kāna bihi uṭum li-B. l-Naḍīr 'āmmatan*).[48] The term *uṭum*

[47] The existence of these two types of fortifications was noticed by 'Abd al-Qaddūs al-Anṣārī, *Āthār al-Madīna al-munawwara*, Damascus 1353/1953, 42; H.Z. Hirschberg, *Yisra'el be-'Arav*, Tel-Aviv 1946, 185 [in Hebrew]; and 'Ubayd al-Madanī; cf. al-Madanī's "Uṭūm al-Madīna l-munawwara", 214, 216–17. Cf. about the *āṭām* Qays b. al-Khaṭīm, *Dīwān*, ed. T. Kowalski, XV–XX; on p. XV it is inaccurately stated (following Wellhausen, see above, 12n) that they were "für gewöhnlich unbewohnt". This is only true of the special fortifications in the 'Āliya.

[48] Samh., II, s.v. Fāḍija; I, 163; *Maghānim*, s.v. Jifāf, 89 (the definition in the latter source, *mawḍi' amāma l-'Awālī*, seems to relate to the [later] 'Awālī village). Yaq., s.v. Fāḍija, wrongly says that Fāḍija was a name of an *uṭum* of Naḍīr in Medina, and Fīrūzābādī (*Maghānim*, s.v., 310) corrects this to: it is an orchard in Medina containing a fortress belonging to the Naḍīr as a whole. In Fīrūzābādī's time (he died in 817/1415) it lay in ruins and in its place there was a date-palm-grove called al-Fāḍija (*sic*, with an article), in al-Jifāf (again, with an article), "behind" (*warā'a*) the '*Awālī* (= the later 'Awālī village). The people of Medina identify Jifāf with Qurbān between Qubā' and the 'Awālī village; see *Khulāṣat al-wafā*, 533n.; *Maghānim*, 454.

in itself is of course not indicative of the type of fortification we have here since it usually designates an ordinary fortress or tower-house found everywhere in the Medina area.

A late non-Medinan source uses the term *qalʿa* to designate the fortresses of the Naḍīr and Qurayẓa, and Samʿānī (d. 562/1167) conceives of the Naḍīr and Qurayẓa as inhabiting two fortresses near Medina. Qurayẓa, he says, was a man whose children (or descendants) settled in a fortified stronghold (*qalʿa ḥaṣīna*) near Medina which was named after them.[49] The same details are provided about Naḍīr: he was a man whose children (or descendants) settled in a *qalʿa* near Medina.[50] Al-Madanī[51] notes the spaciousness of the Naḍīr fortress. In this context he rightly refers to Ibn Ubayy's suggestion (whether or not it is historical is beside the point) that he enter the Naḍīr's fortress with two thousand men of his own clan and "other Arabs".[52]

2. Qurayẓa: While the name of the Naḍīr's fortress is still unknown,[53] that of the central fortification of the Qurayẓa is known to be al-Muʿriḍ. The fortress, we are told, was not used as a dwelling, but the Qurayẓa sought shelter in it in times of fear (*uṭum B. Qurayẓa lladhī kānū yaljaʾūna ilayhi idhā faziʿū*). It was located between "the great tree with spreading branches" (*al-dawḥa*) in the Baqīʿ of Qurayẓa (*baqīʿ* is "a spacious piece of land with trees"), and "the date-orchard from which the torrent (*sayl*) issues".[54]

---

[49] Samʿānī, s.v. al-Quraẓī: ... *Qurayẓa, wa-huwa smu rajul nazala* [add: *awlāduhu*, from Ibn al-Athīr, *Lubāb*, s.v.] *qalʿa ḥaṣīna bi-qurbi l-Madīna fa-nusiba* [read: *fa-nusibat*] *ilayhim*.

[50] See s.v. al-Naḍīrī in Samʿānī and s.v. al-Naḍarī in Ibn al-Athīr, *Lubāb*. The latter source uses *ḥiṣn* in both cases instead of *qalʿa*.

[51] "Uṭūm al-Madīna l-munawwara", 217.

[52] See, e.g., *Sīra Shāmiyya*, IV, 456: *fa-inna maʿī alfayni min qawmī wa-ghayrihim mina l-ʿarabi yadkhulūna maʿakum ḥiṣnakum.*

[53] It may have been identical with one of the fortresses, the names of which are known to us, e.g., al-Buwayla, Samh., I, 163; or Manwar, Samh., II, s.v.

[54] Samh., s.v. al-Muʿriḍ. Note that there were a few other Baqīʿs in Medina, one of which was the famous cemetery Baqīʿ al-Gharqad. Note also that this fortress had a namesake in the Sāfila, a fortress of the Sāʿida. See *Maghānim*, s.v. Muʿriḍ, 386. On the stronghold of the Qurayẓa cf. Kister, "The massacre of the Banū Qurayẓa", 87, 90, 92.

Two Arab clans in the ʿĀliya had similar fortifications and both were part of the Aws subdivision called Aws Allāh.

3. Khaṭma: Their court was adjacent to that of the Naḍīr. We know this from an interchange of two place-names: when the Prophet besieged the Naḍīr, he prayed the afternoon prayer in the Naḍīr's open space (*faḍā'*). Elsewhere we are told that he prayed in the court (*dār*) of the Khaṭma. In addition, "the small mosque of the Khaṭma" was later built on the site of the Prophet's tent during the siege on the Naḍīr. Also, the heads of several Jews of the Naḍīr, killed while raiding the Muslims, were reportedly thrown into one of the Khaṭma's wells.[55]

The fortress of the Khaṭma, *uṭum* Ḍaʿ Dharʿ, did not have dwelling-places in it since they built it as a *ḥiṣn* to shelter them in times of war (*laysa bihi buyūt, jaʿalūhu ka-l-ḥiṣni lladhī yataḥaṣṣanūna fīhi li-l-qitāl*). It also belonged to the Khaṭma as a whole. The fortress was near "the hollowed stone from which one performs the ablution" (*mihrās*) of the Khaṭma and was named Ḍaʿ Dharʿ because it was near the Khaṭma well called Dharʿ.[56]

In a few instances pre-Islamic fortresses were transformed into tribal mosques or rebuilt as such mosques. In the case of the Khaṭma, the problem of the fortress/mosque is very complicated and, while their mosque was certainly close to their central fortification, it is not clear whether the two were identical. Both their fortress and mosque are linked with their well: the fortress Ḍaʿ

[55] Waq., I, 370:–3, 371:8, 372:11. Ibn Saʿd, II, 57 reports that the houses of the Naḍīr were in the al-Ghars area (east of Qubā') which "today" corresponds to the cemetery of the Khaṭma. Cf. *Maghānim*, s.v. Bi'r Ghars, 46 and Samh., II, 978 (Samhūdī corrects the *Maghānim*'s reading "Ḥanẓala" to "Khaṭma"). The well called Bi'r Ghars is half a mile east of the Mosque of Qubā' in the Qurbān village, in an orchard carrying the well's name. Al-ʿAyyāshī locates it half a mile north-east of the Qubā' Mosque; al-Jāsir, *Muqtaṭafāt min riḥlat al-ʿAyyāshī*, 145 (vocalized: Ghurs; perhaps the pronunciation underwent changes).

[56] Samh., I, 197; s.v. Ḍaʿ Dharʿ in *Maghānim*, 231; *uṭum ... shibhu l-ḥiṣn* is Fīrūzābādī's variation of Ibn Zabāla's *jaʿalūhu ka-l-ḥiṣni*; Samh., 1257; *Khulāṣat al-wafā*, 577. On Bi'r Dharʿ see Samh., II, 966–67. Concerning the name Ḍaʿ, cf. perhaps the noun *ḍwʿ* in Sabaic which means "alarm, state of emergency"; A.F.L. Beeston, M.A. Ghūl, W.W. Müller and J. Ryckmans, *Sabaic Dictionary*, Louvain-la-Neuve 1982, 42.

Dharʿ was named, as already mentioned, after their well, Dharʿ, which was near it, whilst the well, which was still known at the time of Samhūdī, was in the mosque's courtyard (*finā'*).[57] But this circumstantial evidence is insufficient to establish that the two structures were in fact one and the same.

The following passage in Samhūdī (quoted from Ibn Zabāla) does not help in resolving the problem but is nevertheless relevant for us here and is certainly unique:

> The Khaṭma were dispersed in their fortresses and none of them lived in the heart of their court (perhaps: in its fortified stronghold, *qaṣabat dārihim*[58]). When Islam came, they built their mosque. One of them built a house near the mosque in which he lived and they would inquire about him every morning for fear that the wild beasts had attacked him [i.e., the mosque was in an isolated area]. Then they multiplied in the court [i.e., in the formerly uninhabited area near their mosque] until it was called [literally: until they were called] "Gaza", i.e., it was likened to the Gaza of Palestine because of its many inhabitants.[59]

The formerly isolated area of the *qaṣaba* was some distance from the fortresses of the Khaṭma. This area became important in Islamic times after the Khaṭma's mosque was built there. Perhaps the mosque was on the site of their fortress, or part of the fortress was transformed into a mosque.

4. Wāqif: Along with other fortresses, the Wāqif, who were also a clan of the Aws Allāh, built a fortress called Raydān which belonged to the whole clan (*kāna lahum ʿāmmatan*). It was to the

[57] Samh., II, 872–73, 966–67.

[58] *EI*², s.v. Ḳaṣaba (A. Miquel).

[59] Samh., I, 198: *wa-kāna B. Khaṭma mutafarriqīna fī āṭāmihim, lam yakun fī qaṣabati dārihim minhum aḥad. Fa-lammā jā'a l-islāmu ttakhadhū masjidahum, wa-'btanā rajulun minhum ʿinda l-masjid baytan sakanahu fa-kānū yas'alūna ʿanhu kulla ghadātin makhāfata an yakūna l-sabʿ ʿadā ʿalayhi. Thumma kathurū fī l-dār ḥattā kāna yuqālu lahum Ghazza, tashbīhan bi-Ghazzati l-Shāmi min kathrati ahlihā.*

south of "the Mosque of Date Wine" (*masjid al-faḍīkh*), otherwise known as "the Mosque of the Sun", and east of Qubā'.[60]

We come across four constructions of a special type in the 'Āliya not found elsewhere in Medina: fortresses built strictly for military purposes which belonged to the whole clan. The clans owning them were prepared to withstand a prolonged siege. Two of the fortresses belonged to the main Jewish tribes and the other two to Arab clans of the Aws Allāh group. All four fortresses were in the eastern part of the 'Āliya, presumably within a short distance of each other. No similar fortification was to be found in the western part of the 'Āliya, namely in Qubā' and al-'Aṣaba. This made the eastern 'Āliya the most fortified area in Medina then,[61] which is a conclusion of major importance to understanding Medinan politics at the time of the Prophet.

[60] In Samh., I, 195–96 it is erroneously called: al-Zaydān, but Raydān (without the article) is the correct name; Samh., II, s.v. Raydān, 1226 and in *Khulāṣat al-wafā*, s.v., 560. Samhūdī saw the ruins of the dwellings of the Wāqif to the south of "the Mosque of Date Wine". They included *āṭām*, a village and a huge fortress (*ḥiṣn 'aẓīm*); see Samh., I, 196. *Masjid al-faḍīkh* is east of the Mosque of Qubā' and north-east of the 'Awālī village, roughly three kilometres from the Mosque of the Prophet; *Maghānim*, 458. For another mosque called *Masjid al-shams* between Ḥilla and Karbalā', see Goldziher, *Muslim Studies*, II, 301; *EI*², s.v. Masdjid, 650a (J. Pedersen).

[61] Cf. Watt, *Medina*, 165, who describes the Aws Allāh as "a heterogeneous collection of old groups whose strength was declining. They lacked both genealogical and geographical unity .... They carried little weight in the Medina that Muḥammad found".

CHAPTER TWO

THE AWS ALLĀH CLANS

The conversion of the Aws Allāh to Islam

Our focus shifts now to the clans of the Aws Allāh group which lived in the eastern part of the ʿĀliya. This chapter concentrates on their role at the time of the Prophet, and particularly on their relatively late conversion to Islam.[1] It will be shown that *sīra* literature provides reliable information on this sensitive issue.

Our point of departure are the several fundamentally significant reports that the Aws Allāh embraced Islam only after the Battle of the Ditch, that is, not earlier than 5 A.H.[2] Hence, of all

---

[1] R. Paret, "Toleranz und Intoleranz im Islam", in *Saeculum* 21 (1970), 344–65, at 347, seems to be unaware of the fact that the conversion of Medina to Islam was a rather lengthy process: "Etwa die Hälfte der ortsansässigen Bevölkerung nahm innerhalb kurzer Zeit den Islam an, soweit sie sich nicht schon vor dem Eintreffen der mekkanischen Emigranten dazu entschlossen hatte. Es waren die sogenannten *Anṣār*, die 'Helfer'". The other half were the Jews. Cf. *idem*, *Mohammed und der Koran. Geschichte und verkündigung des arabischen Propheten*, Stuttgart 1957, 102–103, 124–25. Th. Nöldeke, *Das Leben Muhammed's*, Hannover 1863, 48–49, did mention that after Muḥammad had sent Muṣʿab b. ʿUmayr to Medina, Islam quickly spread ("...mit reißender Schnelle breitete sich der Islâm unter den beiden sonst so feindlichen Stämmen aus"). But he did not fail to notice the slow acceptance of Islam by the Aws Allāh, and wrote (55–56) that: "...noch längere Zeit nach seiner [= the Prophet's] Ankunft ein Theil der Medînenser dem alten Götzendienst treu blieb — wie z. B. von einem großen Geschlechte, den Aus-allâh, berichtet wird, daß sie sich unter dem Einfluß des Dichters Abû Kais noch Jahre lang von dem Islam fern hielten ...". Far less accurate is Wellhausen, *Skizzen* IV, 15: "Mit wunderbarer Schnelligkeit verbreitete sich der Islam bei ihnen [= the Anṣār]; noch ehe der Prophet selber kam, waren sie schon fast alle für seine Lehre gewonnen".

[2] See, e.g., Ibn Ḥazm, *Ansāb*, 345; Rubin, "Ḥanīfiyya", 89. Watt (*EI*[2], s.v. al-Madīna, 994) explains the late conversion to Islam as follows: "It is probable that before the arrival of any Jews there were some Arabs at Medina, doubtless the ancestors of those found subordinate to the Jews at the time of the settlement of al-Aws and al-Khazradj. It was probable [*sic*] because

the Arab clans of Medina, the Aws Allāh were the last to embrace Islam. Their close proximity to the Jewish tribes of the ʿĀliya no doubt played a major role here. It becomes clear that for at least five of his ten years of activity in Medina the Prophet had no access at all to the eastern ʿĀliya which was inhabited by the Naḍīr, the Qurayẓa and the clans of the Aws Allāh.[3]

We begin with Ibn Isḥāq's account as quoted by Ibn Hishām. At the end of a report on the mission of Muṣʿab b. ʿUmayr, whom the Prophet sent from Mecca to Medina before the Hijra, a clear distinction is made between early and late converts to Islam. Together with his Medinan aide and host, Asʿad b. Zurāra, Muṣʿab was active propagating Islam among the ʿAbd al-Ashhal and Ẓafar clans of the Nabīt group (Aws). The report clearly shows that the clans making up the Aws Allāh group, which also belonged to the Aws, were late to embrace Islam. Ibn Isḥāq's sources are ʿUbaydallāh b. al-Mughīra b. Muʿayqīb and ʿAbdallāh b. Abī Bakr b. Muḥammad b. ʿAmr b. Ḥazm.[4] Hence, Ibn Isḥāq received the same report from both informants. The following

---

of this close relation to the Jews that certain small Arab clans (Khaṭma, Wā'il, Wākif, Umayya b. Zayd, sections of ʿAmr b. ʿAwf) did not at first accept Muḥammad as prophet". It should be remarked that while we do not know whether these groups were large or small, the available genealogical information presents them as part of the *Aws*, not of the old population of Medina.

[3] Contrast Watt, *Medina*, 178 who estimates that what he terms "the pagan opposition" was never "of prime importance in the affairs of Medina" (on p. 179 he speaks of "the bankruptcy of paganism"). The term "pagan" is infelicitious (besides being incongruous to some extent with Watt's correct remarks about the close links between the Aws Allāh and the Jews as the backdrop to their opposition to the Prophet). Watt says: "Those who remained pagans were bitter about the advance of Islam"; but ʿAṣmā' bint Marwān of the Aws Allāh was Jewish (below, 38), and the same is true of Abū ʿAfak of the ʿAmr b. ʿAwf (below, 52). Cf. N.A. Stillman, *The Jews of Arab Lands*, Philadelphia 1979, 13 ("Two pagan poets, one an old man, the other a woman with an infant at her breast, were assassinated for having written satirical verses about him" [= the Prophet]). Also see Watt, "Muḥammad", in P.M. Holt, A.K. Lambton and B. Lewis (eds.), *Cambridge History of Islam*, I, 46; Watt, *Medina*, 328 (in the context of "the alleged moral failures" of the Prophet): "the individuals who were assassinated had forfeited any claim to friendly treatment by Muḥammad through their propaganda against him".

[4] Ibn Hishām, II, 77–80.

passage is introduced by the verb *qālā*, which again indicates that it too reached Ibn Isḥāq from these two sources.

> By God, by the evening every man and woman in the court of the ʿAbd al-Ashhal embraced Islam. Asʿad and Muṣʿab returned to the house of Asʿad b. Zurāra and he [the former] stayed with him, calling upon the people to embrace Islam, until no court of the Anṣār was without Muslim men and women in it. The only exceptions were the courts of the Umayya b. Zayd, Khaṭma, Wā'il and Wāqif, i.e., the Aws Allāh, who are part of the Aws b. Ḥāritha. The reason was that among them was Abū Qays b. al-Aslat [al-Aslat, "one whose nose has been cut off"], whose name was Ṣayfī. He was one of their poets and a leader whose orders they would hear and obey. He prevented them from embracing Islam and they remained like this until the Messenger of God (ṣ) emigrated to Medina and the battles of Badr, Uḥud and the Ditch had taken place.[5]

In this passage, the ʿAbd al-Ashhal are singled out for their quick and total conversion to Islam. The *Sīra Shāmiyya* contains a fuller version of Ibn Isḥāq's report with an important addition which relates to a member of a Jewish clan called B. Zaʿūrā':

[5] Cf. Rahman, "The conflicts between the Prophet and the opposition in Madina", 264 f, where she deals with the "Arab Opposition" to the Prophet without once referring to Abū Qays b. al-Aslat. Also, read Iyās instead of Ayās on p. 267. Saʿd b. Muʿādh and Usayd b. Ḥuḍayr were not "the young leaders of the Aws and Khazraj" (p. 268): they both belonged to the Aws (more precisely, to the ʿAbd al-Ashhal). Read Kulthūm b. al-Hidm instead of Kulthūm b. al-Hadam; read Saʿd b. Khaythama instead of Saʿd b. Khutaym; and Abū Ayyūb instead of Abū Ayūb (269); read al-Mujadhdhar b. Dhiyād instead of al-Mundhir b. Dhiyād (272); read ʿAmr b. Umayya instead of ʿĀmir b. Umayya (283, 284); read Fazāra instead of Fizāra (285). The correct names should first be established.

As we have seen, Abū Qays' name was Ṣayfī. The *Lisān al-ʿarab*, end of s.v. *ṣ.f.y.*, says that the name of Abū Qays b. al-Aslat al-Sulamī(?) was Ṣafī. This seems to be an error, although the mysterious relative adjective, al-Sulamī, may be an attestation to uniqueness and genuineness. Other versions concerning his name are ʿAbdallāh, al-Ḥārith (*TMD* MS, VIII, 392:2,11; *Istīʿāb*, II, 734; IV, 1734) and Ṣirma (*Iṣāba*, VII, 334). On Abū Qays see *GAS*, II, 287.

> By God, by the evening every man and woman in the court of the ʿAbd al-Ashhal became Muslim, except al-Uṣayrim ["the poor little man with a numerous family"],[6] i.e., ʿAmr b. Thābit b. Waqsh.[7] His conversion to Islam was delayed until the Day of Uḥud. Then he embraced Islam and was killed in the Way of God without prostrating himself before God in prayer even once. And the Messenger of God (*ṣ*) said that he was of the people of Paradise.[8]

The information given about al-Uṣayrim/ʿAmr's tribal affiliation shows that he was a member of the Zaʿūrāʾ, a Jewish clan incorporated into the ʿAbd al-Ashhal.[9] His affiliation to the Zaʿūrāʾ of course provides a new context for his refusal to convert to Islam when the rest of the ʿAbd al-Ashhal did so. Obviously, a Medinan audience, which was familiar with these individuals and clans, knew that al-Uṣayrim was a Jew, and so the fact that he only converted at a late date did not tarnish the reputation of the ʿAbd al-Ashhal. His status among the ʿAbd al-Ashhal can be deduced from that of his brother, al-Ḥārith, who was a client (*ḥalīf*) of the Anṣār (i.e., of the ʿAbd al-Ashhal); the same should have been true for him.[10]

---

[6] This is probably a pejorative nickname. He is Uṣayrim B. ʿAbd al-Ashhal; Ibn al-Kalbī, *Jamhara*, 636. There is a lacuna in the text (it also exists in the manuscript of the *Jamhara*) which can be filled with the help of Ibn al-Kalbī, *Nasab Maʿadd*, I, 378: ʿAmr (b. Thābit) was not the brother of Salama b. Salāma b. Waqsh, but of Salama b. Thābit b. Waqsh; in the last-mentioned source read Waqsh instead of Qays, and Zughba instead of Zaghba; see *Iṣāba*, III, 144 (quoting Ibn al-Kalbī); Ibn Durayd, *Ishtiqāq*, 444 f (read ʿAmr instead of ʿUmar).

[7] His grandfather is sometimes called Wuqaysh or Uqaysh.

[8] *Sīra Shāmiyya*, III, 274. Cf. Samh., I, 227–28; Tab., II, 359 [I, 1217]; Ibn Saʿd, III, 118.

[9] Lecker, "Muḥammad at Medina", 44–46; *Iṣāba*, IV, 608–10; *Istīʿāb*, III, 1167; *Usd al-ghāba*, IV, 90–91; Ibn Qudāma, *Istibṣār*, 223; Lecker, "Ḥudhayfa b. al-Yamān and ʿAmmār b. Yāsir, Jewish converts to Islam", the end of section 1.

[10] Under "ʿAmr b. Uqaysh" (omitting the father's name in pedigrees was not uncommon) we find this apologetic explanation of his delayed conversion to Islam: in the Jāhiliyya he was owed money with interest and did not like to embrace Islam before collecting it; Ibn Qudāma, *Istibṣār*, 232 (< Abū

Having discussed these more marginal matters we now return to the Aws Allāh. The lateness of their conversion to Islam is mentioned in different contexts. Some of the reports to be quoted below may admittedly be variations of one and the same report rather than independent pieces of evidence. But then the historical reliability of these reports is confirmed by other evidence to be discussed later in this chapter.

One of the accounts tells us about Medina during the first year or so after the Prophet's arrival:

> And the Messenger of God (ṣ) stayed in Medina from the time of his arrival in the month of Rabīʿ al-Awwal to Ṣafar of the following year, until his mosque and houses had been built for him and the conversion to Islam of the Anṣār had been accomplished. There was no court of the Anṣār whose people did not embrace Islam, except Khaṭma, Wāqif, Wā'il and Umayya; and these are the Aws Allāh, a group of the Aws, who remained pagan.[11]

Dāwūd). This is followed in the *Istibṣār* by an entry on al-Ḥārith b. Uqaysh, who was obviously 'Amr's brother, wrongly said to have been of the 'Ukl or the 'Awf(!) and a *ḥalīf* of the Anṣār. (The *Usd al-ghāba*, I, 315 explains that 'Uklī and 'Awfī are the same thing.) Ibn Sa'd, VII, 67 mentions al-Ḥārith among the Companions of the Prophet who settled in Baṣra; *Istīʿāb*, I, 282. Like 'Amr himself, his brother was of course of the Za'ūrā'. The 'Awf/'Ukl version presumably originates from the confusion caused by the occurrence of "Uqaysh" in the name of the B. Zuhayr b. Uqaysh of the 'Ukl; see Ibn Mākūlā, I, 105.

We also know of yet another Jewish client of the 'Abd al-Ashhal, namely the Jew Yūshaʿ. See, e.g., Abū Nuʿaym al-Iṣfahānī, *Dalā'il al-nubuwwa*[2], ed. Muḥammad Rawwās Qal'ajī and 'Abd al-Barr 'Abbās, Beirut 1406/1986, 79, 74; Suyūṭī, *Khaṣā'iṣ*, I, 66 (*lam yakun fī banī 'Abdi l-Ashhal illā yahūdī wāḥid yuqālu lahu Yūshaʿ*, etc.); Balādh., *Ansāb*, I, 286:1 (*wa-kāna yubashshiru bi-l-nabī [ṣ] fa-lammā buʿitha āmana bihi B. 'Abd al-Ashhal siwāhu*).

[11] *Fa-aqāma rasūlu llāhi (ṣ) bi-l-Madīna idh qadimahā shahra rabīʿi l-awwali ilā ṣafar mina l-sanati l-dākhila ḥattā buniya lahu fīhā masjiduhu wa-masākinuhu wa-'stajmaʿa lahu islāmu hādhā l-ḥayyi mina l-anṣār. Fa-lam yabqa* (*sic*, one expects *tabqa*) *dār min dūri l-anṣār illā aslama ahluhā, illā mā kāna min Khaṭma wa-Wāqif wa-Wā'il wa-Umayya, wa-tilka Aws Allāh, wa-hum ḥayy mina l-Aws, fa-innahum aqāmū 'alā shirkihim*; Ibn Hishām, II, 146.

Wāqidī, in a combined report from four different accounts, again singles out the Aws Allāh clans for not embracing Islam, together with the Khazraj and the rest of the Aws (i.e., the clans belonging to the Nabīt and the ʿAmr b. ʿAwf). For this, Abū Qays b. al-Aslat is blamed:

> By the time the Messenger of God came to Medina, the Khazraj and groups of the Aws had already converted to Islam. [They were the following:] All of the ʿAbd al-Ashhal, Ẓafar, Ḥāritha, Muʿāwiya [these four clans were subdivisions of the Nabīt[12]], and ʿAmr b. ʿAwf. In contrast, the clans of the Aws Allāh, i.e., Wā'il, Khaṭma, Wāqif and Umayya b. Zayd, were with Abū Qays b. al-Aslat. He was their leader as well as a poet and an orator and he used to lead them in war. And he nearly embraced Islam.[13]

Finally, in his genealogical work, Ibn Ḥazm makes a somewhat obscure reference to the conversion of the Aws Allāh. This is found in the section about certain clans of the Aws Allāh group, namely the Murra b. Mālik b. al-Aws. The Murra included the clans of Umayya, Wā'il and ʿAṭiyya. The text is not very smooth and may include an inaccurate gloss printed below in italics:

> And from the descendants of Wā'il: Ṣayfī, the poet, who was [also known as] Abū Qays b. al-Aslat. His conversion to Islam was delayed until the Battle of the Ditch had taken place. And the same was the case with the conversion to Islam of all the Khaṭma, i.e., the Jusham b. Mālik b. al-Aws, all the Wāqif, i.e., the Imru'u l-Qays b. Mālik b. al-Aws, and the Aws Allāh [in general], *who were these clans of the descendants of*

[12] The Muʿāwiya were originally of the ʿAmr b. ʿAwf; Lecker, "Muḥammad at Medina", 44.

[13] Ibn Saʿd, IV, 384: *fa-lammā qadima rasūlu llāhi (ṣ) l-Madīna wa-qad aslamati l-Khazraj wa-ṭawā'ifu mina l-Aws: B. ʿAbd al-Ashhal kulluhā wa-Ẓafar wa-Ḥāritha wa-Muʿāwiya wa-ʿAmr b. ʿAwf, illā mā kāna min Aws Allāh, wa-hum Wā'il wa-B. Khaṭma wa-Wāqif wa-Umayya b. Zayd, maʿa Abī Qays b. al-Aslat, wa-kāna ra'sahā wa-shāʿirahā wa-khaṭībahā wa-kāna yaqūduhum fī l-ḥarb wa-kāna qad kāda an yuslima.* On this claim see Appendix C.

> *Murra b. Mālik b. al-Aws.*[14] The Salm b. Imri'i l-Qays were, however, clients of the 'Amr b. 'Awf b. Mālik b. al-Aws and all of them embraced Islam together with their "brothers", the 'Amr b. 'Awf b. Mālik b. al-Aws, before the Hijra and at the early stages (literally: the beginning) of the Hijra.[15]

When Ibn Ḥazm says that Abū Qays embraced Islam after the Battle of the Ditch (how long after that battle we do not know), we should infer from it that the same is true for the Aws Allāh in general. The role ascribed to Abū Qays b. al-Aslat seems to have been exaggerated. A tribal leader in Medina was no tyrant and the town's conversion to Islam was often a matter of challenging the old, established leadership.[16]

There is evidence of military cooperation before Islam between the Aws Allāh under Abū Qays and the Jewish tribes. In the pre-Islamic War of Sumayr, the Aws Allāh clans (Khaṭma, Wāqif, Wā'il and Umayya), having entered into an alliance with the Jewish Naḍīr and Qurayẓa, fought under the command of Abū Qays. The Jews (i.e., other Jewish clans), we are told, entered into alliances with the clans of the Aws and Khazraj. However,

---

[14] This is inaccurate; as we have seen, the descendants of Murra were only part of the Aws Allāh. Elsewhere Ibn Isḥāq states, in two separate reports, that Abū Qays was a member of the Wāqif and of the Khaṭma, respectively. Both statements seem to be wrong and Ibn Hishām's claim (I, 302; cf. Wellhausen, *Skizzen* IV, 25 n. 1), that the Arabs sometimes related a man to his ancestor's brother if the brother was better known, is an unconvincing attempt to harmonize the conflicting evidence.

[15] Ibn Ḥazm, *Ansāb*, 345: ... *Ṣayfī al-shā'ir, wa-huwa Abū Qays b. al-Aslat, wa-'smu l-Aslat 'Āmir b. Jusham b. Wā'il b. Zayd b. Qays b. 'Āmir b. Murra b. Mālik b. al-Aws, wa-kāna sayyid qawmihi fa-ta'akhkhara islāmuhu ilā an maḍā yawmu l-khandaq. Wa-ta'akhkhara islāmu jumhūri B. Khaṭma ... wa-islāmu jumhūri B. Wāqif ... wa-islāmu Aws Allāh, wa-hum hā'ulā'i l-buṭūn, wa-hum min wuld Murra b. Mālik b. al-Aws, illā anna B. al-Salm b. Imri'i l-Qays kānū ḥulafā' B. 'Amr b. 'Awf ... fa-aslamū kulluhum bi-islāmi ikhwatihim B. 'Amr b. 'Awf ... qabla l-hijra wa-fī awwali l-hijra.* Also see Ibn al-Kalbī, *Jamhara*, 644; Ibn al-Kalbī, *Nasab Ma'add*, 385: *wa-l-Salm, baṭn, ḥulafā' fī B. 'Amr b. 'Awf.* The preposition *fī* prompts me to render *ḥulafā'* as "clients" rather than "allies".

[16] On Abū Qays see also Appendices B and C. Cf. Lecker, "Idol worship in pre-Islamic Medina (Yathrib)", 336 f, 343.

the Qurayẓa and Naḍīr had not made alliances with any of the Aws or Khazraj prior to that battle. Both the Aws and Khazraj sought the aid of the Qurayẓa and Naḍīr who chose to join the Aws. Those Aws who formed an alliance with the Qurayẓa and Naḍīr were the Aws Allāh, viz., Khaṭma, Wāqif, Umayya and Wā'il.[17]

On the late conversion to Islam, a rather dubious report by Ibn al-Qaddāḥ, which is on the whole favourable to Abū Qays, deviates only slightly from the above details. He says: "Badr and Uḥud had taken place and none of the Aws Allāh had embraced Islam except four of the Khaṭma.[18] All of them participated in the Battle of Uḥud and in the later battles and because of this [i.e., because the Aws Allāh were absent from Badr], the Khazraj were more numerous among the participants in the battle" (*fa-li-dhālika dhahabati l-Khazraj bi-l-'idda fīman shahida Badran*).[19] Now, even if we assume that these Khaṭmīs participated in the Battle of Uḥud, this would not change the historical picture.[20]

[17] *Wa-kānat yahūdu qad ḥālafat qabā'ila l-Aws wa-l-Khazraj illā B. Qurayẓa wa-banī l-Naḍīr fa-innahum lam yuḥālifū aḥadan minhum ḥattā kāna hādhā l-jam' ... wa-'llatī ḥālafat Qurayẓa wa-l-Naḍīr mina l-Aws: Aws Allāh, wa-hiya Khaṭma wa-Wāqif wa-Umayya wa-Wā'il, fa-hādhihi qabā'il Aws Allāh*; *Aghānī*, II, 169; Wellhausen, *Skizzen* IV, 38–39. See also Horovitz, "Judaeo-Arabic relations in pre-Islamic times", 178 n. 3 (where the reference is wrong), 179.

[18] They were Khuzayma b. Thābit b. al-Fākih (written: al-Fāṭima), 'Umayr b. 'Adī b. Kharasha, Ḥabīb b. Ḥubāsha and Ḥumayḍa (written: Khamīṣa) b. Ruqaym.

[19] *TMD* MS, VIII, 392; *TMD, Tahdh.*, VI, 456 (who repeats the mistakes in the names). One wonders whether the mention of these Khaṭmīs as participants in Uḥud should be credited to the *mawlā* of the Khaṭma, Abū Sa'd Shuraḥbīl b. Sa'd, an early authority on the *Maghāzī* (d. 123/741); about him see J. Horovitz, "The earliest biographies of the Prophet and their authors", in *Islamic Culture*, 1 (1927), 535–59; 2 (1928), 22–50, 164–82, 495–526, at 1, 552; also *GAS*, I, 279 (instead of Shuraḥbīl b. Sa'īd, read: Shuraḥbīl b. Sa'd).

[20] The above passage contains the only mention of Ḥumayḍa b. Ruqaym; it is quoted from Ibn al-Qaddāḥ in *Usd al-ghāba*, II, 55 and *Iṣāba*, II, 130 (he is called al-Qaddāḥ in the latter source) and al-'Adawī (the compiler of *Nasab al-anṣār*; *Iṣāba*, IV, 446), who obviously have the same text. Unlike the other three, Ḥumayḍa is not mentioned in the section about the Khaṭma in Ibn al-Kalbī, *Jamhara*, 642 f and Ibn Ḥazm, *Ansāb*, 343 f. The three are not said by the two genealogists to have participated in Uḥud, while 'Umayr's

A fifth member of the Aws Allāh said to have participated in the Battle Uḥud was none other than Abū Qays' eldest son,

---

brother, al-Ḥārith b. 'Adī b. Kharasha, is said by both to have been killed in Uḥud. (In Ibn Ḥazm, 343:–2 the words *min shuhadā' Uḥud* are repeated, due to a scribal error, after the mention of 'Umayr b. 'Adī.) However, there is no unanimity about al-Ḥārith. Wāqidī (I, 301 f) does not mention him among the Anṣār killed in Uḥud. The same is true for Ibn Isḥāq, and al-Ḥārith was added by Ibn Hishām (III, 133). A possible source for the claim concerning 'Umayr is his son, 'Abdallāh (or 'Adī), who was one of 'Urwa b. al-Zubayr's informants; *Iṣāba*, IV, 722; cf. *op. cit.*, 200.

As for Khuzayma, his is a special case: besides the claim that Uḥud was his first battle on the Prophet's side (al-Ḥākim al-Naysābūrī, in *Usd al-ghāba*, II, 114:11, having quoted from Ibn al-Qaddāḥ the Uḥud claim, notes the disunity concerning this: *wa-ahlu l-maghāzī lā yuthbitūna annahu shahida Uḥudan, wa-shahida l-mashāhida ba'dahā*), we are even told that he participated in Badr and the later battles; *Iṣāba*, II, 278. A search for his name in the lists of Badrīs would be of no avail (Waq., I, 157 f; Ibn Hishām, II, 342 f); in other words, the claim that he was a Badrī never gained wide acceptance. Possible sources of the Badr claim are Khuzayma's son, 'Umāra b. Khuzayma, and his grandson, Muḥammad b. 'Umāra, who are both quoted regarding him; *Iṣāba*, II, 279. Khuzayma's support for 'Alī (he was killed in Ṣiffīn fighting on his side; see, e.g., *Iṣāba*, II, 279) is plausibly behind the claim that he was a Badrī. Khuzayma's Shī'ite sympathies clearly account for the claim, which should be categorized as anti-Shī'ite, that there were two Khuzayma b. Thābit; one of whom was the famous Companion (nicknamed *Dhū l-Shahādatayni*, "the one whose testimony was declared by the Prophet to have been equivalent to that of two persons"), and another who was in 'Alī's camp. In order to "remove" this prominent Anṣārī from the list of 'Alī's supporters it was vital to "kill" him before the time of Ṣiffīn, so it was claimed that he died at the time of 'Uthmān; *Iṣāba*, II, 279 f.

That the claim concerning the participation of the above Khaṭmīs in Uḥud was not mentioned by the genealogists does not mean that they did not know it, but rather that they did not accept it as historical; cf. the dispute between Ibn al-Kalbī and al-'Adawī in Ibn al-Kalbī, *Jamhara*, 632.

Note that some disputed the Companion status of Ḥabīb b. Ḥubāsha; *Istī'āb*, I, 324 (who calls him Ḥabīb b. Khumāsha; cf. the name Khumāsha already in Ibn Sa'd, IV, 381, s.v. 'Umayr b. Ḥabīb b. Ḥubāsha); admittedly, it was not disputed by Ibn al-Kalbī and Ibn Ḥazm. In the above-mentioned entry in the biographical dictionary of Ibn Sa'd, the Baṣran Ḥammād b. Zayd quotes Abū Ja'far al-Khaṭmī < his father < his grandfather, 'Umayr b. Ḥabīb. Abū Ja'far was 'Umayr b. Yazīd b. 'Umayr b. Ḥabīb b. Khumāsha/ Ḥubāsha al-Khaṭmī; Yaḥyā b. Ma'īn, *Ma'rifat al-rijāl*, ed. Muḥammad Kāmil al-Qaṣṣār, Damascus 1405/1985, II, 112 (cf. 191); *Tahdh.*, VIII, 151 (it is claimed that his grandfather, 'Umayr b. Ḥabīb, and his great-grandfather on

Qays.[21] But this assertion merits no more confidence than the others.

We may safely assume that many Khazrajīs had already committed themselves to the cause of Islam before the Hijra. There were Muslims among the Aws from the Nabīt and the ʿAmr b. ʿAwf.

Early converts to Islam among the Aws Allāh

Not all the Aws Allāh converted to Islam after the Battle of the Ditch. There were two tribal groups of the Aws Allāh that had converted at an earlier date. But these groups do not weaken the reliability of the statements on the delayed conversion of the other Aws Allāh groups. On the contrary, both groups no longer lived in the territory of the Aws Allāh, and it is this fact which explains their different attitude to the Prophet.

THE CASE OF THE SALM

As we have just seen, Ibn Ḥazm wrote that the B. al-Salm b. Imriʾi l-Qays were clients of the ʿAmr b. ʿAwf and that all of them embraced Islam with their "brothers", the ʿAmr b. ʿAwf, before the Hijra and at the early stages of the Hijra. The Salm's move from the territory of the Aws Allāh in the eastern ʿĀliya to Qubāʾ in the western ʿĀliya led them to become clients of the ʿAmr b. ʿAwf. The shift was reportedly a result of a breach between the two brother-clans, Wāqif and al-Salm, following a quarrel between their two eponyms. It is reported that al-Salm and Wāqif shared the same court. They then quarrelled, and the younger brother al-Salm settled among the ʿAmr b. ʿAwf (i.e., in Qubāʾ), amongst whom his children remained.[22]

---

his mother's side, al-Fākih b. Saʿd, were Companions; it is not hard to guess the source of this claim).

[21] *TMD* MS, VIII, 392:-3.

[22] Samh., I, 196:3 (printed: al-Salam). Wellhausen, *Skizzen* IV, 25 says: "Einige Sippen der Mar'alqais jedoch, namentlich die Salm, hatten sich den Thaʿlaba von Amr b. Auf angeschlossen, welche in der Mitte zwischen Ausallah und Amr b. Auf wohnten und eine Art Übergang zwischen den beiden Gruppen bildeten". In a footnote he mentions: "In dem Verzeichnis der Badrkämpfer werden indessen die Ghanm b. al-Salm b. Mar'alqais als eigenes

The Salm reached Qubā' long enough before the Hijra to build a fortress there since Ibn Zabāla reports that the Salm had a *ḥiṣn* to the east of the Mosque of Qubā'.[23] As might be expected, the Salm married into the 'Amr b. 'Awf: some ten years before the Hijra Sa'd b. Khaythama married into what was probably the most important family in Qubā'. Sa'd's wife Jamīla was the daughter of Abū 'Āmir al-Rāhib of the B. Ḍubay'a and she bore him a son, 'Abdallāh, who participated in the expeditions of Ḥudaybiyya and Khaybar (at the end of 6 and the beginning of 7 A.H., respectively).[24]

When the Prophet came to Qubā', the Salm were there; we have been told that their conversion to Islam occurred "before the Hijra and at the beginning of the Hijra". Sa'd b. Khaythama of al-Salm, for example,[25] was in Qubā'.[26] Sa'd was an important figure. He was one of the five members of the 'Amr b. 'Awf who participated in the great 'Aqaba meeting where he is said to have been a *naqīb*.[27]

Geschlecht angesehen und den Tha'laba beigeordnet". I could not find Wellhausen's source for the statements that the Salm were specifically linked with the Tha'laba and that the latter were located as he says. Cf. the list of Badrīs in Ibn Hishām, II, 347; Wāqidī, I, 161.

[23] Samh., I, 196.

[24] See Lecker, "The Anṣārī wives of 'Umar b. al-Khaṭṭāb and his brother, Zayd" (forthcoming), section 2.2 (Jamīla bint Abī 'Āmir). 'Abdallāh b. Sa'd b. Khaythama married a granddaughter of Ibn Ubayy, Umāma bint 'Abdallāh b. 'Abdallāh b. Ubayy b. Salūl; Ibn Sa'd, IV, 382.

[25] Whose mother was of the Aws Allāh clan B. Khaṭma; Ibn Sa'd, VIII, 354.

[26] See, e.g., Ibn Hishām, II, 122.

[27] The list of 'Aqabīs in Ibn Hishām, II, 99 mentions among the *naqībs* both Sa'd b. Khaythama of the Salm and Rifā'a b. 'Abd al-Mundhir of the 'Amr b. 'Awf subdivision named Umayya b. Zayd, implying that they were both in charge of the 'Amr b. 'Awf. This may well be the result of Ibn Isḥāq's harmonization of contradictory claims made by the two respective families (or clans). Cf. Ibn Sa'd, VIII, 354: Sa'd was the *naqīb* (by implication: the only *naqīb*) of the 'Amr b. 'Awf. The claim that Sa'd was a *naqīb* comes unambiguously from his family: al-Mughīra b. Ḥakīm (al-Ṣan'ānī al-Abnāwī; *Tahdh.*, X, 258) asked 'Abdallāh b. Sa'd b. Khaythama whether he had participated in Badr. 'Abdallāh replied: "Yes, and in the 'Aqaba as well. I rode behind my father on the back of his camel, and he was a *naqīb*"; *Iṣāba*, III, 55. But cf. *Iṣāba*, IV, 108 (where Badr is replaced by Uḥud). On Badr see also Ibn Ḥabīb, *Muḥabbar*, 403.

On the whole, the evidence shows that the Salm preserved their original Aws Allāh genealogy even after they were separated from the Aws Allāh and settled in Qubā'. In their genealogical works, Ibn al-Kalbī and Ibn Ḥazm list the Salm as members of the Aws Allāh.[28] The list of Awsī women who pledged their allegiance to the Prophet is concluded with the names of women of the Aws Allāh, the very last being from among al-Salm b. Imri'i l-Qays b. Murra (!) b. Mālik b. al-Aws.[29]

---

[28] Ibn Ḥazm, *Ansāb*, 345; Ibn al-Kalbī, *Jamhara*, 644.

[29] Ibn Sa'd, VIII, 358. It is true that in Ibn Isḥāq's list of *nuqabā'* in the 'Aqaba meeting, Sa'd b. Khaythama is given a pedigree (unfortunately, it is partial) going back to 'Amr b. 'Awf. (In Ibn Isḥāq's list of the Muslims killed at Badr, Sa'd b. Khaythama is a member of the 'Amr b. 'Awf; Ibn Hishām, II, 364.) Ibn Hishām gives Sa'd the old Aws Allāh pedigree (...b. Ghanm b. al-Salm b. Imri'i l-Qays). He rejects the 'Amr b. 'Awf pedigree given by Ibn Isḥāq, remarking that Sa'd was in fact of the Ghanm b. al-Salm. Ibn Hishām's argumentation is convincing. He explains that often when a man was included in the fighting unit of a certain clan (literally: when his battle-cry was "within" a certain clan) and he lived in its court, he was (wrongly) considered one of them; Ibn Hishām, II, 99: *wa-nasabahu bnu Isḥāq fī B. 'Amr b. 'Awf, wa-huwa min B. Ghanm b. al-Salm, liannahu rubbamā kānat da'watu l-rajuli fī l-qawm wa-yakūnu fīhim fa-yunsabu ilayhim.* For entries on Sa'd see the following Companion dictionaries: *Iṣāba*, III, 55; *Usd al-ghāba*, II, 275; *Istī'āb*, II, 588. The last two refer to the dispute over his pedigree. And see the fragments recorded in Ṭabarānī, *Kabīr*, VI, 29f (the entry on Sa'd): the list of 'Aqaba participants going back to Zuhrī (via Mūsā b. 'Uqba) mentions Sa'd as a *naqīb* of the 'Amr b. 'Awf. Another report in Ṭabarānī, *having the same isnād*, again going back to Mūsā b. 'Uqba < Zuhrī, is a fragment from the list of Badrīs. We are told here that Sa'd was of the 'Amr b. al-Salm b. Mālik b. al-Aws (this genealogy is enigmatic). Of special interest are two fragments from the list of Badrīs going back to 'Urwa b. al-Zubayr via Ibn Lahī'a. (Also the rest of their *isnād* is identical.) These fragments make contradictory claims concerning Sa'd's pedigree: in one he is a member of the 'Amr b. 'Awf, while in the other he belongs to the Ghanm b. al-Salm b. Mālik b. al-Aws b. Ḥāritha (printed: Jāriya). Assuming that 'Urwa was really the source of the two conflicting reports, we may conclude that Sa'd's genealogy was already disputed towards the end of the first century A.H.

Cf. the pedigree of a female Companion from this very clan showing her to be a member of the Aws Allāh: Khayra bint Abī Umayya of al-Salm b. Imri'i l-Qays (or of al-Ghanm b. al-Salm); *Iṣāba*, VII, 629; Ibn Sa'd, VIII, 358. The same is true of the Companion al-Mundhir b. Qudāma b. 'Arfaja; *Iṣāba*, VI, 218; *Istī'āb*, IV, 1451; *Usd al-ghāba*, IV, 419 (of the Ghanm b. al-Salm, etc.).

Because by the time of the Hijra the Salm had long ceased to be part of the Aws Allāh, who remained indifferent if not hostile to the Prophet, the former took part in the major events of the nascent Islamic community. They sheltered some of the Muhājirūn in Qubā', and participated in battles and in the *mu'ākhāt*, or "brothering", between the Muhājirūn and the Anṣār. Five of the Salm took part in Badr, including Sa'd b. Khaythama who was killed in the battle. They appear in the list of participants with their Aws Allāh pedigree (B. Ghanm b. al-Salm b. Imri'i l-Qays b. Mālik b. al-Aws) between two subdivisions of 'Amr b. 'Awf.[30] The rest of the Aws Allāh (with the exception of the group discussed below) had no role in the 'Aqaba or any other Islamic activity during the first half of the Prophet's Medinan period.

The Salm steadily declined and the last of them perished at the time of Hārūn al-Rashīd[31] or, more precisely, in the year 200 A.H.[32]

THE CASE OF THE SA'ĪD B. MURRA

The other Aws Allāh group which took part in the major events prior to the Battle of the Ditch was the Sa'īd b. Murra b. Mālik b. al-Aws. As in the case of the Salm this shift away from the policies of the Aws Allāh towards the Prophet can be explained with reference to the fact that at some stage before the Hijra, the Sa'īd stopped being part of the Aws Allāh.

Three brothers from among the Sa'īd b. Murra participated in the Battle of Uḥud. Ḥājib, Ḥubāb and Ḥabīb, the sons of Zayd b. Taym b. Umayya b. Bayāḍa b. Khufāf b. Sa'īd b. Murra, took part in the Battle of Uḥud and Ḥabīb was killed there.[33]

---

[30] Waq., I, 161; Ibn Hishām, II, 347. Similarly, the lists of Badrīs by Wāqidī, 'Abdallāh b. Muḥammad b. 'Umāra al-Anṣārī (Ibn al-Qaddāḥ, *GAS*, I, 268) and Ibn al-Kalbī provide the Aws Allāh pedigree; Mūsā b. 'Uqba and Ibn Isḥāq, while listing the participants of the Ghanm b. al-Salm (= the Salm), do not go beyond their fathers; see Ibn Sa'd, III, 481.

[31] Ibn Ḥazm, *Ansāb*, 345.

[32] Ibn Sa'd, III, 481.

[33] Ibn Qudāma, *Istibṣār*, 275. Ḥubāb was killed in the Battle of Yamāma during the *ridda* wars. Ibn al-Kalbī, *Jamhara*, 648 only mentions Ḥubāb killed in Yamāma, but a MS of the *Jamhara* (Br. Lib. Add. 22346, 56b) also refers to

The participation of three members of the Saʿīd b. Murra in the Battle of Uḥud, and presumably their conversion and the conversion of others of the Saʿīd to Islam, indicate that they allied themselves with the Prophet when the rest of the Aws Allāh were still hostile (or at least indifferent) to him. This does not contradict the report that the Aws Allāh as a whole converted only after the Battle of the Ditch. The conversion of the Saʿīd b. Murra, probably one of the smallest and least important clans in Medina, should be explained with reference to the geography of Medina and the genealogy of the Aws, and more specifically the divisions within the Murra b. Mālik b. al-Aws.[34] The information on the Murra includes two prominent elements: the place-name "Rātij", and the tribal appellative "al-Jaʿādir(a)". Ibn al-Kalbī says:

> And Murra b. Mālik b. al-Aws bore ʿĀmira and Saʿīd,[35] and they [i.e., the descendants of Saʿīd] are the people of Rātij, a fortress in Medina (*wa-walada Murra b. Mālik b. al-Aws ʿĀmira wa-Saʿīd wa-hum ahl Rātij, uṭum bi-l-Madīna*).

Ḥubāb's brother Ḥabīb who was killed in Uḥud. The Companion dictionaries report, in the entries on the above-mentioned Ḥājib, about his participation in Uḥud (< Ṭabarī); see *Iṣāba*, I, 561 which quotes, besides Ṭabarī, also Ibn Shāhīn (who correctly calls Ḥājib "al-Awsī", adding: *thumma al-Bayāḍī*, as if he were a member of the Khazrajī B. Bayāḍa [!]); *Usd al-ghāba*, I, 315 (who wrongly calls him al-Khazrajī al-Bayāḍī); *Istīʿāb*, I, 281. In the entries on Ḥabīb it is mentioned that he was killed in Uḥud; see *Iṣāba*, II, 19, quoting Ibn Shāhīn; *Usd al-ghāba*, I, 370; *Istīʿāb*, I, 319 (in all three entries, instead of Tamīm read: Taym; instead of Usayd read: Umayya; also, contrary to what we are told in the entries, Ḥabīb was not of the Bayāḍa). For entries on al-Ḥubāb see *Iṣāba*, II, 8 (Ibn Shāhīn: he participated in Uḥud and was killed in Yamāma; but Ibn Ḥajar objects to this, saying that Ibn al-Kalbī does not report that he was killed in Yamāma [!]); *Usd al-ghāba*, I, 363 (both the *Iṣāba* and *Usd al-ghāba* have a full pedigree going back to Saʿd b. Murra/Saʿīd b. Murra, respectively); *Istīʿāb*, I, 317.

[34] See a discussion on this clan in Lecker, "Muḥammad at Medina", 47–48. The following conclusions are slightly different from those of the above-noted article.

[35] In Ibn al-Kalbī, *Jamhara*, 646, 648 and Ibn al-Kalbī, *Nasab Maʿadd*, I, 387, 389 the name is vocalized Suʿayd.

He goes on:

> And ʿĀmira bore Qays, and Qays bore Zayd, a *baṭn* [i.e., a small and autonomous tribal group[36]] and Zayd bore Wāʾil, a *baṭn*. Wāʾil b. Zayd bore Jusham, and Jusham bore ʿĀmir, nicknamed al-Aslat. And [Zayd also bore] Umayya, a *baṭn*, and ʿAṭiyya, another *baṭn*. And they are the Jaʿādir. [He also bore] Sālim, who died childless (*daraja*). One of the Wāʾil was the poet Abū Qays Ṣayfī[37] b. al-Aslat/ʿĀmir b. Jusham who had a brother called Waḥwaḥ.[38]

Ibn al-Kalbī's wording indicates that the Jaʿādir(a) were the descendants of Zayd b. Qays b. ʿĀmira b. Murra and his three sons, Wāʾil, Umayya and ʿAṭiyya. In other words, they were the subdivisions (*buṭūn*) of the ʿĀmira branch, not the Saʿīd branch, of the Murra. A passage in a compilation by the genealogist of the Anṣār, Ibn al-Qaddāḥ (ʿAbdallāh b. Muḥammad b. ʿUmāra) who died towards the end of the second Islamic century,[39] points in the same direction. He wrote that Murra b. Mālik had three sons, ʿĀmira, Saʿīd and Māzin.[40] ʿĀmira bore Qays and Qays had Zayd, about whom Ibn al-Qaddāḥ says: *wa-kāna yuqālu lahu Jaʿdar*. This is not mentioned elsewhere. Ibn al-Qaddāḥ continues: Zayd had Wāʾil, Umayya and ʿAṭiyya. This we already know from the other sources, but what follows concerns us

[36] Ibn Zabāla's information on the tribal territories in Medina is arranged according to tribal subgroups which he calls *buṭūn*; see, e.g., Samh., I, 207: *wa-ammā B. ʿAdhāra b. Mālik b. Ghaḍb b. Jusham, fa-kānū aqalla buṭūn B. Mālik b. Ghaḍb ʿadadan ...fa-qatalū qatīlan min baʿḍ buṭūn B. Mālik b. Ghaḍb ....* Note the association between *baṭn* and *masjid* with regard to the *buṭūn* of Kinda that settled in Kūfa; M. Lecker, "Kinda on the eve of Islam and during the *ridda*", in *JRAS* 1994 (forthcoming), section 2.4.

[37] The MS has "b. Ṣayfī", but the "b." is superfluous.

[38] A few other members of this family are mentioned; Ibn al-Kalbī, *Jamhara*, 646 f. The MS of Ibn al-Kalbī's *Jamhara* (which I employed when I wrote "Muḥammad at Medina", Br. Lib. Add. 22346, 56a–b) is almost identical, with ʿĀmir and Saʿīda instead of ʿĀmira and Saʿīd, and al-Jaʿādira instead of al-Jaʿādir (this is simply a variant).

[39] Above, 31n.

[40] The diacritical points are missing; Māzin is of interest because he is not mentioned in the other sources.

more: *wa-hā'ulā'i l-thalātha humu l-Ja'ādira.*[41] Elsewhere, we find confirmation that the Wā'il and the Umayya were part of the Ja'ādir(a).[42] But then we are also told, in contrast to the evidence just adduced, that the Murra as a whole, *including* the Sa'īd b. Murra, were called al-Ja'ādir(a).[43] It seems that the question of whether the tribal appellative, al-Ja'ādir(a), applied to all of the Murra or only to part of them must be left open for the time being.

The key to the problem of the Sa'īd b. Murra's dissent from the policies of the Aws Allāh is the place-name Rātij. I previously wrote that: "All of the Banū Murra, the descendants of both 'Āmir[44] and Sa'd,[45] inhabited Rātij".[46] I now realize that

---

[41] *TMD* MS, VIII, 392. Ibn Ḥazm inaccurately says (*Ansāb*, 345) that the Murra b. Mālik were the Ja'ādira; cf. the text, which is not smooth, in Ibn al-Kalbī, *Nasab Ma'add*, I, 364: *wa-Murra, wa-hum ahlu l-Ja'ādir, laqab, kāna yulaqqabu Ja'daran.* In fact, as we have seen the Ja'ādir(a) were only the descendants of 'Āmir/'Āmira.

[42] Each of the following reports relates to family links between the Ja'ādir(a) and the Ḥanash, a subdivision of the 'Amr b. 'Awf: a woman of the *Wā'il* b. Zayd (who married a Ḥanashī) is said to have been of the Ja'ādir(a); Ibn Sa'd, VIII, 352; the mother of Sahl b. Ḥunayf of the Ḥanash was of the *Umayya* b. Zayd, of the Ja'ādir(a). (The last-mentioned woman was also married in the Ḍubay'a of the 'Amr b. 'Awf: she was the mother of 'Abdallāh and al-Nu'mān, the sons of Abū Ḥabība b. al-Az'ar b. Zayd b. al-'Aṭṭāf b. Ḍubay'a; Ibn Sa'd, III, 471. Cf. the links between the Ḥanash and the Ḍubay'a in connection with the Ḍirār Mosque; below, Ch. 4.)

[43] "Muḥammad at Medina", 47. Also Ibn Qudāma, *Istibṣār*, 204 says that the Murra are the same as Ja'ādira. Cf. Caskel, *Ǧamharat an-Nasab*, II, 248 (the Ja'ādir[a] are the 'Āmira b. Murra but the name is often used to indicate the Murra as a whole). Wüstenfeld, *Medina*, 32 wrongly renders a passage from Samhūdī (I, 176), giving the impression that the Aws Allāh were in fact the Aws as a whole. Samhūdī: *fa-walada l-Aws Mālikan wa-min Mālik qabā'ilu l-Aws kulluhā, fa-wulida li-Mālik 'Amr wa-'Awf wa-Murra, wa-yuqālu lahum Aws Allāh, wa-humu l-Ja'ādira, summū bi-dhālika l-qiṣar fīhim*; translated: "el-Aus hatte nur einen Sohn Mâlik, dieser aber vier Söhne 'Amr, 'Auf, Murra und Ǵuscham [who is not mentioned in my edition of Samhūdī; a fifth son of Mālik, Imru'u l-Qays, should also be added], welche zusammen Ausallah genannt werden; sie heissen auch el-Ǵa'âdira d.i. die kleinen, weil sie meist von kleiner Statur werden". Cf. Ibn al-Kalbī, *Jamhara*, 621 (*wa-l-ja'ādir sūd qiṣār*).

[44] Or 'Āmira.

[45] Or Sa'īd or Su'ayd or Sa'īda.

[46] Lecker, "Muḥammad at Medina", 47.

the statement of the 'Āmir (or 'Āmira) having lived in Rātij is mistaken. What Ibn al-Kalbī probably meant (*wa-walada Murra b. Mālik b. al-Aws 'Āmira wa-Sa'īd wa-hum ahl Rātij*), was that the descendants of Sa'īd, but not those of 'Āmira, were "the people of Rātij" (in fact they were one of the components in the population of Rātij). Rātij was *in the Sāfila*; in other words, the branch of the Murra which sent three warriors to Uḥud did not live with the rest of the Murra and the other Aws Allāh clans in the 'Āliya. Being close to the "territorial basis" of the Prophet[47] and surrounded by his supporters, the Sa'īd converted to Islam earlier than the rest of the Aws Allāh. In short, there is no conflict between the case of the Sa'īd and the belated conversion to Islam of the rest of the Aws Allāh.[48] Like other groups living in Rātij, the Sa'īd were "adopted" by the nearby 'Abd al-Ashhal, and this was done by giving them an 'Abd al-Ashhal genealogy.[49]

The case of the Sa'īd shows that an acquaintance with the geography of Medina and the genealogy of its clans can take us beyond the *sīra* accounts.

The late conversion to Islam of the Aws Allāh was a major factor in the politics of Medina during the first five years of the decade the Prophet spent there. When we look at the map of Medina we immediately realize that a significant part of the town was in those years beyond the Prophet's reach. It seems plausible that were it not for the Naḍīr and Qurayẓa, the Aws Allāh would have been unable to withstand the pressure to convert to Islam. It is no accident that the Battle of the Ditch (and, it may be added, the fall of the Qurayẓa immediately after the battle), is given as the last major event before the Aws Allāh's conversion to Islam.

The Aws Allāh clans and the Prophet

The literature on the Prophet's life focuses on clans and individuals who supported him, and on his enemies however great

[47] Lecker, "Muḥammad at Medina", 59.

[48] For marriage links between the Sa'īd b. Murra and the Salima (who also lived in the Sāfila) see Ibn Sa'd, VIII, 358.

[49] Lecker, "Muḥammad at Medina", 47.

or small. Between these groups was a third category which we should be aware of, although it is hardly mentioned: the many non-participants, those who waited on the sidelines to see how things would develop. Perhaps they were a silent majority. They did not stand to gain much if Islam succeeded, and would be little hurt in case of failure.[50] The uneven coverage of Medina in the *sīra* means that no judgement concerning the relative size and strength of its clans can be based on the *sīra* reports.

As we saw above, the Salm participated in the important events of the nascent Islamic community and some of the Saʿīd fought in Uḥud. The rest of the Aws Allāh are simply not mentioned in connection with these events. This strongly supports the account of their belated conversion to Islam. That the Aws Allāh were absent from these events during the first few years of the Islamic era can be seen from the third volume of Ibn Saʿd, which includes entries on the warriors of Badr. It has valuable data on the Muhājirūn's stay after their Hijra with various Anṣār. These data, which are sometimes contradictory, do not relate to the Aws Allāh.[51] With the exceptions noted above, none of them fought on the Prophet's side in any battle (though some fought against him), and none of them is known to have been part of the *mu'ākhāt*, or "brothering", between the Muhājirūn and the Anṣār during the first year after the Hijra. No marriage links could be found between the Aws Allāh and the Muhājirūn. Finally, the Aws Allāh did not share in the spoils from the Qurayẓa immediately after the Battle of the Ditch.[52]

[50] Cf., for example, Ibn al-Kalbi's comment concerning some tribal groups related to the Aws and Khazraj: *kulluhum anṣār bi-l-Madīna, wa-laysa kulluhum naṣara, wa-innamā naṣarat Rifāʿa*, etc.; Ibn al-Kalbī, *Jamhara*, 619.

[51] Cf. Watt, *Medina*, 175, who correctly remarks: "The second or great meeting of al-ʿAqabah was attended by men from all the clans of the Aws and Khazraj with the exception of Aws Manāt" (= Aws Allāh; Wellhausen, *Skizzen* IV, 24, 51).

[52] Other groups of the Aws received their share: one portion went to the ʿAbd al-Ashhal, Ẓafar, Ḥāritha and Muʿāwiya of the Nabīt group. Another went to the ʿAmr b. ʿAwf "and those who remained of the Aws" (it would seem far-fetched to suggest that this ambiguous formulation refers to the Aws Allāh); Waq., II, 521.

In view of all this, one expects to find many of the Aws Allāh in the lists of *munāfiqūn*, yet they include only one. But then *nifāq* was often (though not invariably) a rather mild form of opposition. Moreover, a *munāfiq* is one who declares himself to be Muslim.[53] This was not the case with the alienated Aws Allāh. The single member of the Aws Allāh in the lists of *munāfiqūn* is Qays b. Rifā'a of the Wāqif while most of the *munāfiqūn* among the Aws belonged to the 'Amr b. 'Awf and several to the Nabīt.[54] *Nifāq* may have been an indication of internal differences within the clan itself over the attitude to be adopted towards the new religion. It did not occur when the whole clan refrained from embracing Islam. *Nifāq* was widespread in Qubā' in the western 'Āliya, which was the only part of the 'Āliya not controlled by the Aws Allāh or the Jewish Naḍīr and Qurayẓa. There the Prophet gained a foothold at an early stage, but the internal strife went on for years. The obscure Ḍirār Mosque incident (below, Ch. 4) shows that even as late as 9 A.H. the struggle for Qubā' was not over yet (or, to use the language of the traditional sources, "the *munāfiqūn* there were still numerous"). While it is no doubt true that some of the *munāfiqūn* were simply converted (or outwardly converted) Jews and that the Naḍīr and Qurayẓa had supported the opposition until they were expelled or killed, the continued opposition to the Prophet's authority in Qubā' must have been motivated by factors deeper than sympathy for the vanquished Jewish allies.

As has already been observed, the role given to Abū Qays b. al-Aslat seems exaggerated. It cannot of course be denied that he was the most prominent leader among the Aws Allāh. Reasons for resisting change in the existing order are never in

---

[53] M.J. Kister recently emphasized the economic aspect in the attitude of the *munāfiqūn*, whom he defined as "a group of Medinans who had outwardly converted to Islam, but who had remained loyal to their former allies, faithful to their Jāhilī ideals and their tribal relations"; Kister, "The massacre of the Banū Qurayẓa", 88 (their former allies were the Jews) .

[54] On Qays b. Rifā'a (there are other versions concerning his name) see *GAS*, II, 296–97; Muḥammad b. 'Imrān al-Marzubānī, *Mu'jam al-shu'arā'*, ed. F. Krenkow, Cairo 1354/1935 (bound together with al-Āmidī, *al-Mu'talif wa-l-mukhtalif*), 322. See the lists in Ibn Ḥabīb, *Muḥabbar*, 467–70; Ibn Hishām, II, 166–74; Balādh., *Ansāb*, I, 275–83.

short supply. Besides, the established tribal leaders of Medina realized that the power accumulated by the Prophet minimized their own role in Medinan politics and enabled him to create new leaderships by providing opportunities to people from outside the leading families to gain prestige and influence, either through their unconditional support and loyalty or through valour on the battlefield.

Besides his association with the Jews, Abū Qays b. al-Aslat had close ties with Mecca. Mecca was, for some time at least, his second home. He had a Qurashī wife, Arnab bint Asad b. ʿAbd al-ʿUzzā, and he would stay with his wife in Mecca for years on end.[55]

VERSES REFLECTING A DIVIDED MEDINA AFTER THE HIJRA

The Jewish poetess ʿAṣmāʾ bint Marwān (presumably an Arab proselyte), was assassinated shortly after the Battle of Badr, in the nineteenth month after the Hijra.[56] The bitter and somewhat obscene poetical exchange between her and Ḥassān b. Thābit reflects a Medina split over its attitude to the Prophet.[57]

ʿAṣmāʾ belonged to the Umayya b. Zayd. There were two clans of this name in the ʿĀliya, one in Qubāʾ among the ʿAmr b. ʿAwf, and the other in the eastern ʿĀliya among the Aws

---

[55] Ibn Qudāma, *Istibṣār*, 271: *wa-kāna yuḥibbu Qurayshan, wa-kāna lahum ṣihran, kānat ʿindahu Arnab bint Asad b. ʿAbd al-ʿUzzā, wa-kāna yuqīmu ʿindahumu l-sinīna bi-ʾmraʾatihi.* See also Rubin, "Ḥanīfiyya", 93. Note that her pedigree is not in order (it is too short). Cf. the list of Asad b. ʿAbd al-ʿUzzā's children in Ibn Ḥazm, *Ansāb*, 117; Ibn al-Kalbī, *Jamhara*, 68–69.

[56] Zurqānī, I, 453:17; Balādh., *Ansāb*, I, 373:4. Contrast the Prophet's "firm but gentle handling of the [Muslim] opposition" (i.e., of the *Munāfiqūn*) in Watt, *Medina*, 183 with his "stern attitude towards the Jews when they rejected his appeals" in Watt, *op. cit.*, 204. Watt explains that it "was not simply pique at this rejection, but the reaction of a man in danger to those whose ill will is causing this danger". With a touch of malice I wish to quote in this context Rahman, "The conflicts between the Prophet and the opposition in Madina", 282: "Composing satiric poems was a hazardous occupation. An offended party or individual might have reacted too strongly to an offence" ...

[57] The generous quotations of adversaries' verses reveal the historical consciousness of the Arabs; Nöldeke, "Die Tradition über das Leben Muhammeds", 165–66.

Allāh.[58] One source explicitly states that she belonged to the ʿAmr b. ʿAwf,[59] but in fact ʿAṣmāʾ was of the lesser-known Umayya b. Zayd who were part of the Aws Allāh: first, they were presumably then more hostile to the Prophet; second, she was married to a man of an Aws Allāh clan; and third, Ḥassān b. Thābit responds to her verses by attacking the Aws Allāh clans. Her husband was a member of the Khaṭma and his name was Yazīd b. Zayd b. Ḥiṣn al-Khaṭmī.[60] Her assassin was also a Khaṭmī.[61]

ʿAṣmāʾ's *hijāʾ* verses are purely political and the names of clans they contain reflect the political division of Medina around the time of Badr (2 A.H.). ʿAṣmāʾ attacks the B. Mālik, al-Nabīt, ʿAwf and B. al-Khazraj. Ḥassān responds by assailing the B. Wāʾil, B. Wāqif and Khaṭma, in other words, he attacks the Aws Allāh group. (True, the presumed clan of the poetess herself, the Umayya b. Zayd, is missing; but this is verse, not genealogical evidence.)

The identification of the clans attacked by ʿAṣmāʾ as supporters of the Prophet is less straightforward. She mentions the Khazraj (as a whole) and three other groups. The Nabīt are the well-known Aws group whose main component is the ʿAbd al-Ashhal. The ʿAwf are the ʿAmr b. ʿAwf of Qubāʾ. In other words, between them the verses account for all five branches of the Aws: the Nabīt and the ʿAmr b. ʿAwf are with the Prophet, whilst the three branches of the Aws Allāh oppose him (Murra = "Wāʾil" in Ḥassān's verses, Imruʾu l-Qays = "Wāqif" and Jusham = "Khaṭma").[62]

---

[58] As already noticed by Wellhausen, *Skizzen* IV, 48, n. 1; 61, n. 4; 63, n. 3.

[59] *Istīʿāb*, III, 1218 (quoting al-Hajarī, on whom see Ḥamad al-Jāsir, *Abū ʿAlī al-Hajarī wa-abḥāthuhu fī taḥdīd al-mawāḍiʿ*, Riyāḍ 1388/1968).

[60] Ibn Saʿd, II, 27; Waq., I, 172; Ibn Hishām, IV, 285:14. For another marriage link between these Umayya b. Zayd and the Khaṭma see Ibn Saʿd, IV, 374. (For a marriage link between the Umayya b. Zayd and the Wāqif see Ibn Saʿd, III, 460.)

[61] Ibn al-Kalbī, *Jamhara*, 642; Ibn al-Kalbī, *Nasab Maʿadd*, I, 384 (where the fact that she was Jewish is not mentioned); Ibn Durayd, *Ishtiqāq*, 447. The assassin's name in the last source, Ghishmīr b. Kharasha, could be a *lectio difficilior* for ʿUmayr [b. ʿAdī] b. Kharasha; but no support for this could be found and Ibn Ḥajar (*Iṣāba*, V, 345) argues strongly that Ibn Durayd is wrong.

[62] Waq., I, 172–74; Ḥassān, *Dīwān*, I, 449. The ʿAmr b. ʿAwf were also

There remains the problem of the B. Mālik mentioned by the poetess. The Mālik seem to be superfluous because even without them the clans referred to by the two poets correspond to the subdivisions of the Aws and Khazraj. Mālik is Mālik b. al-Aws, the father of all the branches of Aws. In other words, the Mālik correspond to the Aws as a whole. In a famous verse in a military context, the Aws Allāh leader, Abū Qays b. al-Aslat, boasts of his managing the affairs of the main part of the Mālik (i.e., the Aws):

> *asʿā ʿalā julli Banī Mālikin kulli mriʾin fī shaʾnihi sāʿi*
> "I labour on behalf of the main part of the Children of Mālik every man labours for the cause that is his".[63]

The poem in question relates to the Battle of Buʿāth in which, as Ibn al-Kalbī informs us, the Aws "rested upon Abū Qays their affair" (*qad asnadū amrahum ... ilā Abī Qays b. al-Aslat al-Wāʾilī*).[64] Elsewhere Ibn al-Kalbī interprets the B. Mālik of the above verse as the B. Mālik b. al-Aws.[65] Of course ʿAṣmāʾ

---

referred to as the ʿAwf. Cf., e.g., Ibn Ḥazm, *Ansāb*, 332: *fa-walada Mālik b. al-Aws ...: ʿAwf b. Mālik b. al-Aws wa-hum ahl Qubāʾ*; see the same in Ibn al-Kalbī, *Nasab Maʿadd*, I, 364.

[63] Ch.J. Lyall, *The Mufaḍḍalīyāt: An Anthology of Ancient Arabian Odes*, Oxford 1921–24, II, 226 (no. LXXV^{5}).

[64] *Aghānī*, XV, 161:9. According to another version, the poem relates to the War of Ḥāṭib which preceded Buʿāth; *Mufaḍḍaliyyāt* (Lyall), II, 225.

[65] Ibn al-Kalbī, *Nasab Maʿadd*, I, 364 f (*julli* was corrupted to *jaddi* and *sāʿī* became *shākī*; n. 5 on p. 364 shows that the editor misunderstood the text; al-Salm is the son of Imruʾu l-Qays and the brother of Wāqif, not the son of Mālik b. al-Aws). See also *Mufaḍḍaliyyāt* (Lyall), II, 227: "Mālik is the name of the patriarch of the tribe called al-Aus, of which Abū Qais was the leader". See the verse, e.g., in *Lisān al-ʿarab*. s.v. *s.ʿ.y.*, 386b; al-Mufaḍḍal al-Ḍabbī, *al-Mufaḍḍaliyyāt*, ed. Aḥmad Muḥammad Shākir ʿAbd al-Salām Muḥammad Hārūn, Cairo 1383/1963 (reprint Beirut), no. 75,5; Jumaḥī, I, 227:2 (the editor correctly identifies the Mālik as Mālik b. al-Aws); al-Qurashī, *Jamharat ashʿār al-ʿarab*, ed. al-Bijāwī, Cairo 1387/1967, II, 653. Mālik in the sense of "Aws" can also be found in Qays b. al-Khaṭīm, *Dīwān*, 62 (*wa-salū ṣarīḥa l-kāhinayni wa-Mālikan*, possibly a reference to the alliance between the Naḍīr and Qurayẓa and the Aws) and in a verse by the same poet on the War of Ḥāṭib, again referring to the *kāhināni* and Mālik, 82: *atat ʿuṣabun mi l-kāhinayni wa-Mālikin*.

does not target the Aws as a whole: she immediately specifies that of the Mālik b. al-Aws she only meant to attack the [ʿAmr b.] ʿAwf and the Nabīt.

The verses exchanged between ʿAṣmāʾ bint Marwān and Ḥassān b. Thābit confirm Aws Allāh's hostile attitude to the Prophet shortly after the Hijra and the split in Medinan society caused by the advent of the Prophet. A split in Medinan society was of course no novelty. But unlike the old one between the Aws and Khazraj, the division this time was not along tribal lines since on the Prophet's side we find not only the Khazraj, but also two out of the five Aws branches, namely the Nabīt and the ʿAmr b. ʿAwf.

The Jews of the Aws Allāh

The widespread idol worship on the eve of Islam, in Medina in general and in the ʿĀliya among the Aws Allāh in particular,[66] should not discourage us from looking for Jewish proselytes among the Aws Allāh; after all, no Arab group in Medina was closer than them geographically and politically to the strongest Jewish tribes, the Naḍīr and Qurayẓa. However, evidence of proselytes is meagre, possibly as a result of suppression.

Qays b. Rifāʿa of the Wāqif (above, 37) was a Jewish proselyte.[67] He is satirized by Islamic tradition: among the *munāfiqūn* who belonged to the Aws, Balādhurī mentions the poet Qays b. Rifāʿa of the Wāqif and al-Ḍaḥḥāk b. Khalīfa of the ʿAbd al-Ashhal, both of whom used to frequent the synagogue (presumably an indirect way of telling us that they were Jews). Qays, the report cheerfully continues, was hit by a candle in the synagogue and lost his eye.[68] This is of course an edifying story. Synagogues should be avoided for fear of being hit by flying candles. We are unlikely to find corroborative evidence for the eye injury (it may

[66] Lecker, "Idol worship in pre-Islamic Medina (Yathrib)", section 2.2 (where two idols of the Khaṭma are mentioned).

[67] For mention of the idols of the Wāqif see Lecker, "Idol worship", 335.

[68] Balādh., *Ansāb*, I, 277 (printed: al-Ḍaḥḥāk b. Ḥunayf); Ibn Ḥabīb, *Muḥabbar*, 469:3; see the entry on Qays in *Iṣāba*, V, 468.

well be historical!), but we are assured that Qays was a Jew, and again, it may be observed that where there is one proselyte we should expect to find more.[69]

THE 'AṬIYYA AND THE JEWS

The B. 'Aṭiyya b. Zayd were the brothers of the B. Wā'il b. Zayd and the B. Umayya b. Zayd. A curious genealogical and geographical link existed between the 'Aṭiyya and the Jewish Qaynuqā'.

The Qaynuqā' (or part of them) and the 'Aṭiyya lived in the same area. We know this from the reports concerning their courts as both inhabited a place called Ṣafīna or Ṣafna between Qubā' and the territory of the Ḥublā or Sālim subdivisions of the 'Awf (Khazraj).[70] This geographical detail would be of little significance without the following genealogical detail: Shās (rather, Sha's) b. Qays of the 'Aṭiyya[71] is identical with Shās b. Qays in the list of the Prophet's adversaries who were of the Qaynuqā'.[72]

All this can now be taken a little further with evidence from Ibn al-Kalbī's *Jamharat al-nasab.* In the paragraph about the 'Aṭiyya we read:

> Shās b. Qays b. 'Ubāda b. Zuhayr b. 'Aṭiyya b. Zayd was one of the eminent persons of the Aws in the Jāhiliyya. He converted to Judaism and was one of their leaders (*min ashrāfi l-Aws fī l-jāhiliyya wa-kāna qad tahawwada wa-kāna ra'san fīhim*).[73]

[69] Qays' father was presumably Abū Qays b. Rifā'a whom al-Jumaḥī lists in his *Ṭabaqāt fuḥūl al-shu'arā'* among the Jewish poets; Jumaḥī, I, 288.

[70] Cf. Wellhausen, *Skizzen* IV, 41, n. 1 (where al-Ṣufayna should be replaced by al-Ṣafīna/Ṣafna); *Maghānim*, 220, n. 1. Ṣafna was along the route of the supplies reportedly sent by the Qurayẓa to the Qurashī army besieging Medina during the Battle of the Ditch. The supply caravan was at Ṣafna on its way to the 'Aqīq Valley, when it was intercepted by troops of the 'Amr b. 'Awf who were on their way home, i.e., to Qubā'; *Sīra Shāmiyya*, IV, 539–40.

[71] He appears once as the owner of a fortress of the 'Aṭiyya called (after him) Shās; Samh., I, 198.

[72] See already Lecker, "On the markets of Medina", 137–38.

[73] Ibn al-Kalbī, *Jamhara*, 648; see already Caskel, *Ǧamharat an-Nasab*, II, 528. His conversion to Judaism is not mentioned in Ibn al-Kalbī, *Nasab Ma'add*, I, 389; Ibn Durayd, *Ishtiqāq*, 448 and Ibn Ḥazm, *Ansāb*, 346. On Shās, see also Ibn Hishām, II, 204–205, 216:3, 219:5.

The fact that Shās converted to Judaism indicates that the ʿAṭiyya are not identical with the Jewish Qaynuqāʿ. It seems plausible that the ʿAṭiyya were the clients of their neighbours, the Qaynuqāʿ.

We also have evidence associating the ʿAṭiyya with the Naḍīr. In connection with the Battle of the Ditch we are told that the Naḍīr and some of their Arab allies incited Quraysh and certain Bedouin tribes to besiege Medina. The details of the Arab allies are of interest to us here because they relate to Jewish proselytes among the Wā'il b. Zayd and, more to the point, their brother clan, the ʿAṭiyya b. Zayd. Ibn Isḥāq writes that *a group of Jews*, including Sallām b. Abī l-Ḥuqayq, Ḥuyayy b. Akhṭab and Kināna b. Abī l-Ḥuqayq of the Naḍīr, as well as Hawdha b. Qays and Abū ʿAmmār, both of the Wā'il, together with some of the Naḍīr and Wā'il, set out to Mecca to incite the Quraysh against the Prophet.[74] Another source concludes the above list with the remark: *wa-hum kulluhum yahūd.*[75] Yet another report mentions from among the Naḍīr the following: Ḥuyayy, Abū

---

[74] Ibn Hishām, III, 225 (*anna nafaran mina l-yahūdi, minhum ...*). Gil, "The origin of the Jews of Yathrib", 214 confuses the above-mentioned Wā'il, who were of the Aws Allāh, with Wā'il's namesake, a subdivision of the Judhām. On the same page (n. 36) he also confuses them with the Wā'il who "acted (*sic*) for the kings of Ḥīra as *dhawū ākāl*"; but these recipients of fiefs from the kings of Ḥīra were of the (Bakr b.) Wā'il. Cf. Gil, "The creed of Abū ʿĀmir", 29.

[75] Ibn ʿAbd al-Barr, *al-Durar fī khtiṣār al-maghāzī wa-l-siyar*, Beirut 1404/1984, 121. According to Mūsā b. ʿUqba's *Maghāzī*, Ḥuyayy went to Mecca and Kināna went to the Ghaṭafān, whom he promised half of Khaybar's date produce that year; see Zurqānī, II, 103:15. Waq., II, 441 mentions the following amongst the Naḍīr: Ḥuyayy, Kināna b. Abī l-Ḥuqayq, one Hawdha b. al-Ḥuqayq (possibly a duplicate), while from the Arabs he mentions Hawdha b. Qays al-Wā'ilī "of the Aws, [more precisely,] of the Khaṭma (*sic*)" and Abū ʿĀmir al-Rāhib. The reference to Khaṭma could reflect later conditions, i.e., the incorporation of the Wā'il into the Khaṭma; cf. the *nisba* al-Anṣārī al-Khaṭmī al-Wā'ilī relating to one of Ibn Isḥāq's informants (Ibn al-Athīr, *Lubāb*, s.v. al-Wā'ilī). The reference to Abū ʿĀmir al-Rāhib in this report seems to be erroneous: an unknown Abū ʿAmmār (or ʿUmāra, or Abū ʿĀmir, see below) could easily have been replaced by the well-known Abū ʿĀmir al-Rāhib. Cf. Rubin, "Ḥanīfiyya", 86 ("Following the expulsion of Banū al-Naḍīr to Khaybar [3H/625], Abū ʿĀmir is again said to have gone to Mecca along with some Jews and certain people of Aws"), 94, 109n.

Rāfiʿ Sallām[76] b. Abī l-Ḥuqayq and al-Rabīʿ b. al-Rabīʿ b. Abī l-Ḥuqayq, and of the Wā'il: Abū ʿAmmār, Waḥwaḥ b. ʿĀmir and Hawdha b. Qays.[77] Waḥwaḥ b. ʿĀmir (i.e., Waḥwaḥ b. al-Aslat; al-Aslat was his father's nickname) was Abū Qays b. al-Aslat's brother.[78]

The Arab allies of the Naḍīr belonged to the Aws Allāh. The statement, *wa-hum kulluhum yahūd*, is of fundamental importance for ʿĀliya politics after the Hijra. With Waḥwaḥ b. al-Aslat/b. ʿĀmir we may stand on firm ground: if he was a Jewish proselyte (or a descendant of one), it seems probable that the same is true for his brother, the Aws Allāh leader, Abū Qays b. al-Aslat. This brings to mind the combination of Jewish faith and tribal leadership in the case of Shās b. Qays of the ʿAṭiyya. Perhaps this combination was typical to the ʿĀliya where the Jews were the dominant power. In other cases, maybe even in most cases, tribal leadership in pre-Islamic Medina was associated with idol worship.[79]

We now turn to Hawdha b. Qays about whom we have contradictory evidence: he was either of the Wā'il or of the Khaṭma. But his most detailed, and hence, I believe most reliable pedigree shows him to be a member of the ʿAṭiyya. We arrive at his pedigree through that of his son, Maʿbad:

> Maʿbad b. Hawdha b. Qays b. ʿUbāda b. Duhaym b. ʿ*Aṭiyya* b. Zayd b. Qays b. ʿĀmir [b. Murra] b. Mālik b. Aws.[80]

[76] Thus vocalized in Ibn Bashkuwāl, *Ghawāmiḍ al-asmā' al-mubhama*, ed. ʿIzz al-Dīn ʿAlī al-Sayyid and Muḥammad Kamāl al-Dīn ʿIzz al-Dīn, Beirut 1407/1987, II, 638.

[77] Ibn Hishām, II, 210; cf. the version of this report in Ṭabarī, *Tafsīr*, V, 85–86 (Abū ʿĀmir instead of Abū ʿAmmār). Suyūṭī, *Durr*, II, 172:6 has: ʿUmāra instead of Abū ʿAmmār.

[78] ʿAbdallāh b. Muḥammad b. ʿUmāra (= Ibn al-Qaddāḥ), quoted in *Iṣāba*, VI, 601, says that he was a Companion and participated in the Battle of the Ditch and later battles. On the apostasy and departure to Mecca of Waḥwaḥ, Abū ʿĀmir al-Rāhib (*sic*) and others see Ṭabarī, *Tafsīr*, III, 242:17 (commentary on Qur'ān 3,86).

[79] Lecker, "Idol worship in pre-Islamic Medina (Yathrib)", 342–43 (Conclusions).

[80] *Iṣāba*, VI, 170; see also *Usd al-ghāba*, IV, 394; *Istīʿāb*, IV, 1428. Also

Preferring the detailed pedigree to the general and contradictory statements concerning him, we may conclude that Hawdha b. Qays, just like Shās b. Qays, was a Jewish proselyte of the ʿAṭiyya. Moreover, Hawdha and Shās were brothers. As we saw, Ibn al-Kalbī gave the following pedigree for Shās:

Shās b. Qays b. ʿUbāda b. Zuhayr b. ʿAṭiyya b. Zayd.

In this pedigree, the name Zuhayr replaces that of Duhaym in the preceding pedigree. The two names are very similar in the Arabic script; Duhaym is preferable because it is a *lectio difficilior.*

Assuming that Arab leaders of the Aws Allāh, or more precisely of the brother clans Wāʾil and ʿAṭiyya, participated in inciting the Prophet's enemies before the Battle of the Ditch, one wonders whether some Arab allies of the Jewish Naḍīr had been expelled together with the Naḍīr. The assumption that they were is not at all far-fetched — after all, some Arabs, presumably Jewish proselytes living among the Qurayẓa, were executed together with the Qurayẓa.[81] In addition, when Khaybar was attacked by the Prophet, Hawdha b. Qays was there.[82]

THE JUDAISED MURĪD OF THE BALĪ

Among the Aws Allāh there lived at least one Judaised clan belonging to the Balī (a tribe of the Quḍāʿa), namely the Murīd (or Murayd).[83] Like the other clans of the Balī that inhabited various

Iṣāba, VI, 587, s.v. Hawdha b. Qays b. ʿUbāda b. Duhaym. For the Murra added in the above pedigree cf. Ibn Ḥazm, *Ansāb*, 346.

[81] See M. Lecker, "On Arabs of the Banū Kilāb executed together with the Jewish Banū Qurayẓa", in *JSAI* 19 (forthcoming).

[82] For Hawdha's role in the defence of Khaybar when it was attacked by the Prophet see Waq., II, 640 (Kināna b. Abī l-Ḥuqayq and Hawdha b. Qays enlist the Ghaṭafānī allies of the Jews, promising them the date produce of Khaybar for one year).

[83] The two forms of the name appear to have existed side by side. For Murayd see Ḥamad al-Jāsir, "Jawla fī al-maghrib al-ʿarabī", no. 6 ("Fī madīnat Tūnis"), in *Majallat al-ʿarab* 7, xii (July 1973), 881–97, at 889–90, where the author quotes a passage from al-Rushāṭī (d. 542/1147), *Iqtibās al-anwār wa-ʾltimās al-azhār fī ansāb al-ṣaḥāba wa-ruwāt al-āthār*: *al-Muraydī fī Balī. Qāla Abū Muḥammad* [= al-Rushāṭī]: *lam ajid hādhā l-nasab fī kitābi bni l-kalbī wa-lā fī ghayrihi wa-laysa ʿindī fīhi siwā mā ḥakāhu Abū ʿAlī l-Hajarī, qāla: Murayd qabīla min Balī, wa-ḥakā bn Hishām qāla: qāla bn Isḥāq: qālati*

parts of Medina, the Murīd were there before the arrival of the Aws and Khazraj. They appear in two independent (though to some extent overlapping) lists of clans. One list is of Arab clans who were clients of the Jews before the arrival of the Aws and Khazraj.[84] The other is a list of the Jewish clans that *remained* in Medina after the Aws and Khazraj had settled there (*wa-kāna mimman baqiya mina l-yahūd ḥīna nazalat ʿalayhimi l-Aws wa-l-Khazraj ...*).[85] The Murīd lived "in [the territory of] the Khaṭma and Nāʿimat Ibrāhīm b. Hishām", and they had a fortress (*uṭum*) with a well in it; the fortress was called after them ("the fortress of the Murīd").[86] The Murīd were not, however, the clients of the Khaṭma, but of another Aws Allāh clan, the Umayya b. Zayd.[87]

---

mraʾa mina l-muslimīna min B. Murayd, baṭn min Balī, kānū ḥulafāʾ B. Umayya b. Zayd etc. (see below). Cf. E.M. López and J.B. Vilá, *Al-Andalus en el kitāb iqtibās al-anwār y en el ijtiṣār iqtibās al-anwār*, Madrid 1990 (Fuentes Arábico-Hispanas 7).

[84] *Aghānī*, XIX, 95:14 (printed Marthad); Samh., I, 162:16. Wüstenfeld, *Medina*, 29 has: "Muzeid" (= Muzayd) remarking that elsewhere their name is Marthad or Yazīd.

[85] The wording seems to suggest that some clans went into exile following the settlement of the Aws and Khazraj. See already Lecker, *The Banū Sulaym*, 102. I wish to correct here an erroneous English usage in the monograph just mentioned. I now realize that the term "clients" is more appropriate than the term "confederates" which I used; when a small, alien, group attaches itself to a bigger, settled, group (on which, we may assume, it depends for its protection), we should speak of clientage, not confederation. Cf. below, 103.

[86] Samh., I, 163:–2,–1. This is the Murīd fortress said elsewhere to have belonged to the Khaṭma (i.e., the masters of the Murīd); Yaq., s.v. Murayd [*sic*]; Ḥāzimī, *Amākin*, MS Laleli 2140, fol. 175 has: Murīd. Cf. the Muʿāwiya who were "in" (*fī*) the Umayya b. Zayd; Lecker, *The Banū Sulaym*, 102, n. 15.

[87] Ibn Hishām, III, 57:2 *Murayd, baṭn min Balī, kānū ḥulafāʾa fī B. Umayya b. Zayd.* Ibn Hishām seems to suggest that the Murīd were identical with the Jaʿādir(a). See *Iṣāba*, VIII, 132; Ibn Qudāma, *Istibṣār*, 283: the poetess Maymūna bint ʿAbdallāh was of the Murayd (*sic*), a *baṭn* of the Balī who were called the Jaʿādira and were the clients (*ḥulafāʾ*) of the Umayya b. Zayd of the Anṣār. But this seems to be wrong and is incompatible with the definitions of the appellative Jaʿādir(a) discussed above. The text in Ibn Hishām is not smooth and is presumably misleading: the Umayya, not the Balawīs, are meant here; cf. Lecker, "Muḥammad at Medina", 47–48. Note that Ibn Qudāma includes the entry on Maymūna in the section on the Umayya b. Zayd who were a subdivision of the ʿAmr b. ʿAwf; however, there is little doubt that he is wrong and that she was associated with the Umayya b. Zayd who were a subdivision of the Aws Allāh.

This apparent discrepancy may have been caused by changing circumstances: before Islam and in its early days, the Murīd lived in an area known as the court of the Umayya b. Zayd. Later in the Islamic period the area came to be named after the Khaṭma. This assumption is corroborated by the mention of the orchard called Nā'imat Ibrāhīm b. Hishām. Ibrāhīm b. Hishām was the governor of Medina under Hishām b. 'Abd al-Malik. He was the Caliph's maternal uncle and belonged to the Quraysh clan of Makhzūm.[88] The place-name, "Nā'imat Ibrāhīm b. Hishām", is a mixture of new and old. Al-Nā'ima, a luxuriant orchard in the 'Āliya, had belonged to the Naḍīr. There was another orchard near it, al-Nuway'ima ("the small Nā'ima"). Hence the name al-Nawā'im (plural), designating the place (*al-mawḍi'*).[89] "Al-Nawā'im" appears in a description of Naḍīr's territory. Again, it is a mixture of new and old perfectly intelligible for an inhabitant of Medina in the second Islamic century with some knowledge of his hometown. The description contains a reference to the *qaṣr* of Ibrāhīm b. Hishām and the territory of the Umayya b. Zayd of the Aws Allāh, who were the masters of our Murīd:

> The Naḍīr inhabited al-Nawā'im and one of their fortresses, the one belonging to 'Amr b. Jaḥḥāsh, was in the Zuqāq [= lane of] al-Ḥārith, at the back (*dubra*) of *qaṣr* [Ibrāhīm] Ibn Hishām, behind (*dūna*) the B. Umayya b. Zayd.[90]

A few words concerning 'Amr b. Jaḥḥāsh may be in place here. We know 'Amr b. Jaḥḥāsh b. Ka'b from the story of Naḍīr's alleged plot to assassinate the Prophet: 'Amr was the one who volunteered to carry this out.[91] His ownership of a fortress and

[88] On Ibrāhīm's market cf. Lecker, "On the markets of Medina", 140 f. On Ibrāhīm see Balādh., *Ansāb*, VIb, Index.

[89] Samh., s.v. al-Nā'ima.

[90] Samh., I, 163:14 (printed: 'Umar b. Jaḥḥāsh).

[91] Ibn Hishām, II, 212:1 (vocalized: Jiḥāsh); Suyūṭī, *Durr*, II, 266:11 (printed: 'Umar b. Jaḥḥāsh b. Ka'b). See also Waq., I, 364:-1, 367:14 (printed: Jiḥāsh). Ibn Sa'd, II, 57:9 calls him 'Amr b. Jiḥāsh b. Ka'b b. Basīl. Instead of Basīl, read perhaps: Shibl: Waq., III, 994:11 mentions a relative of 'Amr b. Jaḥḥāsh whom he calls Yāmīn b. 'Umayr b. Ka'b b. Shibl (see

the Prophet's instruction to assassinate him, allegedly for his role in the plot, seem to indicate that 'Amr was a prominent figure among the Naḍīr.

The man chosen by the Prophet for the job was Ibn Yāmīn, 'Amr's cousin (*ibn 'amm*) and brother-in-law: Ibn Yāmīn's sister, al-Ruwāʿ bint 'Umayr, was 'Amr's wife. Ibn Yāmīn himself was not directly involved in the assassination; he hired a man of the Qays (i.e., Qays 'Aylān) to carry out the deed.[92] From the sister's name we learn that Ibn Yāmīn's father was in fact named 'Umayr (Ibn Yāmīn/Yāmīn being an Arabized form of the common Hebrew name Binyamin). That his father's name was 'Umayr is confirmed by the report about the two members of the Naḍīr who converted to Islam on the eve of the Naḍīr's surrender. The two were Yāmīn b. 'Umayr[93] and Abū Saʿd b. Wahb.[94]

It is doubtful whether the Murīd, the Judaised clients of the Balī who lived in the middle of the 'Āliya and were dependent on the Aws Allāh, could adopt an independent policy towards the Prophet. Yet there are some indications that they did so. Verses by Umāma al-Murīdiyya, which are perhaps authentic, support the assassination in 2 A.H. of Abū 'Afak, an old Jewish poet of the 'Amr b. 'Awf (see below, 52).[95] Another poetess of the Murīd, Maymūna bint 'Abdallāh, answers Kaʿb b. al-Ashraf's verses which lamented the Qurashīs killed at Badr.[96]

---

below). 'Amr b. Jaḥḥāsh is listed among the adversaries of the Prophet who belonged to the Naḍīr; Ibn Hishām, 160:15.

[92] Waq., I, 374:2.

[93] Some sources have: Yāmīn b. 'Amr; and cf. *Usd al-ghāba*, V, 99: Yāmīn b. Yāmīn.

[94] Waq., I, 373:–3. Ibn Isḥāq's informant for this story is a member of Yāmīn's family (*baʿḍ āl Yāmīn*; Ibn Kathīr, *Tafsīr*, Beirut n. d., IV, 332:8; *Iṣāba*, VI, 641). That Yāmīn was indeed the cousin of 'Amr b. Jaḥḥāsh b. Kaʿb (not his uncle; cf. Ibn Kathīr, *loc. cit.*) is seen from the fact that the grandfather of both was Kaʿb: the entry in the *Iṣāba* is entitled: Yāmīn b. 'Umayr b. Kaʿb Abū Kaʿb. See also above, 47n.

[95] See *Iṣāba*, VII, 505; *Usd al-ghāba*, V, 400–401; Zurqānī, I, 456:6; Waq., I, 175 (*wa-qālat al-Nahdiyya* [!] *fī dhālika, wa-kānat muslimatan*); Ibn Hishām, IV, 285 (Umāma al-Muzayriyya!).

[96] Ibn Hishām, III, 57. Ibn Hishām remarks, however, that most authorities on poetry deny the authenticity of her verses and of Kaʿb's poetical reply.

In the above chapter the focus fell on the Aws Allāh who lived in the eastern ʿĀliya near the Naḍīr and Qurayẓa. Concentrating on the clans and their territories, rather than on events (without, however, losing sight of the historical context) is a useful way of making progress in the study of the Prophet's biography.

With few well-accounted for exceptions, the Aws Allāh embraced Islam only after the Battle of the Ditch. Our sources can be trusted on this point; the Aws Allāh were absent from the events which amalgamated the small community of devout Muslims surrounding the Prophet during the earliest and most difficult phases of his struggle for power. A correlation has been found between the general statement about their delayed conversion and the detailed information. We have seen that the readiness of our sources to provide detailed accounts of the opposition to the Prophet is a remarkable feature of the *sīra* literature.

The historical conclusions arrived at in this chapter inspire guarded confidence in the source material. The amount and quality of our data do facilitate sound and serious work on the Prophet's biography. It would be absurd to argue that the fine, detailed information we have on certain aspects of early Islamic Medina is unusable or entirely the outcome of later inventions. Students of Islam are often perplexed by contradictory evidence and there is clearly an appalling amount of forged material. Certainly many questions will never be answered. Yet, in time a solid foundation of facts may be established whilst we simultaneously improve our analytical tools for this difficult, but by no means inaccessible literature.

CHAPTER THREE

QUBĀ': MUSLIMS, JEWS AND PAGANS

There were two villages on the western side of the 'Āliya, Qubā' and the much smaller al-'Aṣaba. A comparison between the information available to us about each of the two sides of the 'Āliya could lead to the conclusion that the western side was more populous than the eastern side; but this impression may be wrong since, quite understandably, the Prophet's supporters, who were far more numerous in the western 'Āliya, received more attention in the Islamic literature than those who opposed him.

The 'Amr b. 'Awf of the Aws were referred to as "the people of Qubā'", but this only signifies that they were the dominant group there, though not the only one. While some evidence exists of Naḍīrī presence in Qubā',[1] during the Prophet's time, clans of the Balī (Quḍā'a) were an important component of the Qubā' population and, as we shall see in the following chapter, they had a role to play in the Ḍirār incident. The Balī, both those who lived in Qubā' and in other places in the Medina area, arrived at Medina before the Aws and Khazraj immigrated there. The Balawīs then became the clients of the Aws and Khazraj, a state of affairs which continued to the Islamic era. (Before they became clients of the Aws and Khazraj they may well have been the clients of the Jews.)

Besides the 'Amr b. 'Awf and the Balī, there were in Qubā' clans from the Salm of the Aws Allāh (above, 25) who settled in Qubā' before Islam. There were also Khazrajīs (of the Zurayq).[2]

---

[1] Regarding the three fortresses owned by a Jew (said to have been of the Naḍīr) in the heart of Qubā', see below, 133.

[2] See Samh., I, 207 about the shift of the 'Adhāra b. Mālik b. Ghaḍb b. Jusham b. al-Khazraj (above, 33n) to Qubā' which involved client status and marriage links: *fa-kharajū ... ḥattā nazalū Qubā'a 'alā B. 'Amr b. 'Awf fa-ḥālafūhum wa-ṣāharūhum.* The 'Adhāra are identical with the Ka'b b. Mālik b. Ghaḍb b. Jusham said to have been *ḥulafā' B. 'Amr b. 'Awf*; Ibn Ḥazm, *Ansāb*, 356. The 'Adhāra remained among the 'Amr b. 'Awf to

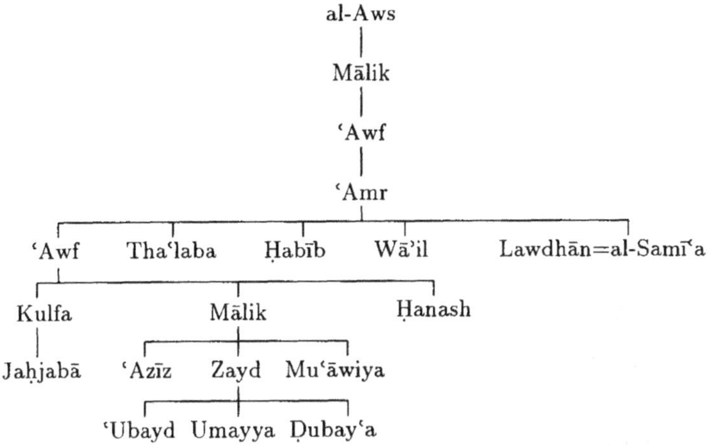

The ʿAmr b. ʿAwf

It should be added that some of the ʿAmr b. ʿAwf, for example the Muʿāwiya, left Qubāʾ before the Islamic era and when the Prophet arrived were living outside Qubāʾ.

Much of what we know about the fortresses of pre-Islamic Medina comes from Ibn Zabāla, the author of a history of Medina entitled *Akhbār al-Madīna*. In this book, which survived only as extracts found in Samhūdī and other sources, there was a chapter on the settlement of the Aws and Khazraj. Ibn Zabāla presented the data about the different clans using this unchanged pattern: "The B. so-and-so settled in such-and-such place and built the fortress called so-and-so". While our knowledge of Qubāʾ and its inhabitants may not be complete, we do have a fair amount of

160/777. When the Caliph al-Mahdī assigned a portion in the register of soldiers or pensioners to the Anṣār, the ʿAdhāra moved their register to the Bayāḍa (i.e., they returned to their Khazrajī relatives); Samh., I, 208 (*fa-lam yazālū ka-dhālika ḥattā faraḍa l-Mahdī li-l-anṣār sanata sittīna wa-miʾa fa-ʾntaqalū bi-dīwānihim ilā B. Bayāḍa*). See already Wellhausen, *Skizzen* IV, 24, who wrongly calls them Ghudāra, following Wüstenfeld, *Medina*, 45, 46. Caskel, *Ǧamharat an-Nasab*, I, no. 192 and II, 275, calls them Ghirāra.

Yaʿqūbī's statement (*Buldān*, ed. M.J. de Goeje, Leiden 1892, 313:11) that before Islam the houses of the Aws and Khazraj were located in Qubāʾ is problematic; the text is possibly not in order (*wa-mina l-Madīna ilā Qubāʾ sittatu amyāl wa-bihā kānat manāzilu l-Aws wa-l-Khazraj qabla l-islām*).

detailed information of fundamental importance, as will become clear from the following discussion.[3]

CONVERTS TO JUDAISM AMONG THE ʿAMR B. ʿAWF

There appear to have been more Jewish converts among the ʿAmr b. ʿAwf than among the Aws Allāh (above, 41). In any case, the numbers are small. The results are based on casual evidence and may not be indicative of the actual state of affairs.[4]

The following converts were found:

1. Ibn Hishām's list of the Jewish adversaries of the Prophet includes Qardam b. ʿAmr of "Yahūd B. ʿAmr b. ʿAwf".[5]

2. The poet Abū ʿAfak, assassinated after the Battle of Badr, was a Jewish proselyte belonging to the ʿAmr b. ʿAwf,[6] or more precisely, to the ʿUbayd b. Zayd.[7]

3. Before the Islamic era, a Quraysh man married a woman from amongst the *yahūd al-anṣār*. She belonged to the ʿAmr b. ʿAwf but it is not clear to which subdivision. According to one source, she was of the Jaḥjabā subdivision, while another, more detailed and thus probably more trustworthy pedigree presents her as one of the Ḍubayʿa.[8]

---

[3] Several fortresses of the ʿAmr b. ʿAwf clans are mentioned in the following chapter in connection with the Ḍirār Mosque.

[4] For idol worship among the ʿAmr b. ʿAwf, see Lecker, "Idol worship in pre-Islamic Medina (Yathrib)", 332, 334.

[5] The interpretation of this difficult phrase is a key issue in the ʿ*Ahd al-Umma* (the so-called "Constitution of Medina"). Qardam was either of the ʿAmr b. ʿAwf or their client (in the latter case he does not belong here).

[6] Ibn Saʿd, II, 28; Balādh., *Ansāb*, I, 373; Zurqānī, I, 455:-4; Gil, "The origin of the Jews of Yathrib", 211. According to an extraordinary report, ʿAlī killed him; Balādh, *Ansāb*, I, 374:1. The Jewish poetess, ʿAṣmāʾ, who was also assassinated after Badr, was not of the ʿAmr b. ʿAwf but of the Aws Allāh; above, 38.

[7] In Ibn Hishām, IV, 284–85 read ʿUbayd instead of ʿUbayda. "Abū ʿAfak", "father of stupidity", was certainly not his *kunya* or his name (it may, however, be a mutilated form of his name).

[8] Lecker, "A note on early marriage links", 26 = Ibn al-Kalbī, *Jamhara*, 69. Mālik b. Ama b. Ḍubayʿa, etc. can be traced in the genealogy of the Ḍubayʿa; see *op. cit.*, 622.

4. Al-Jumaḥī concludes the section on the Jewish poets in his *Ṭabaqāt fuḥūl al-shu'arā'* with a mention of Dirham b. Zayd; while some call him al-Awsī, Ibn al-Kalbī is more specific as he includes him in the section on the Ḍubay'a. Ibn al-Kalbī calls him Dirham b. Zayd b. Ḍubay'a, remarking that he was a *jāhilī*.[9] Dirham's pedigree as quoted above is too short and several ancestors are presumably missing between him and his clan's eponym, Ḍubay'a, who could not have been Dirham's grandfather.[10]

[9] Jumaḥī, I, 294–96 = Ibn al-Kalbī, *Jamhara*, 624; also *Nasab Ma'add*, I, 367. It is noteworthy that a verse attributed to Dirham includes a pagan oath formula ("by 'Uzzā and by Allāh, before whose house [that is the Ka'ba] Sarif is located", *innī wa-rabbi l-'Uzzā l-sa'īdati wa-'llā hi lladhī dūna baytihi Sarifu*); Ibn al-Kalbī, *al-Aṣnām*, ed. Aḥmad Zakī Bāshā, Cairo 1343/1924, 19:16. But perhaps such oaths were a matter of poetic convention. On Sarif see Yaq., s.v. The verse is connected to the War of Sumayr. Another version of the verse (*Aghānī*, II, 168:4; Ḥassān, *Dīwān*, II, 38) does not mention al-'Uzzā, but the Ka'ba remains (*innī la-'amru lladhī yaḥujju lahu l-nā su wa-man dūna baytihi Sarifu*). The Jew 'Abdallāh b. Salām reportedly told the Jewish leaders of Medina that he wished to visit "the mosque of our father Abraham"; Rubin, "Ḥanīfiyya", 109. In Rubin's opinion, 'Abdallāh "seems to have been closer to the *ḥanīf*s than to the majority of the Jews in this, that he regarded the Ka'ba as the House of Abraham". (In Watt, *Medina*, Index, s.v. and Paret, *Mohammed und der Koran*, 104, read Salām instead of Sallām; see Ibn Mākūlā, IV, 403; and see already M. Steinschneinder, *Polemische und apologetische Literatur in arabischer Sprache zwischen Muslimen, Christen und Juden*, Leipzig 1877, 110, n. 1.)

Incidentally, Rubin, *op. cit.*, 109, n. 111 says: "Christians as well may have venerated the Ka'ba, towards which some of them reportedly used to pray". He refers to Suyūṭī, *Durr*, I, 143: ... *ṣallat al-Naṣārā naḥwa l-Ka'ba ḥawlayni qabla qudūmi l-nabiyyi (ṣ)*. But this must be a misprint: one expects here "al-Anṣār", not "al-Naṣārā", because *qudūm al-nabiyyi* can only be a reference to the Hijra. On the link between Abraham and the Ka'ba cf. Kister, *EI*^{2}, s.v. Maḳām Ibrāhīm.

[10] Dirham's brother Sumayr gave the Sumayr War its name (it was also called *Yawm Sumayḥa*). He started it by killing a client of Mālik b. al-'Ajlān; *Aghānī*, II, 167f. This dates the brother's lifetime roughly three generations before the Prophet's time. The eponym Ḍubay'a lived roughly five generations before the Prophet's time; see the pedigrees in Ibn Ḥazm, *Ansāb*, 333. The pedigree of 'Āṣim b. Thābit b. Abī l-Aqlaḥ has seven generations, but in Ibn al-Kalbī, *Jamhara*, 622–23 there are only six. In the story of the above-mentioned war (Ḥassān, *Dīwān*, II, 36:4, 40:8,12) Sumayr is called Sumayr b. Zayd b. Mālik. (Cf. Jumaḥī, *loc. cit.*, n. 3.) His grandfather, Mālik, was possibly identical with Ḍubay'a's grandson Mālik who appears in the pedigree of Abū 'Āmir al-Rāhib: Abū 'Āmir b. Ṣayfī b. al-Nu'mān b. *Mālik* b. Umayya

5. Abū ʿĀmir al-Rāhib of the same subdivision, Ḍubayʿa, was probably the most important leader in Qubāʾ. In a report on the Ḍirār Mosque (below, 88) the early Qurʾān commentary by Muqātil calls him Abū ʿĀmir al-Yahūdī. He was referred to as *al-rāhib* ("the God-fearing"),[11] Muqātil says, because he applied himself to acts of devotion and sought (religious) knowledge. The epithet "al-Yahūdī" with regard to Abū ʿĀmir is rare and was not found elsewhere. As we saw in the preceding chapter, there were people of note who were Jewish proselytes among the Aws Allāh in the eastern part of the ʿĀliya. If accurate, this detail about Abū ʿĀmir's faith would be another example of a link between Jewish faith and tribal leadership in pre-Islamic Medina.

It is interesting to note in this context that in later times some conceived of Abū ʿĀmir's threat to nascent Islam (on which see below, Ch. 4) as being a continuation of the threat posed by the Jewish Qurayẓa. This is reflected in the story that the Prophet lamented the untimely death of Saʿd b. Muʿādh, the Anṣārī who gave the verdict on the Qurayẓa, which occurred before he could take care of "the calf which was to be set up in the heart of Islam, similar to the calf of the people of Moses". The Prophet anticipated the whole incident and foretold that it would only achieve partial success (*wa-yastamirrūna bi-baʿḍi tadbīrihim, thumma llāhu yubṭiluhu*).[12]

6. There was a Jewish convert among the ʿAzīz b. Mālik subdivision of the ʿAmr b. ʿAwf: before the Islamic era, the Meccan dignitary, al-Walīd b. ʿUtba b. Rabīʿa b. ʿAbd Shams, married a Jewish woman from among the ʿAzīz. It is noteworthy in this context that al-Walīd's brother, Abū Ḥudhayfa, was married to a woman of the ʿAmr b. ʿAwf, or more accurately of the ʿUbayd b. Zayd (but she is not said to have been Jewish).[13] This pre-Islamic marriage, as well as similar marriages (see above, no. 3),

---

b. Ḍubayʿa.

[11] It cannot be rendered "the monk" in this context; see below.

[12] *Biḥār al-anwār*, XXI, 257. H. Busse, "The Arab conquest in revelation and politics", in *Israel Oriental Studies* 10 (1980), 14–20, at 17, mentions that "numerous elements taken from the biography of Moses have been transferred to the biography of Muḥammad".

[13] Lecker, "A note on early marriage links", 22–23.

reveal an important aspect of the relations between Mecca and Medina before Islam.

THE JAḤJABĀ MOVE FROM QUBĀ' TO AL-'AṢABA

The population of early Islamic Qubā' was to some extent patterned by an event of two or three generations before the Hijra, namely the shift of the 'Amr b. 'Awf subdivision called Jaḥjabā from Qubā' to the nearby al-'Aṣaba to its west. The number of fortresses involved in this event makes it a major occurrence in the history of Qubā'. It was reportedly connected to the payment of blood-wit to another subdivision of the 'Amr b. 'Awf, the Umayya b. Zayd.[14] The Jaḥjabā, we are told, had to leave Qubā' and settle in al-'Aṣaba because one of them killed a member of the Umayya b. Zayd named Rifā'a b. Zanbar.[15] The following friendly conversation allegedly took place between two members of the clans involved:

> Sa'd b. 'Amr al-Jaḥjabī said to Bishr b. al-Sā'ib:[16] "Do you know why we settled in al-'Aṣaba"?
> Bishr: "No".
> Sa'd: "Because we killed one of you in the Jāhiliyya".
> Bishr: "By God, I wish you killed another of us and settled behind 'Ayr", i.e., [= a gloss] the mountain to the west of al-'Aṣaba.[17]

Elsewhere, in a more detailed account of the incident, two slain men are mentioned (which is of course incongruous with the above conversation):

[14] Cf. above, 38. For a dispute between the Jaḥjabā and the Zayd see Wellhausen, *Skizzen* IV, 37. Considering the scale of this shift, one expects some fighting between the two clans to have occurred; cf. the siege and expulsion of the Ḥāritha; Lecker, *The Banū Sulaym*, 104.

[15] b. Zayd b. Umayya [b. Zayd] b. Mālik b. 'Awf b. 'Amr b. 'Awf.

[16] Instead of Bishr, presumably read Bashīr; the alleged conversation should be dated to the second half of the first century A.H.: Bashīr b. al-Sā'ib was the grandson of the famous Abū Lubāba of the Umayya b. Zayd; see below, 117.

[17] Samh., I, 193–94; Wellhausen, *Skizzen* IV, 25, n. 5 (where the place-name is vocalized al-'Aṣba, as elsewhere in Wellhausen's book).

> The Jaḥjabā came from Qubā' after they killed Rifā'a b. Zanbar and Ghanm who were of the 'Amr b. 'Awf. They settled in al-'Uṣba [= al-'Aṣaba][18] and Uḥayḥa b. al-Julāḥ built a fortress in it called al-Ḍaḥyān.[19]

Uḥayḥa b. al-Julāḥ lived three generations before the Prophet's time. He was the great-grandfather of the Companion al-Mundhir b. Muḥammad b. 'Uqba b. Uḥayḥa.[20] Uḥayḥa was also the great-grandfather of another Companion, 'Iyāḍ b. 'Amr b. Bulayl b. Uḥayḥa,[21] and of 'Amr b. Bulayl b. Bilāl b. Uḥayḥa.[22] This conforms with the fact that Uḥayḥa lived during the lifetime of the Prophet's great-grandfather, Hāshim b. 'Abd Manāf: the mother of the Prophet's grandfather, Salmā, had been married to Uḥayḥa before she married Hāshim.[23] Roughly the same chronology is suggested by the pedigrees of the Companion Abū Lubāba and his brothers: the slain man (or one of the two slain men), Rifā'a b. Zanbar, was their grandfather.[24]

The following fortresses in Qubā' are linked to this event:

1. Wāqim had belonged to Uḥayḥa b. al-Julāḥ and became the property of the B. 'Abd al-Mundhir b. Rifā'a as blood-wit for

---

[18] Other forms of this place-name are al-'Uṣaba, al-Mu'aṣṣab and the above-mentioned al-'Aṣba.

[19] *Maghānim*, s.v. Ḍaḥyān, probably quoting al-Zubayr b. Bakkār, *Akhbār al-Madīna: aqbala B. Jaḥjabā min Qubā' ḥīna* (printed: *ḥattā*) *qatalū Rifā'a b. Zanbar* (printed: *Zubayr*) *wa-Ghanman* (vocalized: *wa-Ghunman*) *akhaway* (printed: *akhawā*) *'Amr b. 'Awf fa-sakanū l-'Uṣbata, fa-'btanā Uḥayḥa b. al-Julāḥ bihā* (printed: *bihimā*) *uṭuman yuqālu lahu al-Ḍaḥyān*, etc. Cf. Samh., I, 193–94. On Uḥayḥa see *GAS*, II, 284–85. Of the fortresses of Medina only two remain to this day: *Ḥiṣn* Ka'b b. al-Ashraf and *uṭum* al-Ḍaḥyān; Kaḥḥāla, *Jughrāfiyyat*, 185.

[20] See, e.g., Ibn al-Kalbī, *Nasab Ma'add*, I, 371. The *Iṣāba*, VI, 219 calls him al-Khazrajī (!). On Uḥayḥa see Lecker, *The Banū Sulaym*, 105.

[21] *Usd al-ghāba*, IV, 164 (where "Mulayk" is a misprint of "Bulayl"); *Iṣāba*, IV, 756. In Ibn Qudāma, *Istibṣār*, 315 Bulayl is missing.

[22] *Iṣāba*, IV, 607 (printed: Balīl); Ibn Mākūlā, I, 354–55. But cf. Ibn Ḥazm, *Ansāb*, 336 (... 'Amr b. Bilāl b. Bulayl b. Uḥayḥa).

[23] Lecker, "A note on early marriage links", 28.

[24] See, e.g., Ibn Qudāma, *Istibṣār*, 278. About one of Rifā'a b. Zanbar's daughters, see Ibn Sa'd, VIII, 316. See also *op. cit.*, 343.

their grandfather, Rifāʿa b. Zanbar.[25] The Wāqim fortress remained in the hands of the same family for generations and we know that it was owned by the descendants (*Āl*) of Abū Lubāba.[26]

2. Al-Mustaẓill near the Ghars well once belonged to Uḥayḥa before it became the property of the B. ʿAbd al-Mundhir.[27]

3. Kans Ḥuṣayn, near the ablutions washstand (*mihrās*) in Qubāʾ, belonged to Ḥuṣayn b. Wadaqa b. al-Julāḥ (Uḥayḥa b. al-Julāḥ's nephew) before it became the property of the B. ʿAbd al-Mundhir as blood-wit for their grandfather, Rifāʿa b. Zanbar.[28]

4. Also, al-Khaṣī near the Mosque of Qubāʾ presumably belongs here.[29]

---

[25] Samh., I, 193. For the payment of blood-wit in the form of landed property cf. an incident between two Jews in pre-Islamic Medina: a man whose hand had been cut off demanded an orchard as compensation; Samh., I, 164. For land given by the Zurayq (Khazraj) as blood-wit (*al-nāḥiya llatī wadat B. Zurayq*) see Samh., I, 207:1.

[26] *Maghānim*, s.v., 425. There was later a court called Wāqim on the site of this fortress; Samh., s.v. Wāqim, II, 1329. Also ʿUwaym b. Sāʿida's father owned a fortress in Qubāʾ called Wāqim (below, 67n). Samhūdī (s.v. Wāqim) suggests that there were two fortresses in Qubāʾ called Wāqim, one, in al-Maskaba, belonged to ʿUwaym b. Sāʿida's father, and another, "in the place of the court called Wāqim which had belonged to Uḥayḥa before he shifted to al-ʿAṣaba". But there was probably only one Wāqim in Qubāʾ as we are dealing in both cases with the territory of the Umayya b. Zayd: ʿUwaym was a client (*ḥalīf*) of the Umayya and his mother was from among them; see below, 65n.

[27] Samh., I, 193; Samh., s.v.

[28] *Maghānim* and Samh., s.v. Kans Ḥuṣayn. Abū ʿUbayd al-Qāsim b. Sallām, *Gharīb al-ḥadīth*, Hyderabad 1384/1964–1387/1967, IV, 185 interprets *mihrās* as *ḥajar manqūr mustaṭīl ʿaẓīm ka-l-ḥawḍ yatawaḍḍaʾu minhu l-nās lā yaqdiru aḥad ʿalā taḥrīkihi*. See also Lane, *Arabic-English Lexicon*, s.v.: "A stone hollowed out, oblong, and heavy ... in which one bruises, brays, or pounds, and from which one performs the ablution called *wuḍūʾ*; a hollowed stone, of oblong shape ... consisting of a bulky stone, which several men cannot lift nor move because of its weight, capable of holding much water".

[29] It was not the only ʿAmr b. ʿAwf fortress mentioned in connection with the Mosque of Qubāʾ: the minaret of the Qubāʾ Mosque was built in the place of the Ghurra fortress; Samh., s.v. Ghurra, II, 1278. Also *Maghānim*, s.v., 303: *uṭum bi-l-madīna li-B. ʿAmr b. ʿAwf buniya (sic) makānahu manāratu masjid Qubāʾ*. There is some uncertainty about the fortress' name. According to Samhūdī (*loc. cit.*), it appears that the name was also pronounced with an *ʿayn* (i.e., instead of a *ghayn*) because, Samhūdī continues, al-Majd (= Majd

Al-Khaṣī was built by the ʿAmr b. ʿAwf (more specifically, it seems, by the Jaḥjabā) near the Wāqim fortress.[30] It had once belonged to the Jaḥjabā or, we are told, the Salm b. Imriʾi l-Qays b. Mālik b. al-Aws, and later became the property of the B. ʿAbd al-Mundhir as part of the blood-wit they received for their grandfather. The Salm seem to be irrelevant here: al-Khaṣī was built by the ʿAmr b. ʿAwf while the Salm (above, 28) were of the Aws Allāh. This fortress was presumably part of the blood-wit settlement.

Al-ʿAṣaba

When the Jaḥjabā left Qubāʾ, they went to al-ʿAṣaba west of Qubāʾ. Al-ʿAṣaba was the site of al-Ṣafāṣif, one of the four markets of pre-Islamic Medina.[31] There was an easy access to al-ʿAṣaba from the ʿAqīq Valley, and those coming from Mecca did not have to cross Medina first. When the Prophet in his famous

---

al-Dīn al-Fīrūzābādī) mentions the fortress in both places. Indeed, in the *Maghānim* we find another entry, obviously relating to the same fortress: "ʿAzza is a fortress put up by the ʿAmr b. ʿAwf which was located on the site of the (later) minaret of the Qubāʾ mosque. It belonged to the Ḥabīb b. ʿAmr b. ʿAwf, the clan (*raht*) of Suwayd b. al-Ṣāmit"; *Maghānim*, 262. The words of an unspecified scholar quoted elsewhere in the same book (*Maghānim*, 328) are clearer about the replacement of the fortress by the minaret: "One of the scholars mentioned that at the place where the minaret of the Qubāʾ Mosque was built there had been a fortress of the ʿAmr b. ʿAwf called ʿAzza. It had been destroyed and the minaret of the mosque was built in its place". It is unlikely that the fortress was called both ʿAzza and Ghurra. Perhaps the less common ʿAzza was the correct name, the more so since like the names of many fortresses in Medina it connotes strength. On the Ḥabīb see Ibn Ḥazm, *Ansāb*, 337–38; Ibn al-Kalbī, *Nasab Maʿadd*, I, 374 f; Ibn al-Kalbī, *Jamhara*, 632–33. In the early days of Islam this group existed more in Anṣārī genealogical theory than in reality: the member of the Ḥabīb executed at the Prophet's time in retaliation for the murder of a Muslim was "the last of them", and prior to that the group numbered two or three; Ibn al-Kalbī, *op. cit.*, 633.

[30] Also called Waqār([?], *yuqālu lahu Waqār*); variant in *ʿUmdat al-akhbār*, 274:3: Warqā. According to al-Zubayr b. Bakkār, al-Khaṣī is east of the Mosque of Qubāʾ; one of the mosque's columns (he gives precise details of its location) was placed on Biʾr al-Khaṣī (i.e., the well of this fortress); *Maghānim*, Samh. and *ʿUmdat al-akhbār*, s.v. al-Khaṣī.

[31] Lecker, "On the markets of Medina", 134.

Hijra came to the ʿAqīq (more specifically, in al-Jathjātha, south of Ḥamrāʾ al-Asad), he asked to be shown a way that could bring him to the ʿAmr b. ʿAwf without approaching Medina. Both the Muhājirūn (i.e., those who had arrived at Medina before the Prophet) and the Anṣār, we are told, used to wait for him on Ḥarrat al-ʿAṣaba, or the lava-field of al-ʿAṣaba.[32] The same route was taken by ʿUmar b. al-Khaṭṭāb and ʿAyyāsh b. Abī Rabīʿa when they arrived at Medina: from the ʿAqīq they went straight to Qubāʾ via al-ʿAṣaba.[33]

The distance between al-ʿAṣaba and Qubāʾ was so small that al-ʿAṣaba was sometimes considered part of Qubāʾ. In a report on the arrival of the first Muhājirūn to al-ʿAṣaba it is said to be "a place in Qubāʾ".[34] The distinction between the two places which existed in early Islam disappeared in later periods. Having studied the reports on the vicinity of Qubāʾ, Samhūdī concludes that al-ʿAṣaba and the well called Ghars were in fact part of Qubāʾ and formed its western and eastern boundaries, respectively. (He could find no record concerning the northern boundary of Qubāʾ, but only details on the distance between Qubāʾ and Medina.[35])

That the distinction between Qubāʾ and al-ʿAṣaba was lost can also be demonstrated by what we know about the Unayf (see below). They were clients of the Jaḥjabā and lived between Qubāʾ and al-ʿAṣaba. However, Samhūdī remarks that their dwellings at Biʾr ʿAdhq and its environs were in fact in Qubāʾ.[36]

[32] Ibn Saʿd, I, 233. The Prophet's alleged wish not to approach Medina smacks of polemics and should probably be associated with the dispute between the ʿAmr b. ʿAwf (Aws) and the Khazraj about the Prophet's stay in Qubāʾ.

[33] Ibn Saʿd, III, 271. See also Waq., I, 341; II, 454–55. On a visit by al-Walīd b. ʿAbd al-Malik to the mosque of al-ʿAṣaba see *Aghānī*, XIII, 119 (printed: al-Qaṣaba!). The Mosque of Qubāʾ was one of those rebuilt by al-Walīd b. ʿAbd al-Malik; Anon., *al-ʿUyūn wa-l-ḥadāʾiq fī akhbār al-ḥaqāʾiq*, ed. M.J. de Goeje, Leiden 1871, 12 (*aḥdatha* means "rebuilt" in this context).

[34] Samh., s.v. al-ʿUṣba; Bakrī, s.v. al-Muʿaṣṣab, IV, 1244.

[35] Samh., s.v. Qubāʾ, II, 1284. For more on the problem of the northern boundary of the ʿĀliya in general see above, 6. For Wadi Rānūnā which flowed in al-ʿAṣaba see Lecker, "On the markets of Medina", 136.

[36] Samh., I, 194, and see 162–63; II, 875. Al-Zubayr (b. Bakkār) says that the Balī clans al-ʿAjlān, Unayf and Ghuṣayna were clients of the ʿAmr b. ʿAwf. (This information is accurate only with regard to the first two groups: the

We now follow the Jaḥjabā into al-ʿAṣaba. As is common in our information on tribal territories in pre-Islamic Medina, the central theme is fortress-building. The dominant figure among the Jaḥjabā was Uḥayḥa b. al-Julāḥ. He would have been called today an agricultural entrepreneur. He is portrayed as a niggardly landowner who sold his products for postponed payment at interest. He controlled almost all the estates of the Medinans and employed ninety-nine camels when irrigating his land. He had a palm-grove in al-Jurf (three miles north of Medina) and used to go out and check it almost daily.[37] In addition, he owned a village in the territory of the Sulaym called Ḥanadh.[38] This is a slightly exaggerated description of a successful businessman who lived in Medina a few decades before the Islamic era.

Uḥayḥa built the Ḍaḥyān fortress (cf. above, 56) in al-ʿAṣaba, and one assumes that he built it after the Jaḥjabā had left Qubāʾ. It is possible though that Uḥayḥa simultaneously owned three

Ghuṣayna were clients of the ʿAwf b. al-Khazraj; see Ibn Mākūlā, I, 184–85: ... *B. Ghuṣayna ... wa-ḥilfuhum fī B. ʿAwf b. al-Khazraj.*) Al-Zubayr adds (or perhaps it was Ibn ʿAbd al-Barr) that these were whole clans of the Balī among the Anṣār (*wa-hiya qabāʾil bi-asrihā min Balī fī l-Anṣār*). Later in the same passage, the statement that they were clients is refuted, probably by Ibn ʿAbd al-Barr: *wa-lam yakun ʿashāʾir hāʾulāʾi ḥulafāʾ*; Ibn ʿAbd al-Barr al-Namarī, *al-Inbāh ʿalā qabāʾil al-ruwāt*, in *Majmūʿat al-rasāʾil al-kamāliyya fī l-ansāb*, Ṭāʾif: Maktabat al-Maʿārif, n. d., no. 2, 49–122, at 120. This refutation by the 5th/11th century Andalusian scholar is reminiscent of the remark made by his Andalusian contemporary Ibn Ḥazm with regard to the client status of Abū l-Haytham b. al-Tayyihān, one of the *nuqabāʾ* at the ʿAqaba meeting: "It was said that the two [i.e., Abū l-Haytham and his brother] were clients of the Anṣār from Quḍāʿa. This is no doubt wrong, because none of the *nuqabāʾ* was a client. On the contrary, the *nuqabāʾ* were the most excellent of their people, men of pure genealogy" (*mina l-ṣamīmi l-ṣarīḥ*); Ibn Ḥazm, *Ansāb*, 340. See also Lecker, "Muḥammad at Medina", 52, n. 152 (where "confederate" [*ḥalīf*] should be replaced by "client"; above, 46n). Since there were Balawīs in al-Andalus (Ibn Ḥazm, *Ansāb*, 443) it stands to reason that problems relating to their prestige and image, rather than lack of accurate genealogical and historical information, are behind the refutations of client status.

[37] *Aghānī*, XIII, 123: *wa-kāna rajulan ṣanīʿan li-l-māl shaḥīḥan ʿalayhi yabīʿu* (printed: *yatbaʿu*; and see *Khizāna*, III, 358) *bayʿa l-ribā bi-l-Madīna ḥattā kāda yuḥīṭu bi-amwālihim. Wa-kāna lahu tisʿun*(!) *wa-tisʿūna baʿīran* (*Khizāna*: *biʾran* [!]) *kulluhā yanḍaḥu ʿalayhā.*

[38] Lecker, *The Banū Sulaym*, 105.

fortresses: al-Mustaẓill and Wāqim in Qubā' (above, 56 f), and al-Ḍaḥyān in al-ʿAṣaba (i.e., that he had a fortress in al-ʿAṣaba even before he left Qubā'). Al-Mustaẓill and Wāqim were presumably in the court of the Jaḥjabā clan, while al-Ḍaḥyān was in Uḥayḥa's own estate outside the clan's court.[39] Indeed, one verse (or, rather, one version of a verse) suggests that al-Ḍaḥyān (here called: Ḍāḥin) was built on Uḥayḥa's estate in al-ʿAṣaba.[40]

The name al-Ḍaḥyān, "the one exposed to the sun", is of course the negative of the name of al-Mustaẓill, "the one shaded from the sun". These names may be indicative of the topography. Al-Ḍaḥyān was located in an elevated place (possibly for better defensibility), since we know that it could be seen from a great distance. Al-Ḍaḥyān is defined as "the black fortress of al-ʿAṣaba" (the definition is clearly aimed at Medinans familiar with the fortresses of their town). It was a square fortress with a width almost the same as its length, and built twice; the first time being when Uḥayḥa constructed it from "the white stones of the lava flows", but it crumbled.[41]

---

[39] The estate in question is called "al-Ghāba", which is probably a *lectio facilior*; *Aghānī*, XIII, 123–24. Other versions concerning this place-name are al-Qubāba (Yaq., s.v. Ḍaḥyān; Yaq., s.v. al-Qubāba and *Maghānim*, s.v., 331–32 say only that it was one of the fortresses of Medina); also Qanān/Qinān (Samh., s.v. Ḍaḥyān, quoting Yāqūt); probably also al-Qunāba (Yaq., s.v., defines it as a fortress [!] belonging to Uḥayḥa b. al-Julāḥ). Bakrī, s.v. al-Qunāba, says: *uṭum min āṭāmi l-Madīna.* Wellhausen, *Skizzen* IV, 43 has wrongly: al-ʿIbâba (his source, the above-mentioned passage from the *Aghānī*, has al-Ghāba).

[40] "I built, *after* Mustaẓill, Ḍāḥin I built it in ʿUṣba with my money"; *Aghānī*, XIII, 123–24: *wa-kāna lahu uṭumāni, uṭum fī qawmihi yuqālu lahu l-Mustaẓill ... wa-uṭumuhu al-Ḍaḥyān fī arḍihi llatī yuqālu lahā l-Ghāba (sic) ... banaytu baʿda Mustaẓillin Ḍāḥiyā banaytuhu bi-ʿUṣbatin min māliyā.* Uḥayḥa reportedly took shelter in al-Mustaẓill when he fought Tubbaʿ Asʿad Abū Karib al-Ḥimyarī. But elsewhere we are told that when he fought against Tubbaʿ, he was in al-Ḍaḥyān; *Aghānī*, XIII, 120; *Khizāna*, III, 355, 356–57. The Dār al-Kutub edition of the *Aghānī* similarly has al-Ghāba (variant: al-ʿ.nāya, al-ʿ.nāna, al-ʿ.bāya, al-ʿĀliya); *Aghānī*, XV, ed. ʿAbd al-Salām Hārūn, Cairo 1379/1959, 47–48.

[41] Samh., I, 194 (*banāhu awwalan min bathra bayḍā' fa-saqaṭa, yaʿnī min ḥijārati l-ḥirāri l-bīḍ, wa-kāna yurā mina l-makāni l-baʿīd*). See *Lisān al-ʿarab*, s.v. *b.th.r.*: *al-bathru, arḍ ḥijāratuhā ka-ḥijārati l-ḥarra illā annahā bīḍ*; *Maghānim*, s.v. Ḍaḥyān. According to the *Aghānī*, XIII, 124:2, the black

The Jaḥjabā (together with a group called Majdaʿa) built al-Hujaym fortress in al-ʿAṣaba "near the mosque in which the Prophet prayed". The well of al-Hujaym was named after the fortress.[42] The mosque mentioned is *Masjid al-tawba* ("the Mosque of Repentance"). Samhūdī did not know why it was given this name.[43]

Finally, another fortress in al-ʿAṣaba was between al-Ṣafāṣif (where the above-mentioned market was located) and the Wadi (i.e., probably Wadi Rānūnā). During the Islamic period, it was given the name of ʿUdayna after a woman who lived in it.[44]

Thus, when the Prophet and the Muhājirūn came to Medina, the Jaḥjabā had already been in al-ʿAṣaba for two or three generations.

The Balī in the Qubāʾ area

There was a strong Balawī element in Qubāʾ where the Balī clans were clients of the ʿAmr b. ʿAwf.[45]

---

building had two white additions (perhaps later ones): *banāhu bi-ḥijāra sūd wa-banā ʿalayhi nabra bayḍāʾ mithla l-fiḍḍa thumma jaʿala ʿalayhā mithlahā, yarāhā l-rākib min masīrati yawm aw naḥwihi.*

According to a contemporary source (quoted in *Maghānim*, 457), the ruins of al-Ḍaḥyān can now be seen west of Biʾr Shumayla and north of al-ʿAṣaba. Madanī, "Uṭūm al-Madīna l-munawwara", 218–19 reports that the remaining walls of al-Ḍaḥyān are almost fourteen metres high and on the western side the fortress is about ten metres wide. The area surrounding the fortress appears to have included houses. About forty metres south-west of the fortress there is an old and desolate well said to have been that of the fortress. It is assumed, Madanī adds, that it was originally inside the fortress. (He gives some further details.) See also above, 11n.

[42] Samh., I, 194; Samh., s.v. Biʾr al-Hujaym (variant: Hajam). Qaṣr Ibn Māh was "beneath" (*asfal min*) Biʾr Hujaym; see Samh., s.v. Qaṣr Ibn Māh. Ibn Shabba mentions among the wells of Medina one called al-Hujayr, with a *rāʾ* instead of *mīm* and says that it was in the Ḥarra above Qaṣr Ibn Māh; see Samh., s.v. Biʾr al-Hujaym.

[43] Samh., II, 876–77. The famous repentance of Abū Lubāba is usually linked with Qubāʾ, not with al-ʿAṣaba. On mosques built where the Prophet had prayed cf. Goldziher, *Muslim Studies*, II, 279; below, 69n.

[44] Samh., s.v.; *Maghānim*, s.v., 249.

[45] The ʿAjlān of Balī will be discussed in detail in the following chapter in connection with their role in the Ḍirār incident.

The Ḥishna b. ʿUkārima and ʿUwaym b. Sāʿida

We begin with the Ḥishna who were probably among the smallest and least significant groups in Medina. That one of them, the Companion ʿUwaym b. Sāʿida, had a role in the development of Islamic law gained them what little prominence they have in Islamic history. ʿUwaym is also a case-study in double genealogy, as some said that he was a member of the Balī while according to others he was an Anṣārī.

ʿUwaym is given as the source of a report which interprets Qur'ān 9,108: "A mosque that was founded upon god-fearing from the first day is worthier for thee to stand in; therein are men who love to cleanse themselves; and God loves those who cleanse themselves" (trans. Arberry). The report somewhat bluntly portrays the Prophet in the role of a mere medium since he received the revelation from God but did not know what it meant, and had therefore to ask about it the people *in the Mosque of Qubā'*. In other words, the report takes for granted something which is not unanimously accepted: that the unnamed mosque which "was founded upon god-fearing from the first day" was that of Qubā'. It is therefore intrinsically polemical without resorting to the language of polemics.[46]

So the Prophet asked the people in the Qubā' Mosque about the cleanliness for which God praised them in the above verse. They replied (in marked humility): "By God, O Messenger of God, we know nothing, but we had Jewish neighbours and they used to wash their posteriors from the excrement, and we washed the way they did".[47]

---

[46] Saʿīd b. Jubayr favoured this interpretation; see below, 78.

[47] *Wa-'llāhi yā rasūla llāhi lā naʿlamu shay'an illā annahu kāna lanā jīrān mina l-yahūd fa-kānū yaghsilūna adbārahum mina l-ghā'iṭ fa-ghasalnā kamā ghasalū*; Kister (M.J. and Menahem), "On the Jews of Arabia — Some Notes", 237 = ʿAlī b. Abī Bakr al-Haythamī, *Majmaʿ al-zawā'id wa-manbaʿ al-fawā'id*, Beirut 1967, I, 212; and see Ṭabarānī, *Kabīr*, XVII, 140; Ṭabarī, *Tafsīr*, XI, 22–24. The washing, we are told, followed the basic cleaning using stones (*wa-kānū idhā aḥdathū atbaʿū l-ḥijārata bi-l-mā'*); *Lisān al-ʿarab*, s.v. *ṭ.h.r.*, 505a. One source quotes the Prophet as saying that ʿUwaym was one of those meant by the Qur'ān verse. The same source continues, "and ʿUwaym was the first [i.e., the first Muslim] who washed his posteriors with water, according to what became known to us, and God knows best"; Ibn

Similar reports go back to a son (called Muḥammad) and a grandson (called Muḥammad b. Yūsuf) of the famous Jewish convert, ʿAbdallāh b. Salām.[48] M.J. and Menahem Kister suggest that washing or wiping after defecating (*istinjāʾ*), a requirement in Islamic law, was derived from Jewish practice according to its adoption by the Anṣār. They conclude (240):

> This is one of the few cases in which we find explicit testimony of the way a Jewish practice became Muslim law. Should this exceptional case teach us about the common situation,[49] this should instruct us *to be cautious in evaluating the amount of the direct influence of Judaism on the emergence of early Islamic Law.* It seems that sometimes, as in this case, Islam drew more from pre-Islamic local practices, especially from the Anṣār, Muḥammad's supporters in Medina.[50]

It is this assumed Anṣārī medium which mainly concerns us here. In what follows I agrue that this case is, after all, one of *direct* influence from Judaism:[51] ʿUwaym b. Sāʿida was a descendant of a Jewish proselyte.

ʿUwaym b. Sāʿida is usually said to have been a member of the Umayya b. Zayd subdivision of the ʿAmr b. ʿAwf. His pedigree is given as follows: ʿUwaym b. Sāʿida b. ʿĀʾish b. Qays b. Zayd b. Umayya. However, Ibn al-Kalbī, who provides an alterna-

Saʿd, III, 459–60. For a recent survey of "the Jewish/Christian contribution to Islam" see Lewis, *The Jews of Islam*, 68 f.

[48] Kister (M.J. and Menahem), "On the Jews of Arabia—Some Notes", 237, n. 29; Ibn Qudāma, *Istibṣār*, 195; cf. *Usd al-ghāba*, IV, 323:19; G. Vajda, "Juifs et musulmans selon le ḥadīṯ", in *Journal Asiatique* 229 (1937), 57–127, at 66 f.

[49] The authors remark that we do not usually find explicit testimony of the Jewish origin.

[50] See more recently Menahem Kister's Appendix to M.J. Kister's "'Do not assimilate yourselves ...'", 354 f, esp. 355, n. 4.

[51] The mention of a son and grandson of the Jewish convert to Islam, ʿAbdallāh b. Salām, points in this direction.

tive pedigree, says that 'Uwaym belonged to the Balī.[52] The Balawī pedigree is supported by Ibn Isḥāq who calls him 'Uwaym b. Sā'ida b. Ṣal'aja,[53] adding that he was a member of the Balī and a client (*ḥalīf*) of the Umayya b. Zayd.[54]

Now I assume that whenever we find a clash between Balawī and Anṣārī pedigrees, the former is correct and the latter fake. We even sometimes find the "fingerprint" of family members on the false claim. There is a simple reason for this. Balawī descent equalled client status, an intolerably inferior position in the eyes of later generations as well. Indeed, it was perhaps found to be even more humiliating later in the Islamic period, following the influx of non-Arab *mawālī*. In order to assert their superior status, Arab clients or their descendants claimed Anṣārī pedigrees and repudiated the Balawī ones. Such efforts would not mislead impartial genealogists, but a sympathetic genealogist could occasionally report a family's claim. However, the diversity of the sources usually denies such claims any exclusivity and the Balawī origin finally emerges. Descendants of Balawī Companions were in some cases later assimilated into the Anṣār by adopting a respectable Anṣārī pedigree; but, when an Anṣārī pedigree is claimed with regard to the time of the Prophet, it is false.

The conflicting pedigrees of Balawīs are a case of beneficial contradictory evidence since they reveal that early Islamic society was indeed preoccupied with genealogy. We also get a glimpse of "real life" through the tension between genealogy specialists and family members or descendants of the people who are "genealo-

[52] See Ibn al-Kalbī, *Nasab Ma'add*, I, 368; Ibn al-Kalbī, *Jamhara*, 625–26. Waq., I, 159 mentions him as one of the Umayya b. Zayd without referring to the Balawī version.

[53] Ibn Sa'd remarks: we did not find Ṣal'aja in the genealogical literature.

[54] Ibn Sa'd, III, 459 ('Uwaym's mother was of the Umayya b. Zayd); Ibn Qudāma, *Istibṣār*, 279; *Istī'āb*, III, 1248. Ibn Ḥazm, *Ansāb*, 334:5 calls him 'Uwaymir b. Sā'ida. See verses by his great-grandson, the poet al-Sarī b. 'Abd al-Raḥmān, in Yaq., s.v. Qubā ('Uwaymir) and an entry on the same poet in *Aghānī*, XVIII, 65f ('Uwaym). Al-Sarī received from the Caliph 'Uthmān's grandson, 'Umar b. 'Amr b. 'Uthmān, the proceeds of an estate in Qubā' for as long as he lived; *loc. cit.*, 68. 'Umar was the father of the poet 'Abdallāh b. 'Umar, better known as al-'Arjī; Ibn Ḥazm, *Ansāb*, 84:–4.

gized". We find expressions such as *wa-ahluhu* (often *wa-ahluhā* in cases of descent from a slave-girl which was also a sensitive matter) *yaqūlūna* or *wa-qawmuhu yazʿumūna* as indications that the specialist knows about the contradictory claim and does not accept it.[55]

ʿUwaym's affiliation to the Balī is confirmed by the long report on the dispersion of the Quḍāʿa tribes, including the Balī, which Bakrī quotes from Ibn Shabba:

> Clans (*qabāʾil*) of the Balī settled in an area called Shaghb wa-Badā[56] between Taymāʾ and Medina. They had remained there until war broke out between the Ḥishna b. ʿUkārima b. ʿAwf b. Jusham b. Wadm b. Humaym b. Dhuhl b. Hanī b. Balī and the B. al-Rabaʿa b. Muʿtamm b. Wadm—this is what Ibn Shabba said. But in fact the al-Rabaʿa are the descendants of Saʿd b. Humaym b. Dhuhl b. Hanī b. Balī. They [the Ḥishna] killed some of the Rabaʿa and then sought shelter in Taymāʾ (*laḥiqū bi-Taymāʾ*). But the Jews refused to let them into their fortress as long as they adhered to a different faith, so they converted to Judaism, and they let them enter. They [= the Ḥishna] were with them [= the Jews] for some time, then a group of them set out to Medina. When God made Islam victorious, some of their children were still there. Among them were ʿUwaym b. Sāʿida, whose offspring adopted an ʿAmr b. ʿAwf b. Mālik b. al-Aws pedigree (*wa-qadi ntasaba waladuhu ilā ʿAmr b. ʿAwf b. Mālik b. al-Aws*) and Kaʿb b. ʿUjra, who held to his Balawī pedigree (*kāna muqīman fī nasabihi min Balī*) and later adopted the pedigree of the ʿAmr b. ʿAwf of the Anṣār. The groups (*buṭūn*) of the Ḥishna

[55] This does not mean that we are always able to separate "family materials" from "specialist materials". The two types are often mingled beyond recognition.

[56] On these places see M. Lecker, "Biographical notes on Ibn Shihāb al-Zuhrī", in *JSS* (forthcoming, 1996), the section entitled: "Zuhrī's estate in the region of Shaghb wa-Badā".

> b. 'Ukārima remained in Taymā' until God inflicted upon the Jews of the Ḥijāz his severe punishment and affliction (*min ba'sihi wa-niqmatihi*). [I.e., then they no longer remained there. In other words, this text implies that the Jews of Taymā' were expelled together with the Ḥishna proselytes who were their clients.][57]

In short, 'Uwaym, a prominent figure in connection with the origin of the practice of washing after carrying out one of the body's natural functions, was Jewish before he converted to Islam; this is a case of direct borrowing from the Jews.

The Ḥishna are not in the list of Arab clans that stayed with the Jews in Medina before the settlement of the Aws and Khazraj[58] because they were so few,[59] and more importantly, because they came after the Aws and Khazraj had settled.

Ḥishna's quarters were east of the Mosque of Qubā', in an area called al-Maskaba,[60] and a fortress there called Wāqim belonged to 'Uwaym's father, Sā'ida b. 'Ā'ish.[61]

---

[57] Bakrī, I, 29–30. See already Th. Nöldeke's review of J. Wellhausen's *Reste arabischen Heidentums*, in *ZDMG* 41 (1887), 707–26, at 720, later referred to by Wellhausen, *Skizzen* IV, 13, n. 2; Nöldeke, *Beiträge zur Kenntnis der Poesie der alten Araber*, Hannover 1864, 55; Horovitz, "Judaeo-Arabic relations in pre-Islamic times", 177, 187; Gil, "The origin of the Jews of Yathrib", 210–11. The text in Bakrī is followed by verses by Abū al-Dhayyāl al-Yahūdī of the Ḥishna lamenting the expulsion of the Jews of Taymā'; see also Jumaḥī, I, 29 f; Nöldeke, *op. cit.*, 79. On Abū al-Dhayyāl see *GAS*, II, 297. And see the entries on the place-names mentioned in these verses: Yaq., s.v. Za'bal ("a place near Medina"); Bakrī, s.v. al-Kibs ("a place in Taymā'"). Also Ḥamad al-Jāsir, *Fī shimāl gharb al-jazīra (nuṣūṣ, mushāhadāt, inṭibā'āt)*, Riyāḍ, 2nd. printing, 1401/1981, 389, 536, 586 (where "Ra'bal" is a misprint of "Za'bal"). (The uncommon name Za'bal appears as the name of a *baṭn* belonging to the Ḥārith b. Ka'b; Ibn 'Abd Rabbihi, *al-'Iqd al-farīd*, ed. Aḥmad Amīn *et al.*, Cairo 1384/1965, III, 396:2. For Za'bal as a proper name see Ibn Mākūlā, IV, 79.)

[58] Samh., I, 162 f; Ibn Rusta, 61–62.

[59] Bakrī, I, 29 uses the word *nafar* ("a number of men, from three to ten") to refer to the Ḥishna who came from Taymā' to Medina.

[60] On al-Maskaba cf. Samh., I, 193; above, 57n.

[61] Misprinted: 'Ābis; Samh., s.v. Wāqim; Samh., s.v. al-Maskaba. 'Uwaym had four sons: 'Utba, Suwayd, Qaraẓa and 'Abd al-Raḥmān. The last-

The Unayf

The Unayf of the Balī (according to some, they descended from the Amalekites) were probably the largest Balawī clan in Qubā', as indicated by the abundant information on their territory. They also had a *majlis* of their own (below, 69). The Unayf who settled in Qubā'[62] are included in Ibn Zabāla's list of "the Arabs who were *with* the Jews" (i.e., who were the Jews' clients) before the (arrival of the) Anṣār.[63]

Samhūdī remarks that Ibn Zabāla did not mention the Unayf's territory in the chapter of his book dealing with the fortresses of the 'Amr b. 'Awf in Qubā', providing the convincing explanation that these Balawīs were the clients of the Jews in Qubā' (in other words, as such, they were discussed in the chapter dealing with the Jews' clients). They were, Samhūdī continues, not from the Aws themselves as some argue, but were clients of the Aws (i.e., at a later stage, when they had ceased to be the clients of the Jews), or more precisely of the Jaḥjabā, as can be seen from Ibn Isḥāq's list of the participants in the Battle of Badr.

Their territory is clearly defined as being between the 'Amr b. 'Awf (viz., Qubā') and al-'Aṣaba. The 'Adhq well and al-Qā'im orchard (both in Unayf's quarter) were still known in Qubā' at the time of Samhūdī.[64]

So, by the beginning of the Islamic era the Unayf had become the clients of the Jaḥjabā. One such client was, for example, 'Abd al-Raḥmān b. 'Abdallāh Abū 'Aqīl. The definitions of his status vary: he was 1. a *ḥalīf* (client) of the Jaḥjabā; 2. or *fī 'idād*

---

mentioned was the eldest as 'Uwaym's *kunya* was Abū 'Abd al-Raḥmān; Ibn Sa'd, III, 459. On 'Abd al-Raḥmān and his brother Suwayd see Ibn Sa'd, V, 78.

[62] Bakrī, I, 28.

[63] A poet of the Unayf boasted that if Qubā' could talk, it would have said that they had settled there before the time of 'Ād and Tubba'; Samh., I, 162:–1: *wa-law naṭaqat yawman Qubā'u la-khabbarat bi-annā nazalnā qabla 'Ādin wa-Tubba'i.*

[64] Samh., I, 194. See Ibn Isḥāq's words in Ibn Hishām, II, 347. See also Waq., I, 161.

Jaḥjabā; 3. or *ṣāḥib Jaḥjabā'*,[65] but the conclusion remains the same.

There are rich details on the fortresses and orchards of the Unayf. The al-Mi'a orchard belonged to one of them.[66] Another orchard, al-Qā'im, was south-west of the Mosque of Qubā'.[67] The Unayf owned the fortress of al-Ajashsh near the Lāwa well, two fortresses between the al-Mi'a and al-Qā'im orchards and other fortresses near the 'Adhq well and elsewhere.[68] Two Unayf fortresses called al-Nawwāḥāni were close to their *majlis*.[69] The

---

[65] No. 1: *Iṣāba*, IV, 325; no. 2: Ibn Ḥazm, *Ansāb*, 442; no. 3: Ibn al-Kalbī, *Nasab Ma'add*, II, 708. Incidentally, 'Abd al-Raḥmān appears to have been a name given to Abū 'Aqīl by the Prophet, since in Ṭabarī, *Tafsīr*, X, 135:18 his name is Ḥabḥāb while in *Iṣāba*, IV, 325 his former name is 'Abd al-'Uzzā.

[66] See Samh. and *Maghānim*, s.v.

[67] *Fī qiblati* [add.: *masjid*] *Qubā' mina l-maghrib*; Samh. and *Maghānim*, s.v. Also Samh., II, 875: the court of the Unayf is in Qubā' near the orchard (*māl*) known today as al-Qā'im, south-west of the Mosque of Qubā' and near the 'Adhq well. On the mosque of the Unayf see Samh., II, 875. The mosque was one of those in which the Prophet prayed. It was near the 'Adhq well, west of the Mosque of Qubā', in their court (*dār*; read: *māl*?) known as al-Qā'im; Aḥmad b. Aḥmad al-Qalyūbī, *al-Nubdha al-laṭīfa fī bayān maqāṣid al-Ḥijāz wa-ma'ālimihi al-sharīfa*, MS Nuruosmaniye Kütüphanesi 2935/3442, 29b. At the time of the Prophet there was no mosque there and they later built it where the Prophet had prayed. The elders of the Unayf reported that the Prophet had prayed near their fortress when he visited his ill Companion Ṭalḥa b. al-Barā'; Samh., *loc. cit.* On Ṭalḥa see *Iṣāba*, III, 524–26.

[68] Samh., I, 162; *Aghānī*, XIX, 95:14 (written: Nayf; Wellhausen, *Skizzen* IV, 12); Ibn Rusta, 62:1; Ibn Ḥazm, *Ansāb*, 442:4. According to a contemporary source (quoted in *Maghānim*, 456), Bi'r 'Adhq in Qubā', called now Bi'r al-Ribāṭ, was joined to al-'Ayn al-Zarqā'. On al-Ajashsh see also Samh. and *Maghānim*, s.v. For al-Ajashsh as a proper name of a man of the Quḍā'a see Ibn Sa'd, VIII, 374. There is a variant reading of the name 'Adhq: Naṣr, *Amkina*, 107a has: Bi'r Ghadaq. He says that it is near al-Qā' fortress of the Balawīs. Naṣr's words are quoted by Yaq. in s.vv. Bi'r Ghadaq and Ghadaq (but Naṣr is not mentioned). Cf. Samh. and *Maghānim*, s.v. Bi'r Ghadaq. Note that there was another 'Adhq in the 'Āliya, a fortress belonging to the Umayya b. Zayd of the Aws Allāh, not to the Umayya b. Zayd who lived in Qubā' and were a subdivision of the 'Amr b. 'Awf.

[69] *Maghānim*, 366; Samh., s.v. al-Nawwāḥāni. (Another case of twin fortresses was that of al-Shaykhāni in al-Wālij village between Medina and Uḥud; Samh., s.vv. Shaykhāni, al-Wālij.) For another *majlis* in Qubā' see below, 105n (*Majlis Banī l-Mawālī*). For a *majlis* in Medina in which a tribal idol was placed see Lecker, "Idol worship in pre-Islamic Medina (Yathrib)", 340. See also Suhaylī, *al-Rawḍ al-unuf*, III, 15 (where a fortress called al-Ḥ.m.y.m,

Unayf owned the fortress of al-Qāʿ, appropriately known as *uṭum al-Balawiyyīna*, near the ʿAdhq well.[70] In one source, the Unayfī Companion, Sahl b. Rāfiʿ, is said to have been *ṣāḥib al-Qāʿ*.[71] But *al-ṣāʿ*, not al-Qāʿ, is presumably the correct reading here.[72]

New information is found in a chapter of Fīrūzābādī's *al-Maghānim al-muṭāba fī maʿālim ṭāba* which was not included in Ḥamad al-Jāsir's partial edition of this book. Al-Jāsir's edition contains the fifth and longest chapter of the *Maghānim* which deals with place-names. Fortunately, al-Jāsir provides the following details in a footnote; Fīrūzābādī writes, quoting al-Zubayr b. Bakkār,[73] that the afore-mentioned fortress of al-Ajashsh belonged to Bayjān (wrongly printed: Tayḥān[74]) b. ʿĀmir b. Mālik

possibly belonging to the Unayf, is mentioned). For further details about the fortresses of the Unayf see *Maghānim*, 366n (from al-Zubayr b. Bakkār); see also *ʿUmdat al-akhbār*, 22.

[70] *Maghānim*, Yaq. and Samh., s.v.

[71] Ibn al-Kalbī, *Nasab Maʿadd*, II, 708 (*ṣāḥib al-qāʿ*; the editor refers to the wrong Qāʿs).

[72] The man who donated one of his two *ṣāʿ*s (a *ṣāʿ* is a measure used for measuring grain, etc.) of dates for the cause of Islam was a poor man, not the owner of a fortress. He was one of "those who find nothing but their endeavour" referred to in Qurʾān 9,79 (see below). Ibn Ḥajar, in his entry on Sahl b. Rāfiʿ, quotes Ibn al-Kalbī's *Jamhara* (i.e., from the part of the *Jamhara* that is still missing): "He is the owner of the *ṣāʿ* of whom the *munāfiqūn* spoke ill" (*huwa ṣāḥib al-ṣāʿi lladhī lamazahu l-munāfiqūna*, a reference to the above-mentioned verse: "Those who find fault with the believers who volunteer their free will offerings, and those who find nothing but their endeavour they deride"); *Iṣāba*, III, 199. See also *Istīʿāb*, II, 663; also Ṭabarānī, *Kabīr*, VI, 107 (*ṣāḥib al-ṣāʿayni lladhī lamazahu l-munāfiqūn*); cf. *Usd al-ghāba*, II, 365.

[73] The text is certainly from the latter's *Akhbār al-Madīna*.

[74] The reading Bayjān is confirmed by the pedigrees of some Unayfī Companions; Ibn al-Kalbī, *Nasab Maʿadd*, II, 708 (printed: Bayjān, Bayḥān); Ibn Ḥazm, *Ansāb*, 442; *Iṣāba*, s.v. ʿAbd al-Raḥmān b. ʿAbdallāh al-Balawī (better known as Abū ʿAqīl *ṣāḥib al-ṣāʿ*), IV, 325; VII, 279–80 (another competitor for the title of *ṣāḥib al-ṣāʿ*, Sahl b. Rāfiʿ of the Unayf, was mentioned above, 70n); the *Iṣāba*, III, 198–99 wrongly attaches this claim to Sahl b. Rāfiʿ of the Najjār. Waq., I, 161 has: Bayḥān. The *Istīʿāb*, IV, 1717–18 has three entries dedicated to Abū ʿAqīl, entitled Abū ʿAqīl *ṣāḥib al-ṣāʿ* and Abū ʿAqīl al-Balawī al-Anṣārī (twice). In one of the latter entries he is said to have been a client of the Thaʿlaba b. ʿAmr b. ʿAwf and in the other, of the Jaḥjabā. The same person is obviously meant. Another member of the Unayf, ʿAbdallāh b. Ṣayfī b. Wabara, was a cousin of the above-mentioned Ṭalḥa b. al-Barāʾ

b. ʿĀmir b. Unayf who lived three generations before the Islamic era.[75]

By the time of the Prophet, the Unayf had become the clients of the Jaḥjabā after having been clients of the Jews, and they lived between Qubā' and al-ʿAṣaba, the latter being the territory of their masters, the Jaḥjabā.

This impressive amount of information on the Unayf and their territory indicates the existence of a silent majority (above, 36) in the Prophet's Medina. Nothing in the evidence on the insignificant role of the Unayf during the Prophet's time suggests massive Unayf presence in the vicinity of Qubā'. Ibn al-Kalbī mentions only six Companions of this group and a few more can perhaps be added from other sources.[76] This imbalance demonstrates that we cannot rely on the *sīra* and the sources related to it (such as the Companion dictionaries) for a full or even satisfactory picture of Medinan society during the Prophet's time.[77]

The Quṣayṣ

Very little is known about the B. al-Quṣayṣ who lived in Qubā', and the texts relating to them are in a poor condition. They belonged to "the Jewish groups which remained in Medina after the settlement of the Aws and Khazraj". Samhūdī's abridged

(69n) and a client of the ʿAmr b. ʿAwf; *Iṣāba*, IV, 134.

[75] *Maghānim*, Introduction, section 3; 366n. Also Caskel, *Ǧamharat an-Nasab*, II, 542 has Tayḥān (and Bayḥān as a variant). On al-Zubayr b. Bakkār see *GAS*, I, 317 f.

[76] Ibn al-Kalbī, *Nasab Maʿadd*, II, 708.

[77] Contrast Watt, *Medina*, passim. E.g., his remarks on p. 170 (introducing a table of the first Muslims, divided by clans). Having noted that the figures refer to Muslims, he adds: "But, except where a clan had a special reason for tending to accept or to reject Islam, we may, in default of better evidence, take these figures as a rough guide to the relative strength of the clans". In my opinion, the figures should not be relied on for a description of Medinan society because they merely reflect the amount of support given to the Prophet by the Medinan clans and, to some extent, the tendentious contributions of tribal historians to the *sīra*. Considering the attitude of the Aws Allāh to the Prophet (above, Ch. 2), it is not surprising that the only reference to them in Watt's table is through the biographies of twelve women of the Khaṭma who pledged their allegiance to the Prophet.

quotation from Ibn Zabāla does not make it clear where they lived and suggests perhaps that they, like the Nāghiṣa (about whom see below) were the clients of the Unayf.[78]

The Nāghiṣa

The Nāghiṣa[79] were also from among the Jewish groups that remained in Medina when the Aws and Khazraj settled there, and they were "with the Unayf in Qubā'";[80] i.e., they were their clients. In other words, the Unayf, who were themselves clients, had clients of their own. No fortress belonging to the Nāghiṣa could be found. Moreover, the report on their location is probably wrong because it is incongruous with the fact that they were in Qubā': some said that they were a clan (*ḥayy*) from the Yemen and lived in the Shiʿb ("the road", or "the watercourse") of the Ḥarām, until ʿUmar b. al-Khaṭṭāb transferred them from the territory of the Ḥarām to *Masjid al-fatḥ*, where their *āthār* (i.e., the ruins of their houses) could be seen in later times.[81] The Ḥarām are a subdivision of the Salima (Khazraj) and lived in the Sāfila. *Masjid al-fatḥ* was also in the Sāfila, not far from their territory.

---

[78] *Wa-kāna mimman baqiya mina l-yahūd ḥīna nazalat ʿalayhimi l-Aws wa-l-Khazraj jamāʿāt, minhā B. al-Quṣayṣ wa-B. Nāghiṣa, kānū maʿa B. Unayf bi-Qubā'*; Samh., I, 163. In the *Aghānī*, XIX, 95:11 they are called B. al-Fuṣayṣ, while Ibn Rusta, 62:9 has al-Quṣayṣ. See also *ʿUmdat al-akhbār*, 341:8, quoting al-Zubayr b. Bakkār: *kāna bi-Qubā B. al-Q.ṣ.ṣ. wa-kāna lahumu l-uṭumu lladhī fī sharqiyyi mirbad (sic)*. The text is truncated at this point so we turn to the *Maghānim*, 331: "In Qubā' there were the B. al-Quṣayṣ who owned the fortress east of the *mirbad* of Muslim b. Saʿīd b. al-Mawlā". The owner of the *mirbad*, Muslim b. Saʿīd, could not be identified. In *ʿUmdat al-akhbār* this is followed by details on the fortress of a Jew named al-Muʿtariḍ b. al-Ashwas (see below, 133), then by what appears to be further details on fortresses in Qubā' owned by the B. al-Q.ṣ.ṣ. In addition to the one east of the *mirbad* they owned one called al-Aʿnaq in al-Bardaʿa orchard (*māl*), and another, Ḥ.ṣ.y.y.h., in al-Samna orchard. All three fortresses became the property of Salama b. Umayya of the ʿAmr b. ʿAwf; *ʿUmdat al-akhbār*, 341. The sentence which then follows (*wa-kānat manāziluhum fī shiʿb B. Ḥarām ḥattā naqalahum ʿUmar b. al-Khaṭṭāb [r] ilā masjidi l-fatḥ, wa-āthāruhum hunāka*) does not belong here and relates to the Nāghiṣa (see below).

[79] Elsewhere they are called B. Bāʿiṣa/Bāʿiḍa.

[80] Samh., I, 163.

[81] *Maghānim*, 331; Samh., I, 163.

The few clans of the Balī discussed above, then, did not play an important role in the history of Islam, and other clans justifiably received the limelights. Yet they were an important and often overlooked section of Qubā''s population. It is possible that the 'Amr b. 'Awf, while being the dominant element in Qubā' in the Prophet's time, were outnumbered by their Balī clients.

CHAPTER FOUR

THE ḌIRĀR MOSQUE (9 A.H.)

Qubā' was the scene of the obscure incident of the Ḍirār Mosque in 9 A.H. On his return from Tabūk, the Prophet ordered the destruction of a mosque usually called *Masjid al-ḍirār* in reference to a Qur'ān verse related to this incident. Less common names of this mosque are *Masjid al-shiqāq* and *Masjid al-nifāq*. It was built by members of the 'Amr b. 'Awf, some of whom were prominent figures. The reports on the incident shed further light on Qubā' and its inhabitants and led to some observations about the *sīra* literature in general.[1]

The verse in question, which includes a reference to *ḍirār*, is Qur'ān 9,107:

> *wa-'lladhīna ttakhadhū masjidan ḍirāran wa-kufran wa-tafrīqan bayna l-mu'minīna wa-irṣādan li-man ḥāraba llāha wa-rasūlahu min qablu wa-la-yaḥlifunna in aradnā illā l-ḥusnā wa-'llāhu yashhadu innahum la-kādhibūna.*
>
> And those who have taken a mosque in opposition (*ḍirāran*) and unbelief, and to divide the believers, and as a place of ambush for those who fought God and His Messenger aforetime — they will swear 'We desired nothing but good'; and God testifies they are truly liars (trans. Arberry).

The reports on this incident often refer to this verse (and to the one that follows it). While some marginal details in the evidence may have had an exegetical origin, the incident is no doubt historical.

[1] Part of this chapter was presented in May 1991 at a seminar in Princeton organized by Prof. Avrom Udovitch and Prof. Michael Cook. I wish to thank them both and the participants, above all Mr. Khaled Abou el-Fadl, for their thoughtful critique of my work. Throughout this chapter I often refer to (and at times disagree with) the conclusions reached by Prof. Moshe Gil in his article "The Medinan opposition to the Prophet".

THE DIVERSITY OF THE ACCOUNTS

The Ḍirār story exists in a number of independent versions, all relating to the same event, which sometimes overlap. At other times they differ. The differences are important because they define the sovereignty of the single version. We cannot tell exactly when each version was created, but they probably originated more or less simultaneously and independently of each other.

Accounts of the incident agree on the outline of events but reveal significant differences, both agreements and disagreements being equally important. The agreed outline (the building of the mosque by individuals mentioned by name; the Prophet's initial approval to the building and his later objection following a Qur'ān revelation; and the destruction of the mosque on the Prophet's orders), represent the common denominator and have a strong claim for historicity. But we should concern ourselves more with the disunity and diversity revealed by the following accounts because they faithfully reflect the earliest, formative stages of the *sīra* literature. As we shall see, there are widely divergent interpretations of the builders' motives. On this, our sources voice the different interpretations expressed, which ranged from the benign to the dangerous. Unlike the basic undisputed facts, the motives ascribed to the builders show the biased ingenuity of these accounts' creators. From the researcher's point of view, the dispute is as helpful as the accepted historical framework because through it he gains a fine viewpoint on the emergence of the *sīra* during the first Islamic century.

The Ḍirār incident is a purely Anṣārī, and more specifically, an Awsī problem, and even more specifically, an ʿAmr b. ʿAwf problem. Of these three points of specificity, the first seems to be the most relevant to the way in which the story was told by different Islamic authorities. A benign account is "friendly" to the builders of the mosque and hence pro-Anṣārī, whilst an "unfriendly" one is anti-Anṣārī. Obviously, the name given to the mosque, *ḍirār*, is Qur'anic, which means that from the inception of Islamic historiography the story of the mosque was associated with a particular Qur'ān verse. This did not make life easier for a pro-Anṣārī tribal historian. The authorities quoted below

(Sa'īd b. Jubayr, 'Urwa b. al-Zubayr and Ibn 'Abbās/Ibn 'Umar) are either the actual or the alleged creators of the accounts; the former possibility should not be ruled out a priori. For this discussion it suffices that we define them as historians of the first century. They represent the earliest stages of Islamic historiography. This point is of fundamental importance because we realize that from the beginning the accounts had a distinct tribal or sectarian colouring.[2]

Sa'īd b. Jubayr: "The envy of the brother-clan"

In the report by Sa'īd b. Jubayr (d. 95/714[3]), which is a *sabab nuzūl* or "occasion of revelation" of Qur'ān 9,107,[4] the whole story is rather benignly presented. He blames the building of the Ḍirār Mosque on a group called the B. Ghanm b. 'Awf, who were the "nephews" of the 'Amr b. 'Awf (i.e., Ghanm and 'Awf, according to him, were brothers):

> The 'Amr b. 'Awf built a mosque and their nephews (*banū ikhwatihim*), the Ghanm b. 'Awf, envied them. They said: "We too built a mosque and invited the Messenger of God to lead our prayer in it[5] as he did in the mosque of our companions. *Perhaps* Abū 'Āmir will pass by us when he comes from Syria and lead our prayer in it". When the Prophet was about to set

[2] Cf. in this context H. Motzki, "The *Muṣannaf* of 'Abd al-Razzāq al-Ṣan'ānī as a source of authentic *aḥādīth* of the first century A.H.", in *JNES* 50 (1991), 1–21. His balanced and careful reasoning brings us back to the first Islamic century as the formative period of Islam's legal tradition. For example, he observes about 'Aṭā' b. Abī Rabāḥ, on the basis of the reports which 'Abd al-Razzāq quotes from him via Ibn Jurayj: "In my opinion, his work can be considered a historically reliable source for the state of legal development at Mecca in the first decade of the second century A.H." (p. 12). Also his conclusion (p. 14) that some of 'Aṭā''s traditions about 'Umar b. al-Khaṭṭāb can be dated "with certainty" before 80 or 70 A.H.

[3] *GAS*, I, 28.

[4] See below, 84.

[5] Printed: *fa-ṣallā*, etc., "and he led our prayer in it"; read: *yuṣallī*.

out to go to them, he had the revelation [prohibiting him to go].[6]

A better and fuller version of Saʿīd's report[7] tells us that the ʿAmr b. ʿAwf built a mosque and invited the Messenger of God to pray in it, and he went to them and did so. Then their brothers,[8] the Ghanm b. ʿAwf, said: "Shall we not build a mosque and invite the Prophet to pray in it as he did in the mosque of our brothers? And *perhaps* Abū ʿĀmir will pray in it" — he was in Syria at that time. So they built a mosque and sent to the Prophet (inviting him) to pray. He stood up in order to go to them, but a number of Qur'ān verses were revealed.

Balādhurī, Ibn Shabba and Samhūdī (who quotes Ibn Shabba) all have a report going back to Saʿīd b. Jubayr. Of these, only Balādhurī mentions nephews of the ʿAmr b. ʿAwf, i.e., the Ghanm b. ʿAwf. Ibn Shabba says: their brothers, the B. Fulān (= so-and-so) b. ʿAwf[9] and Samhūdī has: B. Fulān b. ʿAmr b. ʿAwf. But since the fragments in Ṭabarī (above, n. 7) mention "B. Ghanm b. ʿAwf" and "B. Ghanm" as the builders, respectively, it seems certain that the Ghanm b. ʿAwf belong to Saʿīd b. Jubayr's original report.

---

[6] Balādh., *Ansāb*, I, 282. Cf. *Masālik al-abṣār*, I, 129 ("their brothers, the Ghanm b. ʿAwf, envied them"). More importantly, this source confirms the amendation suggested above: *wa-qālū: nabnī masjidan wa-nursilu ilā rasūli llāhi (ṣ) yuṣallī fīhi wa-yuṣallī fīhi Abū ʿĀmir al-Rāhib idhā qadima mina l-Shām li-yuthbita lahumu l-faḍl wa-l-ziyāda ʿalā ikhwatihim, zaʿamū*. Wāḥidī, 149 has: their brothers, the ʿAmr (!), envied them. The infallibility (*ʿiṣma*) of the Prophet is clearly involved here; cf. *Sīra Shāmiyya*, V, 675:10: *fa-ʿaṣama llāhu tabāraka wa-taʿālā rasūlahu (ṣ) mina l-ṣalāt fīhi*. According to Mūsā b. Jaʿfar (in *Biḥār al-anwār*, XXI, 259 f; Mūsā al-Kāẓim b. Jaʿfar, d. 183/799, was the 7th Imām of the Imāmiyya; *GAS*, I, 534 f), God had informed the Prophet of the real intentions of the *munāfiqūn* before they invited him to pray in their mosque. The Prophet and his Companions intended to go there (or so they pretended), but were hindered by supernatural phenomena.

[7] See Ibn Shabba, *Medina*, I, 52–54; Samh., II, 815; Suyūṭī, *Durr*, III, 276:24; Balādh., *Futūḥ* (Ṭabbāʿ), 8–9. Fragments of Saʿīd's report are also found in Ṭabarī, *Tafsīr*, XI, 19:27, 30.

[8] They were called "nephews" earlier on, but the difference is immaterial.

[9] Adding: *yashukku*, i.e., one of the transmitters was uncertain about their name.

This conclusion creates a serious difficulty: for all the detailed genealogical information we have on Medina, no group called the B. Ghanm b. ʿAwf (or Ghanm b. ʿAmr b. ʿAwf) could be found.[10]

Saʿīd's account is the "friendliest" from the builders' point of view and should be classified as "pro-Anṣārī", "pro-Aws", or "pro-ʿAmr b. ʿAwf". At the same time, it is an ʿIrāqī account.[11] Like its rival accounts it goes beyond the basic facts in offering an insight into the builders' motives. They were driven, we are told, by envy of the ʿAmr b. ʿAwf in whose mosque the Prophet had prayed. This "pious envy" is human and even commendable. The Qur'ān, it is true, taught us that the builders had erred, but this was beyond their control because they built the mosque in good faith and, one could add *al-aʿmāl bi-l-niyyāt*, "deeds are rewarded according to the intentions", as a well-known Islamic adage goes. In this context even their wish to see the Prophet's arch-enemy, Abū ʿĀmir, attend the mosque does not signal hostile intentions towards the Prophet or Islam.[12]

Saʿīd's account of the Ḍirār incident completely plays it down. Since the facts of the matter were presumably too well established in connection with the exegesis of the Ḍirār verse, an interpretation of the builders' intentions remained the only available possibility to create an account which was as harmless as possible.

In the context of Saʿīd's report, it is noteworthy that Saʿīd takes up an "anti-Khazrajī" position in the dispute between the Aws and Khazraj over the identity of "the mosque founded upon god-fearing" (Qur'ān 9,108). He supported the claim that it was the Mosque of Qubā' (above, 63n). The alternative claim names the Mosque of the Prophet which was on Khazrajī soil in the Sāfila of Medina. No wonder that among those who supported the latter claim we find the Khazrajīs Sahl b. Saʿd of the Sāʿida,

[10] Later in this chapter I argue that the possibility that this group was of the Khazraj has to be ruled out.

[11] Perhaps it should also be classified as Kūfan after its presumable place of origin, although it was later transmitted by the Baṣran scholars Ayyūb al-Sakhtiyānī and Ḥammād b. Zayd. On Ayyūb see Dhahabī, *Nubalā'*, VI, 15–26; on Ḥammād see Ibn Saʿd, VII, 286–87 (*wa-kāna ʿUthmāniyyan*).

[12] The tone is anything but alarming, e.g., in Ibn Shabba and Samhūdī: *wa-laʿalla Abā ʿĀmir yuṣallī fīhi.*

Ubayy b. Ka'b and Khārija b. Zayd b. Thābit, both of the Najjār and Abū Sa'īd al-Khudrī of the Ḥārith b. al-Khazraj (as well as the Qurashīs Ibn 'Umar and Sa'īd b. al-Musayyab).[13] The identity of the mosque mentioned in Qur'ān 9,108 was disputed by the Aws and Khazraj, or perhaps more specifically, the 'Amr b. 'Awf and the Najjār.

Some comparative material regarding Anṣārī rivalries is linked to the dispute between the Aws (specifically the 'Amr b. 'Awf) and the Khazraj (i.e., the Najjār) about the earliest prayers conducted in Medina after the beginning of the Anṣār's conversion to Islam. The 'Amr b. 'Awf's claim is connected with the beginnings (or alleged beginnings) of the Hijra to Qubā':

> The first Muhājirūn (*al-mutaqaddimūna fī l-hijra*) of the Companions of the Messenger of God and their Anṣārī hosts had built a mosque in Qubā' and prayed in it in the direction of Jerusalem for one year. When the Messenger of God emigrated and arrived at Qubā', he led them in prayer in it. And the people of Qubā' say: "This is the mosque 'founded on the fear of God from the first day'" (Qur'ān 9,108).[14]

The Aws/'Amr b. 'Awf claim which speaks of prayer in general is associated with the early Hijra of Abū Salama al-Makhzūmī.[15] The rival claim of the Khazraj/Najjār refers specifically to the Friday-prayer. It is supposedly inconvenient: As'ad b. Zurāra is said to have led the Anṣār in the Friday-prayer before the Prophet's Hijra. In other words, we are told that this Islamic institution was introduced not by the Prophet but by an Anṣārī before the Prophet's arrival.[16] However, seen against the competing Aws/'Amr b. 'Awf claim, this Khazraj/Najjār contention

[13] Balādh., *Futūḥ* (Ṭabbā'), 10–11. According to Rāzī, *Tafsīr*, XVI, 195, the majority of the people hold that the Mosque of the Prophet is meant.

[14] *'Umdat al-akhbār*, 139:5 (from Aḥmad b. Jābir, i.e., al-Balādhurī).

[15] On his Hijra see Ibn Hishām, II, 112–13.

[16] See M.J. and Menahem Kister, "On the Jews of Arabia — some notes", 244–47, quoting 'Abd al-Razzāq b. Hammām al-Ṣan'ānī, *al-Muṣannaf*, ed. Ḥabīb al-Raḥmān al-A'ẓamī, Beirut 1390/1970–1392/1972, III, 159–60. (J. Pedersen calls the report that the Friday-prayer was observed in Medina before the Hijra "hardly probable"; *EI*^{2}, 655b = Ibn Hishām, II, 77.)

becomes somewhat polemical. It is as if the Najjār, eager to dispute a rival claim and establish their own Islamic "firstness", paid no heed to the wider implications of the claim concerning the origin of an Islamic ritual.

'Urwa b. al-Zubayr: "Contempt and ridicule"

The account of 'Urwa b. al-Zubayr (d. between 91/711 and 101/720[17]) is totally independent of the other reports discussed here, and this is meant as a cautionary note: the common practice of interpreting a vague point in one report by referring to another which is more clearly formulated, should here be applied with great care. It is true that in the Islamic historiography it is not always possible to tell when one report ends and another begins; editorial practices, above all the practice of forming "combined reports", are to blame. These reports blurred the particular contours of the autonomous, and often contradictory, reports.[18] But, whenever possible, the autonomy of the single report must be respected; the inevitable outcome is divergence and disunity, a rather unwelcome consequence for the modern historian of Islam but a true reflection of Islamic historiography in its incipient, formative stages.

'Urwa offers us his own alternative version of the incident. Sa'd b. Khaythama built a mosque. The site once belonged to Libba (*sic*; the parallel texts have: Līna and Liyya[19]), who tethered her donkey there.[20] So the people of *Masjid al-shiqāq* ("the mosque of disunion, disunity, dissension"; the parallel texts have: *Masjid al-ḍirār*), said: "Shall we prostrate ourselves (parallel texts: pray) where Libba's donkey used to be tethered? No,

This gives Suyūṭī (*Ḥujaj mubīna*, 52) an idea for a riddle: *wa-'alā hādhā yulghazu fa-yuqālu: 'ibāda faraḍahā llāhu ta'ālā 'alā rasūlihi fa-ta'akhkhara fi'luhu lahā wa-fa'alahā qablahu 'iddatu jamā'atin* (?) *min aṣḥābihi*. The answer is of course the Friday-prayer. Suyūṭī was fond of riddles; for another riddle see *op. cit.*, 26 f.

[17] For the different dates given see al-Mizzī, *Tahdhīb al-kamāl*, XX, 23–25.

[18] See M. Lecker, "Wāqidī's account on the status of the Jews of Medina: a study of a combined report", 11 f ("The drawbacks of the combined report").

[19] Wüstenfeld, *Medina*, 131 has: Layya.

[20] For Līna as a proper name of a female cf. *Iṣāba*, VIII, 109; perhaps also Tab. Index, s.v. 'Iyāḍ b. Abī Līna al-Kindī.

we shall build a mosque in order to pray in it until Abū ʿĀmir comes and leads us in prayer there" (i.e., functions as our *imām*). He also relates that Abū ʿĀmir "fled from God and His Messenger" to the people of Mecca,[21] then went to Syria and became a Christian. And God revealed: "And those who have taken a mosque in opposition and unbelief, and to divide the believers, and as an ambush place for those who fought God and His Messenger aforetime" (Qur'ān 9,104), that is to say (the report adds) Abū ʿĀmir. Only Balādhurī (but not the parallel texts) follows this with a note (which is introduced by *qālū*, "they said"), according to which on the revelation of this verse the Prophet sent (people) to destroy the mosque.

WHEN WAS THE ḌIRĀR MOSQUE BUILT?

According to the common mainstream version, the Ḍirār Mosque only stood for a few days. Ibn Jurayj, for example, says that it was completed on Friday, and its people prayed in it on Friday, Saturday and Sunday, then it was destroyed on Monday.[22]

But there are good reasons for doubting this chronology. ʿUrwa's account makes an important point in this context: since the Ḍirār Mosque was built as a reaction to the building of a mosque by Saʿd b. Khaythama (i.e., the Mosque of Qubā'; see below), and since Saʿd was killed at Badr, one could expect the Ḍirār Mosque to have been erected before Badr, that means, several

---

[21] Cf. *Sīra Shāmiyya: bari'a mina llāhi wa-rasūlihi*, "he cleared himself of God and His Messenger".

[22] Ṭabarī, *Tafsīr*, XI, 25:6; Rāzī, *Tafsīr*, XVI, 195. Also Qurṭubī, *al-Jāmiʿ li-aḥkām al-qur'ān*, VIII, 253: when the Prophet returned from Tabūk, they came to him, having finished building the mosque and having prayed in it on Friday, Saturday and Sunday. The Prophet asked for his long shirt (*qamīṣ*) in order to dress himself and go to them, when Qur'ān verses were revealed to him concerning the Ḍirār Mosque, so he ordered it burnt down. On the expedition of Tabūk see Buhl, *Leben*, 322 f. For an explicit statement that the mosque was built just before the expedition of Tabūk see also the report of Mūsā b. Jaʿfar in *Biḥār al-anwār*, XXI, 259: "When it was evident that the Prophet was determined to travel to Tabūk, those *munāfiqūn* built a mosque outside Medina which was the Mosque of Ḍirār, wishing to meet in it and pretending that it was meant for praying". But this massive building ("it was large, had high walls .... Its construction was sound"; below, 134) could not have been accomplished in a short time.

years before its destruction in 9 A.H. In this case it appears that the rare, and from the Islamic point of view, problematic reports have a better claim to historicity. There are three further testimonies attesting to an early date of construction. The most straightforward one comes from the early Qur'ān commentator, al-Ḍaḥḥāk (b. Muzāḥim),[23] who says that people of the Anṣār built a mosque near the Mosque of Qubā', "and it became known to us that it was the first mosque built in Islam".[24] Then we are told that when he was on his way to Badr (2 A.H.), the Prophet sent a member of the Balī to the Ḍirār Mosque "because of something [i.e., a plot] which had become known to him about them" (below, 138). Finally, according to 'Abd al-Jabbār (below, 145n), Abū 'Āmir al-Rāhib had built a mosque in order to spread his propaganda against the Prophet in it. This mosque, which must have been built before the Battle of Uḥud (in which Abū 'Āmir already fought against the Prophet), could have been identical with the Ḍirār Mosque, or perhaps it was a more humble predecessor of the same mosque.

According to 'Urwa, Sa'd b. Khaythama built the Mosque of Qubā'. That this was his claim is confirmed by a text in which the corrupt *al-aḍrār* (below, 84) is replaced by "Qubā'": *kāna Sa'd b. Khaythama banā masjida Qubā'*, etc.[25] While some of the parallel texts are somewhat vague about the claim that Sa'd built the mosque where a donkey had been tethered, the *Iṣāba* is clear on it (admittedly, this may be so thanks to a benevolent scribe).[26]

---

[23] *GAS*, I, 29–30.

[24] Suyūṭī, *Durr*, III, 277:8 who quotes al-Ḍaḥḥāk via Ibn Abī Ḥātim's *Tafsīr*: *hum nās mina l-Anṣār btanaw masjidan qarīban min masjid Qubā', balaghanā annahu awwalu masjid buniya fī l-islām.*

[25] Balādh., *Futūḥ* (Ṭabbā'), 9.

[26] *Iṣāba*: *kāna mawḍi' masjid Qubā' li-'mra'a yuqālu lahā Līna kānat tarbiṭu ḥimāran lahā, fa-'btanā fīhi Sa'd b. Khaythama masjidan.* Ibn Shabba and Samh. locate the preposition *fīhi* differently: *kānat tarbiṭu ḥimāran lahā fīhi, fa-'btanā*, etc. See Ibn Shabba, *Medina*, I, 54–55; Samh., II, 815 and *Iṣāba*, VIII, 109 (both quoting Ibn Shabba). In the *Sīra Shāmiyya*, V, 676, instead of *wa-rawā Ibn Abī Shayba wa-'bnu Hishām 'an 'Urwa 'an abīhi*, read: *wa-rawā Ibn Shabba 'an Hishām b. 'Urwa 'an abīhi.*

The claim that Saʿd built the Mosque of Qubāʾ is not the only existing one.[27] The rival claim mentions no other than the Prophet himself (assisted by the Angel Gabriel).[28] This illustrious alternative clearly enhances the importance of the mosque and may be suspected of being an invention of the ʿAmr b. ʿAwf. The Saʿd claim, on the other hand, has a certain appeal: his clan, the B. al-Salm, came to Qubāʾ in the western ʿĀliya from the territory of the Aws Allāh in the eastern ʿĀliya and became the clients of the ʿAmr b. ʿAwf. If Saʿd were to be identified as the builder, this would have suggested that a recent and marginal element in the population of Qubāʾ was the most enthusiastic one in accepting Islam.

ʿUrwa's account implies what Saʿīd's version explicitly states, namely that the dissenters were related to the B. ʿAmr b. ʿAwf as they were supposed to have prayed in the mosque of the ʿAmr b. ʿAwf. Their initiative is, therefore, considered *ḍirār/shiqāq*. There is no trace of the "pious envy" of Saʿīd's account. For ʿUrwa, these arrogant people (whom he quotes in the first person) ridiculed the mosque of the ʿAmr b. ʿAwf because a donkey had previously been tethered there.[29] ʿUrwa in fact says: Did they not know (a rhetorical question; of course they knew) that once consecrated, a mosque removes the previous filth associated with its site? Was not the Prophet's Mosque built on the site of a former pagan cemetery?[30] They were, of course, punished for their arrogance. This is ʿUrwa's account of the background to the building of the Ḍirār Mosque. Abū ʿĀmir, he adds, was at that time in Syria and they intended to pray there until his return.

[27] It should be linked to the statement (in Muqātil, see below) that the Mosque of Qubāʾ was among the Sālim (read: [al-]Salm). Saʿd was of the B. al-Salm; above, 29. Read Salm instead of Sālim also in Ibn al-Kalbī, *Jamhara*, 645.

[28] The Prophet founded the Mosque of Qubāʾ when he stayed there after his Hijra; see, e.g., Ibn Kathīr, *al-Bidāya wa-l-nihāya fī l-taʾrīkh*, Beirut 1974, III, 196 (Zuhrī < ʿUrwa b. al-Zubayr), 209. Elsewhere we are told that the Prophet, who lived outside Qubāʾ, came there to build a mosque; also, the first three caliphs play a role here; Ṭabarānī, *Kabīr*, II, 339 f. On Gabriel see below, 90.

[29] Cf. Abū ʿĀmir's reference to the Mosque of Qubāʾ as a *mirbad*; below, 93.

[30] *EI*², s.v. Masdjid, 645–46 (J. Pedersen).

Sa'īd, we should remember, was somewhat uncertain about this point: *wa-la'alla Abā 'Āmir yuṣallī fīhi.*

That the Sa'īd and 'Urwa reports were independently written, speaks against Prof. Gil's implied working assumption that the former elucidates the latter. He states:

> According to Balādhurī [= the 'Urwa account], what aroused the envy of the Ghanm [the Ghanm appear only in Sa'īd's account; 'Urwa does not specify the identity of the builders, though he mentions Abū 'Āmir; 'Urwa does not refer to any envy] was a mosque called *masjid al-aḍrār* [!] built by Sa'd b. Khaythama on the spot where a certain Libba (versions: Li'a; apparently a woman, perhaps Jewish; perhaps the name of a sub-clan) used to tether her (or its) donkey(s). This the Ghanm thought was disgraceful.[31]

The common practice of using one account to interpret another is unacceptable here for reasons already mentioned.

The report in Balādhurī going back to Hishām b. 'Urwa (the parallel texts add: from his father, 'Urwa) is, like Sa'īd's report, an interpretation, or rather a *sabab nuzūl*, of Qur'ān 9,107. Some further notes on Gil's analysis of this passage will be in place here. He seems to imply that *masjid al-iḍrār* (see below) built by Sa'd b. Khaythama is identical with our Ḍirār Mosque. He notes (p. 73) that Sa'd was of the 'Amr b. 'Awf, participated in the 'Aqaba meeting where he was one of the *nuqabā'*, and was killed in the Battle of Badr. Gil adds: "Thus we have before us a very important personage in the earliest Islamic period. On the other hand, [i.e., although he was positive in any other respect] he had a strong family relation with some of the main dissenters, a fact which makes the unique information in Balādhurī about his building the *masjid al-aḍrār* [*sic*] quite significant and worthy of being regarded as not a mere error".

But Sa'd b. Khaythama was not from among the 'Amr b. 'Awf; he was a member of the Salm, the Aws Allāh clan which

[31] Gil, "The Medinan opposition", 72 = Balādh., *Ansāb*, I, 283 (*tarbiṭu fīhi ḥimārahā*).

migrated to Qubā'. Moreover, implicating him in the Ḍirār incident (9 A.H.) is impossible; his martyr's death at Badr (2 A.H.) is a perfect alibi.

As is often the case with Islamic texts, Balādhurī's version of 'Urwa's account is corrupt. The parallel text in Ibn Shabba[32] makes it clear that the word *al-iḍrār*[33] is either superfluous or corrupt. Ibn Shabba has: *fa-'btanā Sa'd b. Khaythama masjidan, fa-qāla ahl masjid al-ḍirār*, etc. Hence, it is far from being certain that 'Urwa's report included any epithet regarding the mosque built by Sa'd. Alternatively, perhaps *Masjid al-riḍwān* (cf. Qur'ān 9,109), which is another name for the Mosque of Qubā',[34] should be read instead of *Masjid al-iḍrār*: after all, in this report Sa'd is said to have built *the Mosque of Qubā'*, not the Ḍirār Mosque. This had to have happened before his death in the Battle of Badr.

Ibn 'Umar/Ibn 'Abbās: "The hostile stronghold"

The account ascribed to Ibn 'Umar ('Abdallāh b. 'Umar b. al-Khaṭṭāb, d. 73/692–93[35]) or ('Abdallāh) Ibn 'Abbās (d. 68/687–88[36]) is also a *sabab nuzūl* of the Ḍirār verse. Unspecified Anṣār built a mosque. Abū 'Āmir told them:[37] "Build your mosque and ask for as much enforcement as you can in warriors and weapons,[38] because I am going to Qayṣar, the king of the Byzan-

[32] Also in Samhūdī and the *Iṣāba*, both quoting Ibn Shabba.

[33] The Balādhurī MS has: al-Ḍirār. *Iḍrār* could have been a variant of *ḍirār*; see *TMD* MS Br. Lib. Or. 8045, I, 20a: *... qāla 'Umar b. 'Abd al-'Azīz: inna l-Ḥajjāj innamā banā Wāsiṭan iḍrāran bi-l-miṣrayni ya'nī l-Baṣra wa-l-Kūfa.*

[34] See Suyūṭī, *Durr*, III, 279:21.

[35] *EI*[2], s.v. 'Abd Allāh b. 'Umar b. al-Khaṭṭāb (L. Veccia Vaglieri). Others mention the year 74/693–94; al-Mizzī, *Tahdhīb al-kamāl*, XV, 340.

[36] *EI*[2], s.v. 'Abd Allāh b. al-'Abbās (L. Veccia Vaglieri). Others mention the years 69/688–89 and 70/689–90; al-Mizzī, *Tahdhīb al-kamāl*, XV, 162.

[37] I.e., when he was still in Medina. The combined report in the *Sīra Shāmiyya*, V, 675:5 is more specific about it: "And Abū 'Āmir al-Fāsiq ("the sinful, immoral") had told them before he went out to Syria", etc. See also Zurqānī, III, 81:13. And *Masālik al-abṣār*, I, 129 (Abū 'Āmir was fighting the Prophet until the Battle of Ḥunayn took place, and when the Hawāzin were defeated, he fled to Syria).

[38] *Wa-'stamiddū mā* (variant in Ṭabarī: *wa-'sta'iddū bi-mā*; the former seems to be a *lectio difficilior*) *staṭa'tum min quwwa wa-min silāḥ*. This

tines, in order to bring an army from the Byzantines and drive Muḥammad and his friends out". When they completed their mosque, they invited the Prophet to pray in it and invoke God's blessing for them, but God revealed: "Stand there never", etc. (Qur'ān 9,108).[39] In other words, Abū 'Āmir instructed them to build the mosque ("build your mosque") and provided a goal: creating a stronghold for a Byzantine expedition force. This mosque, or rather hostile stronghold, was a component in a dangerous plot to expel the Prophet and the Qurashī Muhājirūn. Against this background, their seemingly bona fide invitation to the Prophet to pray in the mosque sounds sinister indeed.[40]

These three accounts on the Ḍirar incident date back to the earliest stages of Islamic historiography, and differ considerably,

is probably a reference to their allies in Medina (the Jews) and outside (the Bedouin).

[39] *Sīra Shāmiyya*, V, 675 quoting Ibn 'Umar via Bayhaqī, *Dalā'il*, V, 263; but the latter source quotes it from Ibn 'Abbās. Also Ṭabarī, *Tafsīr*, XI, 19:4 provides this report with an *isnād* reaching Ibn 'Abbās through 'Alī (possibly Ibn 'Abbās' son).

[40] In the Shī'ite *Tafsīr* of Ṭabrisī (X, 143) the "hostile stronghold" story is concluded by the remark that the *munāfiqūn* were anticipating the arrival of Abū 'Āmir, but he died before reaching the king of the Byzantines.

It is in a Shī'ite source that the "hostility-version" is taken much further (without, however, reference to the Ḍirār Mosque): after Sa'd b. Mu'ādh's death (cf. above, 54) and the Prophet's departure to Tabūk, the *munāfiqūn* made Abū 'Āmir their leader and commander (*amīran wa-ra'īsan*) and pledged their allegiance to him. They plotted to plunder Medina and take captive the children of the Messenger of God, and the rest of his family, and Companions, and planned a surprise night attack on Muḥammad in order to kill him on the way to Tabūk; *Biḥār al-anwār*, XXI, 257 (from Mūsā b. Ja'far, on whom see above, 77n). The *Biḥār* report is also unique in other respects and merits further discussion. For example, it tells that Abū 'Āmir left Medina, no doubt shortly before the attempt on the Prophet's life, so as not to be implicated in it. We are also told about an exchange of letters between the *munāfiqūn* (who are here depicted as a fifth column) and Ukaydir of Dūmat al-Jandal. This takes us beyond the mere chronological link between the Tabūk expedition and the Ḍirār incident established by the Sunnī sources. In this context it is interesting to note that according to W. Caskel, the Prophet was worried to his very death about a possible Byzantine attack which did not materialize because of the war with the Persians. Caskel disputes W.M. Watt's assumption that the Prophet took a strategic offensive against Byzantium already before Mu'ta; see Caskel's review of Watt, *Muhammad Medina*, in *Deutsche Literaturzeitung* 80 (1959), 1066–72, at 1069.

especially on the builders' motives. The accounts are strongly biased and form independent variations on the subject, something which must be considered when we try to employ one of them to interpret another. It would be wrong in this case to look for an "official" or "standard" version because variance, not unity, is common in the source-material. The earliest records of the Prophet's time are marked by dissension and disunity, not by unanimity and agreement.

It does not necessarily follow, however, that no meaningful study of the Ḍirār incident may be made. On the contrary, as we shall see, our sources abound with reliable information. While in some areas good results can be achieved, in others, given the nature and limitations of the sources, only broad outlines can be drawn, at least for the time being. True, certain questions may never be answered. But arguing that because of this *no* question can be answered seems to me counter-productive and wrong.

Muqātil b. Sulaymān's account

The commentary by Muqātil b. Sulaymān (d. 150/767[41]) on the Ḍirār verse is remarkable in more ways than one. In what follows, the Qur'ān verses are put between curly brackets; points of special interest are in italics (as are the Arabic quotations):[42]

> {And those who have taken a mosque in opposition} [Qur'ān 9,107], i.e., the mosque of the *munāfiqūn*, {and unbelief} in their hearts, meaning the *nifāq*, {and to divide the believers}. It was revealed concerning twelve men of the *munāfiqūn*. *All of them are of*

[41] *GAS*, I, 36–37.

[42] M.M. al-Sawwaf wrote a doctoral thesis on Muqātil (Oxford 1968; I did not consult it) entitled *Muqātil ibn Sulaymān, An Early Zaidi Theologian.* I found the reference in J. van Ess' review of J. Wansbrough's *Qur'anic Studies*, in *Bibliotheca Orientalis* 35 (1978), 351. For the incorporation of later texts into Muqātil's commentary see Versteegh, "Grammar and exegesis", 220 f. Concerning this problem, reference should be made to S. Leder, "Authorship and transmission in unauthored literature: the akhbār attributed to al-Haytham ibn 'Adī", in *Oriens* 31 (1988), 67–81; also to I. Goldfeld, "The *Tafsīr* of 'Abdallāh b. 'Abbās", in *Der Islam* 58 (1981), 125–35, at 126, 135.

the Anṣār, [more precisely] *of the ʿAmr b. ʿAwf ....*[43] *They said: "We shall build a mosque in order to converse in it and be on our own (nataḥaddathu fīhi wa-nakhlū fīhi).*[44] *When Abū ʿĀmir al-Yahūdī*, i.e., the father of Ḥanẓala [the latter being] 'the one washed by the angels', returns from Syria, we shall say to him: 'We built it for you so that you would be our *imām* in it'". This is meant by His saying {and as a place of ambush for those who fought God and His Messenger aforetime}, i.e., Abū ʿĀmir who was called al-Rāhib [the God-fearing, the ascetic] because he applied himself to acts of devotion and was in search of divine knowledge (*kāna yataʿabbadu wa-yaltamisu l-ʿilm*). He died as a non-believer in Qinnasrīn because of the Prophet's curse.[45]

They came to the Prophet and said: "Walking to the prayer[46] *is difficult for us, please allow us"* [i.e., allow us to build a mosque in our own territory]. He allowed them to build a mosque and they finished the building on a Friday. *They asked the Prophet who their imām should be and he said: "A man of them"* [*sic*; one expects here: from you], *and ordered Mujammiʿ b. Jāriya to be their imām.* Then this verse

[43] Seven names are listed: Ḥ.r.ḥ. (read presumably: Baḥzaj) b. Kh.sh.f. (note that the other sources quoted below do not mention the name of Baḥzaj's father), Jāriya b. ʿĀmir (written: Ḥāritha b. ʿUmar) and his son, Zayd b. Jāriya, Nabtal b. al-Ḥārith, Wadīʿa b. Thābit, Khidhām (written: Ḥizām) b. Khālid and Mujammiʿ b. Jāriya (written: Ḥāritha).

[44] Cf. the negative connotation of *khalaw ilā shayāṭīnihim* (Qurʾān 2,14), "they were alone with their devils".

[45] The "searchers of divine knowledge" or "of the true religion" are part of the pre-Islamic history of certain tribes (and at times matters of intertribal disputes). The search, in itself legitimate, could lead them astray. Cf., e.g., Abū Kabsha of the Khuzāʿa who in his "search for the true religion" worshipped Sirius; *EI*^{2}, s.v. Khuzāʿa, 77b (M.J. Kister). Note the dispute (*loc. cit.*) over the identity of the person who introduced the cult of Hubal: some attributed it to ʿAmr b. Luḥayy of the Khuzāʿa and others to Khuzayma b. Mudrika, an ancestor of Quraysh.

[46] Rāzī, *Tafsīr*, XVI, 194 specifies: to the Mosque of the Messenger of God. Cf. below, 96.

was revealed. Mujammiʿ swore that in building this mosque they only meant to do good, so God revealed concerning Mujammiʿ: {They will swear, 'We desired nothing but good'; and God testifies that they are truly liars} in what they swear about. {Stand there never} i.e., [do not stand] for prayer in the mosque of the *munāfiqūn*. *So* [from that moment onwards] *he would not pray in it nor pass by it and he would take another road. He used to pray in it before.* Then He said: {A mosque}, i.e., the Mosque of Qubā' which is the first mosque built in Medina {that was founded} i.e., built {upon god-fearing from the first day}, i.e., from the first time {is worthier for thee to stand in} for prayer, because it was built before (*min qabli*) the mosque of the *munāfiqūn* ....

Then Mujammiʿ b. Jāriya became a good Muslim (*ḥasuna islāmuhu*),[47] and ʿUmar b. al-Khaṭṭāb sent him to Kūfa to teach them [i.e., the Kūfans] the Qur'ān. He taught ʿAbdallāh b. Masʿūd and dictated the Qur'ān to him (*laqqanahu l-qur'āna*). {Why, is he better who founded his building}, i.e., the Mosque of Qubā', {upon the fear of God and His good pleasure}, i.e., with the good and God's pleasure that were desired in it {or he who founded his building}, the base of his building, {upon the brink of a crumbling bank that has tumbled with him into the fire of Gehenna?}, i.e., the building has fallen into the fire of Gehenna. {And God guides not the people of the evildoers}.

When the people finished building the mosque, they asked the Prophet's permission to stand [in prayer] (*sta'dhanū ... fī l-qiyām*) *in that mosque.*[48] *The people of the Mosque of Qubā' came and said: "Messenger of God, we wish you to come to our mosque and pray in it so that we shall follow your example",*

---

[47] Cf. Appendix A.

[48] What follows shows that they wanted the Prophet to pray in their mosque.

[i.e., learn the way you pray]. *And the Messenger of God walked with a group of his Companions heading to the Mosque of Qubā'. This became known to the munāfiqūn and they went out to receive them.*[49] *When he* [the Prophet] *was in the middle of the way* [between the Sāfila and Qubā';[50] i.e., having decided to accept the invitation of the *munāfiqūn*, or having not yet decided in which of the two nearby rival mosques he should pray?], *Gabriel descended with this verse:* {Why, is he better who founded his building upon the fear of God and His good pleasure}, i.e., the people of the Mosque of Qubā', {or he who founded his building upon the brink of a crumbling bank} and when he said {bank}, the Prophet watched the mosque crumbling down to the seventh earth (*naẓara l-nabī [ṣ] ilā l-masjid ḥattā tahawwara fī l-sābi'a*).[51] *The Prophet nearly fainted and hurried back to his place. Afterwards, the munāfiqūn came to apologize. He accepted their outward* [words], *putting his confidence with God concerning their inward* [intentions].[52] And God said:

---

[49] Presumably in an attempt to convince him to come to *their* mosque.

[50] *Al-manṣif*; cf. Lecker, *The Banū Sulaym*, 105, n. 30 ("border point").

[51] "Crumbling" is used figuratively here, since, as we shall see, the mosque was reportedly burnt down; but perhaps agreement should not be imposed where there is variance; above, 87. Cf. Samh., II, 818: *wa-ruwiya anna rasūla llāhi (ṣ) ra'āhu ḥīna nhāra ḥattā balagha l-arḍa l-sābi'a. Fa-fazi'a li-dhālika rasūlu llāhi (ṣ).*

[52] *Fa-qabila 'alāniyatahum wa-wakala sarā'irahum ilā llāhi 'azza wa-jalla.* Cf. the words of Ka'b b. Mālik on the apologies of those who stayed behind (*al-mukhallafūna*) after the Prophet's return from Tabūk: *fa-qabila ... 'alāniyatahum wa-aymānahum wa-yakilu sarā'irahum ilā llāhi ta'ālā*; Waq., III, 1049. The account on Ḍirār and the one on those who stayed behind in the Tabūk expedition also have the place-name Dhū Awān in common: it was both the site in which the Ḍirār verses were revealed and where those who stayed behind wished to meet the Prophet and apologize to him; Waq., III, 1049. Naṣr, *Amkina*, 16b reports that Wadi Dhū Awān is also called Dhāt Awān. (Gil, "The Medinan opposition", renders *mukhallafūna* or *khawālif*: "challengers" [p. 67] and "dissenters" [p. 68, n. 3], referring to "the bulk of tradition concerning what happened at the time of the Tabūk expedition". This rendering is somewhat removed from the original meaning.) J. Pedersen wrongly says (EI^2, 647a) that, according to some

> {The buildings they have built will not cease to be a matter of disquiet (*rība*) within their hearts}, i.e., sorrow and grief in their hearts, because they regretted having built it, {unless it be that their hearts are cut into pieces}, i.e., until death. {God is All-knowing, All-wise}.
>
> The Prophet sent *'Ammār b. Yāsir* and Waḥshī, the *mawlā* of al-Muṭ'im b. 'Adī, to burn it down and it was swallowed up by the fire of Gehenna.[53] *He* [the Prophet] *ordered that it be made a place of sweepings* (*kunāsa*) *and that carcasses be thrown in it. The Mosque of Qubā' was in the* [territory of the] *B. Sālim* [read: (al-)Salm] *and was built a few days after the Prophet's Hijra.*[54]

Muqātil's account, while sharing the outline of the story with the rest of the versions, adds considerably to their testimony. The relatively large proportion of new material in Muqātil's *Tafsīr* demonstrates that a voluntary restriction in the scope of sources for the study of the Prophet's biography deprives one of important source material. *Tafsīr* books in general, and Muqātil's *Tafsīr* in particular, are indeed indispensable. Because the sources

---

traditions, the Ḍirār Mosque was built in Dhū Awān. He elaborates (647b): "If the connection with the Tabūk campaign is correct, the *Masdjid al-Ḍirār* is to be sought north of Medina; the 'mosque founded on piety' would then be the Mosque of Medina rather than that of Ḳubā' which lies to the south of it". In fact, the Ḍirār Mosque was in Qubā'; see below, 129. Gil, *op. cit.*, 71 has a wrong order of events: "The Prophet was invited to come to the mosque and pray there when he was already on his way to Tabūk, in Dhū Uwān" [read: Awān — M.L.]. But this place is mentioned in connection with the *return* from Tabūk. The text in Ibn Hishām includes a flashback: the Prophet returned from Tabūk and camped at Dhū Awān; already before his departure from Medina, the people of the Ḍirār Mosque had gone to him, etc. (*wa-kāna aṣḥābu masjidi l-Ḍirār qad kānū atawhu*). Such a technique can be suspected to be the mark of a combined report; however, this is not the case here. The flashback element belongs to an ordinary, autonomous report which Ibn Isḥāq quotes from an unspecified "reliable man of the 'Amr b. 'Awf". The report survived in Bayhaqī, *Dalā'il*, V, 259 f.

[53] Waḥshī is mentioned in this context in other sources, but 'Ammār b. Yāsir is not.

[54] Muqātil, *Tafsīr*, I, 159b–161b.

are not made of a repetitive mass of unchanging components, the study of the Prophet's history cannot be solely based on Ibn Hishām, Ibn Sa'd and Ṭabarī.

Uniqueness, though, does not equal historicity. Absence of a certain detail from mainstream Islamic literature may well reflect sifting through a critical mechanism applied by compilers who rejected evidence they considered fabricated and unreliable. A unique piece of information has a claim to historicity where there is reason to suspect self-imposed censorship, aiming at protecting the prestige or reputation of a clan or individual, including the Prophet himself. For example, the unique and potentially embarrassing statement that the Prophet actually prayed in the Ḍirār Mosque seems to me historical. The statement, which could not be found elsewhere, that the Prophet appointed Mujammi' b. Jāriya as the *imām* could also be historical,[55] though it may also be a *faḍā'il* tradition invented by Mujammi''s family, or an attempt to "clear his name" (cf. Appendix A). The *sabab nuzūl* given here (Gabriel appearing to him when he was halfway between the Sāfila and the 'Āliya) is an alternative to the Dhū Awān story, which for some unknown reason prevails elsewhere.[56]

In Muqātil's report, Abū 'Āmir is again in the background:[57] the twelve Anṣār who built the Ḍirār Mosque were anticipating the return from Syria of "Abū 'Āmir al-Yahūdī".

The builders of the Ḍirār Mosque wanted a mosque where they could "converse and be on their own" (*nataḥaddathu fīhi wa-nakhlū fīhi*). The same purpose is mentioned in an autobiographical report of 'Āṣim b. 'Adī al-'Ajlānī (on whom, see below).

---

[55] The appointment of *imāms* by the Prophet was a normal practice. A mosque is an Islamic stronghold and the *imām* is a religious and a political representative of the Prophet among clan members.

[56] Gabriel's warning is of course incongruous with the statement found earlier in Muqātil, that the Prophet actually prayed in the Ḍirār Mosque. The source of this incongruity is presumably Muqātil's reliance on different earlier exegetes without synchronizing their reports.

[57] Gil suggests that "Ibn Qutayba is apparently the oldest source having preserved the tradition which connects the building of the mosque with the person of Abū 'Āmir"; Gil, "The Medinan opposition", 72 = Ibn Qutayba, *Ma'ārif*, 343. This should be amended: Ibn Qutayba died in 276/889, while Muqātil (cf. *Tafsīr*, I, 159b) died in 150/767.

Having told the story of the Ḍirār Mosque, ʿĀṣim was asked: "But why did they want to build it?"[58] He replied:

> They would gather in our mosque. However, they would whisper in each other's ear and turn to one another, and the Muslims would look sideways at them. They were distressed by this and wanted a mosque for themselves [literally: a mosque in which they would stay] that would be frequented only by people they wanted, of those who were of the same view. Abū ʿĀmir used to say: "I cannot enter this *mirbad* of yours because Muḥammad's companions look sideways at me and mistreat me". They said: "We shall build a mosque in which we shall talk, in our court" (*naḥnu nabnī masjidan nataḥaddathu fīhi ʿindanā*).[59]

Abū ʿĀmir calls the Qubāʾ Mosque *mirbad* and the context suggests that he means this pejoratively. It will be remembered that the same mosque was referred to (above, 80) as the place where Liyya's donkey was tethered. This could suggest that *mirbad* here should be understood as "an enclosure for domestic animals" rather than "a place in which dates are put to dry in the sun", but it does not seem to have been the case. Elsewhere, the *mirbad* is said to have belonged to Kulthūm b. al-Hidm who reportedly gave it to the Prophet.[60] Now the *mirbad*, which Kulthūm gave the Prophet, is specifically said to have been *al-mawḍiʿu lladhī yubsaṭu fīhi l-tamr li-yajiffa*, "the place in which the dates are

---

[58] Note the narrator's technique of "recording" the interaction between ʿĀṣim, an eyewitness, and his audience who wished to know more about a specific detail of the story.

[59] Waq., III, 1048–49. Similarly, a rather virulent report purports to convey the intentions of Mujammiʿ b. Jāriya, the future *imām* of the Ḍirār Mosque, as he was building it: it was to become a place "for our secret actions and conversations; nobody will push us in it and we shall say what we want while giving Muḥammad's companions the impression that we only want to do good" (*li-sirrinā wa-najwānā wa-lā yuzāḥimunā fīhi aḥad fa-nadhkuru mā shiʾnā wa-nukhayyilu ilā aṣḥāb Muḥammad innamā nurīdu l-iḥsāna*; cf. *al-ḥusnā* in Qurʾān 9,107); Bayhaqī, *Dalāʾil*, V, 259.

[60] Samh., I, 250 (from Ibn Zabāla and others); II, 808. Cf. also the Ḥadīth on the Prophet's *istisqāʾ*; e.g., *Usd al-ghāba*, I, 196: *inna l-tamr fī l-mirbad*.

spread to dry", which appears to rule out its interpretation as "an enclosure for domestic animals".[61]

The builders of the Ḍirār Mosque justified their initiative by reference to the hardships involved in reaching the mosque where they used to pray. This, I argue, was the Mosque of Qubā'. As the common *sīra* story goes, they invited the Prophet to pray in their mosque when he was preparing to go to Tabūk. They said: "Messenger of God, we have built a mosque for the ill and needy, for the rainy and stormy night".[62] They did not intend it to be a shelter for the weaker elements in society. One may interpret their words as follows: the weak among them, and all of them in bad

[61] *Sīra Shāmiyya*, III, 380. The dates interpretation was chosen by J. Pedersen, *EI*^{2}, s.v. Masdjid, 647a—inconsistently, it should be remarked, with his interpretation of another *mirbad*, mentioned in connection with the Prophet's Mosque, which Pedersen described as "a place for keeping camels (and smaller domestic animals)"; *op. cit.*, 645–46 (Pedersen refers to Bukhārī, *wuḍū'*, *Bāb 66: kāna l-nabī [ṣ] yuṣallī qabla an yubnā l-masjid fī marābiḍi l-ghanam*, "...at the nightly lodging-places of sheep"). Pedersen notes (654a), regarding the increase in the sanctity of mosques, the refusal of Baybars to build a mosque on a site for tethering camels while the Prophet's Mosque was built in exactly such a place. However, it appears that also in the case of the Prophet's Mosque, the dates interpretation is the correct one. In Samh., I, 324:1 we find a clear statement that the *mirbad* which was to become the Prophet's Mosque had been "a place in which dates were put to dry in the sun": *wa-kāna mirbadan li-l-tamri*; see also *op. cit.*, 326:-2. A pejorative reference to the Prophet's Mosque as a former *mirbad* can be added here. A *munāfiq* expelled from this mosque complained of having been thrown out of the *mirbad* of the B. Tha'laba; *EI*^{2}, s.v. Masdjid, 646b = Ibn Hishām, II, 175 [ed. Wüstenfeld, Göttingen 1858–60, 362:10]. On this *munāfiq*, 'Amr b. Qays, see Lecker, "Idol worship in pre-Islamic Medina (Yathrib)", 335, n. 25. These Tha'laba were the Tha'laba b. Ghanm b. Mālik b. al-Najjār; see, e.g., Ibn Ḥazm, *Ansāb*, 349:5; Ibn Qudāma, *Istibṣār*, 64.

We saw above how these two mosques, the Mosque of Qubā' and the Prophet's Mosque, competed for "firstness". Now we realize that both were former *mirbads*. The Mosque of Qubā' and the Prophet's Mosque also have in common a divinely-guided she-camel (*ma'mūra*). The theme which is well-known in connection with the Prophet's Mosque appears in a Shī'ite tradition about the Mosque of Qubā'; Samh., I, 251 = Ṭabarānī, *Kabīr*, II, 246. (Pedersen remarked concerning the Prophet's Mosque that "the choice of the site was left to the whim of his mount"; *EI*^{2}, 645b.)

[62] *Qad banaynā masjidan li-dhī l-'illa wa-l-ḥāja wa-l-laylati l-maṭīra wa-l-laylati l-shātiya*; see, e.g., Tab., III, 110 [I, 1704]. Cf. Gil, "The Medinan opposition", 71, n. 12.

weather, could not come to the Prophet's Mosque to attend the Friday-prayer.[63] Put differently: according to this interpretation, they stated that after a rainy night the wadi between Qubā' and the Sāfila would flow, preventing them from descending to the Friday-prayer. Indeed, one commentary claims that the building of the Ḍirār Mosque was aimed as an act against the Mosque of the Prophet.[64] But there are good reasons to assume that this was not so and that it was a matter of two rival mosques in Qubā'. Two of the three accounts quoted above, Saʿīd b. Jubayr's "pious envy" account and ʿUrwa b. al-Zubayr's "contempt and ridicule" account, leave no doubt that we have here a case of local competition between two mosques in Qubā'. We are also told that the twelve *munāfiqūn* built this mosque in an attempt to harm the Mosque of Qubā' (*yuḍārrūna bihi masjid Qubā'*).[65]

In addition, involving the Prophet's Mosque fails to relate to the builders' problem as stated elsewhere, namely that of justifying the building of a mosque not far from the existing Mosque of Qubā' where they were supposed to pray.

This interpretation, which relates to a rivalry between two adjacent mosques, should be upheld, although the available evidence concerning comparable cases in Medina lends it only partial support. One case is that of the mosque built by the *imām* of the ʿAwf b. al-Khazraj (whose territory was not far from Qubā'). The *imām*, the blind (or extremely short-sighted) ʿItbān b. Mālik, complained to the Prophet that the torrents (*suyūl*) were an obstacle interposed between him and the mosque *of his clan*. He asked, therefore, that the Prophet go to him and pray in a certain

[63] Cf. *EI*², s.v. Masdjid, 647a.

[64] See, e.g., the combined report compiled by Ibn Isḥāq from several sources, in Ṭabarī, *Tafsīr*, XI, 18:20: *fa-ta'wīlu l-kalām: wa-'lladhīna btanaw masjidan ḍirāran li-masjid rasūli llāhi (ṣ).*

[65] Rāzī, *Tafsīr*, XVI, 193. Some Shīʿite Qur'ān interpretations are undetermined and include both possibilities, with the Qur'anic *ḍirāran* explained as: *ay muḍārra* [Ṭabrisī adds: *ay li-l-ḍarar*] *bi-ahl masjid Qubā' aw masjidi l-rasūl (ṣ wa-ālihi) li-yaqilla l-jamʿu fīhi*; *Biḥār al-anwār*, XXI, 253 = Ṭabrisī, *Tafsīr*, X, 143. Mūsā b. Jaʿfar (in *Biḥār al-anwār*, XXI, 259) puts in the mouth of the *munāfiqūn* a clear reference to the Mosque of the Prophet, which was too far from them: *inna buyūtanā qāṣiya ʿan masjidika wa-innā nakrahu l-ṣalāta fī ghayr jamāʿa wa-yaṣʿubu ʿalaynā l-ḥuḍūr.*

place in his house (in order to consecrate it), so that he would turn it into a mosque.[66] This points to the need to justify the creation of a mosque not far from another. But a variant version suggests that the Prophet's Mosque is meant: 'Itbān, having lost his sight, complained to the Prophet that he could not pray with him in his mosque (*fī masjidika*, i.e., in the Prophet's Mosque).[67]

The Prophet's Mosque is again referred to by the Salima, a subdivision of the Khazraj residing to the west of Medina. The Salima[68] complained about the distance between their houses and the mosque (i.e., the Prophet's Mosque), or about the fact that a wadi, or torrent (*sayl*), was interposed between them and the Friday-prayer in the Prophet's Mosque.[69] The report on the Salima, and one of the reports concerning 'Itbān, clearly reflect the topography of Medina: the flowing waters in the 'Aqīq Valley could prevent the Salima from going to the Prophet's Mosque as the waters of the Buṭḥān Valley could prevent 'Itbān from going there too. But the Prophet's Mosque is irrelevant for us here since in the case of the Ḍirār Mosque, the rival Mosque of Qubā' is meant. The complaint of its builders is comparable with one version of the report about 'Itbān's complaint, that is to say, the one relating to his clan's mosque.

In Muqātil's report, the builders of the Ḍirār Mosque asked for permission, *in advance*, to build their mosque because "walking to the prayer was difficult for them". Considering the small distance between their mosque and the Mosque of Qubā', their claim must have seemed ridiculous.[70] Elsewhere we are told that in the

---

[66] Ibn Qudāma, *Istibṣār*, 196–97 (*inna l-suyūla taḥūlu baynī wa-bayna masjid qawmī*). The wording in Ibn Shabba, *Medina*, I, 71 is reminiscent of that used for the Ḍirār Mosque: *al-laylatu l-muẓlima wa-l-maṭar wa-l-sayl.* See also Samh., II, 820–21; al-Bukhārī, *Ṣaḥīḥ*, Cairo 1378/1958, II, 74–75 (*kuntu uṣallī li-qawmī bi-B. Sālim wa-kāna yaḥūlu baynī wa-baynahum wādin idhā jā'ati l-amṭār fa-yashuqqu 'alayya jtiyāzuhu qibala masjidihim*); *Fatḥ al-bārī*, I, 433 f; *EI*^{2}, s.v. Masdjid, 649a, 650a (J. Pedersen).

[67] Ṭabarānī, *Kabīr*, XVIII, 27.

[68] An erroneous version has: the Salima and the Ḥarām; but the Ḥarām were a subdivision of the Salima.

[69] Ibn Shabba, *Medina*, I, 77–78; Samh., I, 203–204; II, 838. Cf. Aḥmad, III, 106:18; 182:18.

[70] The Ḍirār Mosque was "on the side" of the Mosque of Qubā'; Diyārbakrī, *Khamīs*, II, 130:24 says: *fa-banaw masjidan ilā janb masjid Qubā'*; Wāḥidī,

beginning "all of them" (i.e., all of the 'Amr b. 'Awf) prayed in the Mosque of Qubā'. Then people of the *munāfiqūn* built the Ḍirār Mosque for Abū 'Āmir, dividing their group (*yufarriqūna bayna jamā'atihim*), since all of them had previously prayed in the Mosque of Qubā'. They told the Prophet: "Messenger of God, the torrent (*sayl*) often comes and cuts us off from the wadi (*yaqṭa'u baynanā wa-bayna l-wādī*), interposing itself between us and the people (*al-qawm*), [i.e., the rest of the 'Amr b. 'Awf]. Shall we pray in our mosque, and then, when the torrent is gone, pray with them?"[71]

The verbs used to designate the competition between the mosques of Qubā' and Ḍirār are *'āraḍa* ("vied, competed, contended for superiority"; also "emulated, imitated"), and *ḍāhā* ("imitated"). Qatāda, the early Qur'ān commentator, reports that *the Prophet* built a mosque in Qubā', *fa-'āraḍahu l-munāfiqūna bi-ākhara*. They then invited him to pray in it but God revealed their plot to him.[72] Qatāda is also quoted elsewhere, but the wording now is different: "Some of the *munāfiqūn* built a mosque in Qubā' in order to imitate the Prophet's Mosque

---

150: ... *wa-huwa qarīb minhu*. J.B. Philby, *A Pilgrim in Arabia*, 86–87, writes: "About half a mile along the road leading through the village from the mosque [of Qubā'] to the edge of the lava-field stand the ruins of a small mosque, without roof, which was identified by Turkish experts sent down at the time of the construction of the Hijaz Railway as the *Masjid al Dhirar* (or *Al Musabbih*), vaguely connected with some incident of the Prophet's time which involved his followers in damage or disaster. This identification of so problematical a site is doubtful, and the scene in which the building stands is as dreary as can well be imagined. On one side lie the tumbled ruins, partly inhabited, of the village, on the other a ten-foot wall of lava fragments dividing the furthermost fringe of the palm-groves from the lava-field beyond, extending to the limit of sight. The mosque building is only ten paces by seven in area, with a prayer-niche in the long south wall and the entrance opposite it. It has neither cupola, nor minaret, nor roof, and may have been an open-air place of prayer for the villagers". See also below, 129.

[71] Ṭabarī, *Tafsīr*, XI, 20:10 (from Ibn Zayd's commentary, i.e., 'Abd al-Raḥmān b. Zayd al-'Adawī al-Madanī, d. 182/798; *GAS*, I, 38).

[72] Suyūṭī, *Durr*, III, 276:–7. For a similar use of *'āraḍa* see al-Qāsim b. Sallām, *al-Khuṭab wa-l-mawā'iẓ*, ed. Ramaḍān 'Abd al-Tawwāb, Cairo 1406/1986, 148: David had been instructed by God to build the Temple (*bayt al-maqdis*) but was later forbidden to do this because he "imitated it in another edifice of his" (*fa-'āraḍahu bi-binā'in lahu*).

(*li-yuḍāhū bihi masjida rasūli llāhi [ṣ]*). They then invited the Prophet to pray in it".[73] "The Prophet's Mosque" here means "the Mosque of Qubā'" (built, according to some, by the Prophet), and not his famous mosque in the Sāfila. The historian of Medina, Ibn al-Najjār, correctly says that the *munāfiqūn* built the Ḍirār Mosque as an imitation (*muḍāhāt*) of the Mosque of Qubā'. They would gather in it, denounce the Prophet and ridicule him.[74] The word *ḍirār* conveys the idea of harm and injury and, on a secondary level, dissent and rivalry.[75]

---

[73] Ṭabarī, *Tafsīr*, 19:-6.

[74] See Ibn al-Najjār (Muḥammad b. Maḥmūd, d. 643/1245; *GAL S*, I, 613), *Durra*, 382; also quoted in Samh., II, 816. The verb *ḍāhā* has an immediate connotation to Jerusalem: in an often-quoted report 'Umar b. al-Khaṭṭāb accuses Ka'b al-Aḥbār: *ḍāhayta wa-'llāhi l-yahūdiyyata yā Ka'b*; Tab., III, 611 [I, 2408]; Lewis, *The Jews of Islam*, 71 ("you are following after Judaism"). Cf. Lane, *Arabic-English Lexicon*, s.v. *ḍāhāhu*: "He resembled, or conformed with, him, or it", and "he imitated him". Obviously, Ka'b's Jewish origins are in the background of this story.

[75] Cf. Lane, *Arabic-English Lexicon*, s.v. *ḍārrahu*: "He harmed him, injured him, or hurt him, in return, or in requital". Also: "He disagreed with, or differed from, him; dissented from him; was contrary, opposed, or repugnant, to him; or he acted contrarily, contrariously, adversely, or in opposition, to him". The man who wanted "to harm" (*an yuḍārra*) 'Ubaydallāh b. 'Abbās invited to 'Ubaydallāh's house, without the latter's knowledge, the notables of Quraysh for dinner; al-Tanūkhī, *al-Mustajād min fa'lāt al-ajwād*, ed. Muḥammad Kurd 'Alī, Damascus 1365/1946, 16. See also Ya'qūb b. Sufyān al-Fasawī, *al-Ma'rifa wa-l-ta'rīkh*, ed. Akram Ḍiyā' al-'Umarī, Beirut 1401/1981, I, 360: Abān b. 'Uthmān married the daughter of 'Abdallāh b. 'Uthmān *ḍirāran li-'bnati 'Abdillāh b. Ja'far*, etc. Cf. *Naqā'iḍ Jarīr wa-l-Farazdaq*, ed. A.A. Bevan, Cambridge 1905, glossary, s.v. ("marriage with two or more wives", "marriage with a husband who has another wife or other wives"). Cf. the expression *qismat al-ḍirār* in *Iṣāba*, VI, 430.

Watt, *Medina*, 190 calls the Ḍirār Mosque: "mosque of dissension"; Gil similarly calls it "the mosque of dissension" and correctly remarks that *ḍirār* might also be interpreted as "harm" or "competition"; Gil, "The Medinan opposition", 70–71; Pedersen, EI^2, s.v. Masdjid, 647a calls this mosque an "opposition mosque". Buhl, *Leben*, 205, 329 calls it "Moschee der Rivalität", "Rivalitätsmoschee". Buhl draws attention to this mosque in connection with Caetani's assumption that the Prophet's Mosque did not yet exist in his own time; Buhl, *Leben*, 204 f. He concludes (205–206) that towards the end of the Prophet's life there was a mosque ("oder mehrere?", Buhl wonders), so the one built (*pace* Caetani, after the Prophet's death) over Muḥammad's grave was not the first Islamic building of this type in Medina. Indeed, there were other mosques: for tribal mosques in Medina at the time of the Prophet see

When *Ḍirār* is given the sense of something that brings one no benefit while harming one's neighbour,[76] it may be suspected that rather than the general meaning of the word, we have here a commentary tailored to the circumstances of this particular case, which was one of rivalry between two adjacent mosques. But while the influence of the Qur'anic usage cannot be denied, the following example may well represent a living usage regarding a land dispute in Medina. A *ḥalīf* of the Anṣār owned part of a palm-grove, most of which belonged to an Anṣārī. He refused to sell it or exchange it for a similar property elsewhere, or give it to the Anṣārī as a present (probably in return for its equivalent in Paradise), and the Prophet told him: *anta muḍārruhu*. He also permitted the Anṣārī to uproot the *ḥalīf*'s palms.[77] Yet another case, from the Umayyad period is when Yazīd b. ʿAbd al-Malik did not succeed in buying a certain court in Medina, and so he built rooms in order to block its front. They were called *abyāt al-ḍirār*.[78]

Qur'anic influence is evident in yet other cases of association between the *ḍirār* and mosques. *Ḍirār* occurs when two mosques face each other, or when the prosperity of one means the demise of the other.[79] Shaqīq (presumably Shaqīq b. Salama al-Asadī al-Kūfī) once arrived late for prayer at the B. ʿĀmir's mosque where

---

below, 100. On the Prophet's Mosque cf. M.J. Kister, "'A booth like the booth of Moses ...'", in *BSOAS* 25 (1962), 150–55.

[76] Qurṭubī, *al-Jāmiʿ li-aḥkām al-qur'ān*, VIII, 254. Cf. the terms *ḥadath* and *ḍarar* used in connection with Muʿāwiya's acquisition of lands in Medina; Kister, "The battle of the Ḥarra", 47.

[77] Maḥmūd b. ʿUmar al-Zamakhsharī, *al-Fā'iq fī gharīb al-ḥadīth*, ed. al-Bijāwī and Muḥammad Abū l-Faḍl Ibrāhīm, Cairo 1971, s.v. *ʿ.ḍ.d.*, II, 442.

[78] Ibn Shabba, *Medina*, I, 257; Samh., I, 723:7. For *dār al-ḍirār* in Mecca see Muḥammad b. ʿAbdallāh al-Azraqī, *Akhbār Makka*, ed. Rushdī Malḥas, Beirut n. d., II, 240:1 (wrongly printed: *dār al-ṣarāra*); ed. F. Wüstenfeld, Leipzig 1858, 452:1 (correctly: *dār al-ḍirār*); cf. Muḥammad b. Isḥāq al-Fākihī, *Akhbār Makka*, ed. ʿAbd al-Malik b. ʿAbdallāh b. Duhaysh, Mecca 1407/1987, III, 288. According to ʿAṭā' b. Abī Rabāḥ, ʿUmar b. al-Khaṭṭāb prohibited the building of two mosques in the same town *yuḍārru aḥaduhumā ṣāḥibahu*; *Masālik al-abṣār*, I, 130.

[79] Abū Bakr Aḥmad b. ʿAbdallāh b. Mūsā al-Kindī al-Nizwī, *al-Muṣannaf*, ed. ʿAbd al-Munʿim ʿĀmir and Jādallāh Aḥmad, ʿUmān 1979, XIX, 37: *idhā kānā mutaqābilayni aw idhā ʿamara hādhā khariba hādhā* (the reference was given to me by Prof. M.J. Kister).

he used to pray. However, he refused to pray in another nearby mosque, saying: *lā uḥibbu an uṣalliya fīhi fa-innahu buniya ʿalā ḍirār.*[80]

The Prophet's Mosque was, of course, a *jamāʿa* mosque. However, the mosques discussed above belong to the category of tribal mosques. It is reported that during the first year after the Hijra, the Prophet ordered the building of mosques in the tribal courts (*bi-an tubnā l-masājid fī l-dūr*; these courts, unlike the ones belonging to individuals, were in fact small villages). One of these courts was Qubā', "the village of the ʿAwf" (or the ʿAmr b. ʿAwf). The Prophet's Mosque, while belonging to another category, was built in the small village of the Mālik b. al-Najjār.[81]

The Prophet approved of the tribal mosques, including that of Qubā'.[82] It is reported that Medina had nine (tribal) mosques, but the Friday-prayer was held with the Prophet (i.e., in his mosque).[83] One must not, though, put together these two pieces of evidence and draw the conclusion that the people of Qubā' held the Friday-prayer in the Prophet's Mosque. The Mosque of Qubā' is not one of the above-mentioned nine mosques: the nine (tribal) mosques, we are told, relied on Bilāl b. Rabāḥ's call to prayer (*kulluhum yuṣallūna bi-adhān Bilāl*). All of the mosques listed were in the Sāfila and the same must have been true for the other, unlisted, mosques.[84] Obviously, Bilāl's call to prayer could not have been heard in Qubā'. The people of Qubā' were not expected to go to the Prophet's Mosque every Friday and only did so on special occasions.[85]

---

[80] Ṭabarī, *Tafsīr*, XI, 20:23; *Masālik al-abṣār*, I, 130.

[81] Dhahabī, *Maghāzī*, 13.

[82] Pedersen (*EI*², s.v. Masdjid, 647b) correctly observes that "there were already at the time of the Prophet several Muslim mosques which had a markedly religious character and were recognized by the Prophet".

[83] Balādh., *Ansāb*, I, 273; Muṭahhar b. Ṭāhir al-Maqdisī, *al-Bad' wa-l-ta'rīkh*, ed. C. Huart, Paris 1899, IV, 85.

[84] Suhaylī, *al-Rawḍ al-unuf*, IV, 198, quoting Abū Dāwūd's *Marāsīl* and al-Dāraquṭnī's *Sunan*.

[85] For the dichotomy ʿAwālī-*balad* cf. above, 4.

THE INDIVIDUALS AND CLANS INVOLVED

Tracing the individuals involved in the Ḍirār incident places us on firm ground. One list (Ibn Isḥāq's) names twelve builders, while another, unspecified, source names eleven. All the participants, some of whom were prominent figures, were of the ʿAmr b. ʿAwf. One expects the number of actual sympathisers among the ʿAmr b. ʿAwf to have been much higher.

Most of the builders were of an ʿAmr b. ʿAwf subdivision called the B. Zayd b. Mālik b. ʿAwf b. ʿAmr b. ʿAwf. The builders belonged to the three clans of the Zayd: the Ḍubayʿa b. Zayd, ʿUbayd b. Zayd and Umayya b. Zayd.

The Ḍubayʿa b. Zayd were by far the dominant group, accounting for eight out of the twelve names listed by Ibn Isḥāq: Muʿattib b. Qushayr, Abū Ḥabība b. al-Azʿar, Jāriya b. ʿĀmir and his sons, Mujammiʿ and Zayd, Nabtal b. al-Ḥārith, Baḥzaj (who was in fact a client of the Ḍubayʿa[86]) and Bijād b. ʿUthmān.[87] One of the builders, Khidhām b. Khālid, in whose court the mosque was put up, belonged to the ʿUbayd b. Zayd. Two were of the Umayya b. Zayd: Thaʿlaba b. Ḥāṭib[88] and Wadīʿa b. Thābit. The odd one out among the builders was ʿAbbād b. Ḥunayf who was "of the ʿAmr b. ʿAwf" (but not of the Zayd subdivision). He originally belonged to the Ḥanash b. ʿAwf b. ʿAmr b. ʿAwf.[89]

There are some differences between this list and that of eleven mentioned above. A third brother of Zayd and Mujammiʿ, Yazīd, is added, together with a son of Khidhām b. Khālid, Wadīʿa (see below); while three, all of whom belonged to the Ḍubayʿa, are

---

[86] Ṭabarī, *Tafsīr*, XI, 18:19: *wa-Bakhdaj* [!] *wa-huwa ilā B. Ḍubayʿa.*

[87] Zurqānī, III, 81:4 erroneously vocalizes: Bajād; see Ibn Mākūlā, I, 204–205: Bijād b. ʿUthmān of the Ḍubayʿa b. Zayd, one of the builders of *Masjid al-shiqāq*.

[88] In fact, he was a client of the Umayya and was originally of the ʿUbayd: *min B. ʿUbayd wa-huwa ilā B. Umayya b. Zayd*; Ṭabarī, *Tafsīr*, XI, 18:16 (a combined report compiled by Ibn Isḥāq). The full pedigree of Thaʿlaba is: Thaʿlaba b. Ḥāṭib b. ʿAmr b. ʿUbayd b. Umayya b. Zayd b. Mālik b. ʿAwf b. ʿAmr b. ʿAwf; *Istīʿāb*, I, 209–10.

[89] Ibn Hishām, IV, 174; Ibn Qudāma, *Istibṣār*, 321–22; Qurṭubī, *al-Jāmiʿ li-aḥkām al-qurʾān*, VIII, 253–54. On ʿAbbād see below, 119.

missing: Muʿattib b. Qushayr, Nabtal b. al-Ḥārith and Baḥzaj.[90] Gil seems unaware that the Zayd b. Mālik were a subdivision of the ʿAmr b. ʿAwf.[91]

All the builders of the Ḍirār Mosque then were of the ʿAmr b. ʿAwf. Muqātil b. Sulaymān (above, 88) explicitly says so, and almost all of them belonged to the three clans making up the subdivision of the ʿAmr b. ʿAwf called Zayd b. Mālik.

The Zayd b. Mālik

The unity revealed by the B. Zayd b. Mālik in the Ḍirār incident is also reflected in various aspects. Let us begin with genealogy. We are told that each of the three eponyms of the clans making up the Zayd had a son called Zayd (i.e., they were given their grandfather's name). The last Tubbaʿ, as the story goes, was met by the noblemen of Medina, among them being the three Zayds (*al-Azyād*), who were cousins: Zayd b. Umayya b. Zayd, Zayd b. Ḍubayʿa b. Zayd and Zayd b. ʿUbayd b. Zayd. Tubbaʿ revenged his son's murder by killing the three Zayds while a fourth nobleman, Uḥayḥa b. al-Julāḥ, escaped.[92]

---

[90] Ibn Qudāma, *Istibṣār*, 322.

[91] He remarks that except for ʿAbbād b. Ḥunayf, who was of the ʿAmr b. ʿAwf, the rest of the builders were of clans belonging to the Zayd b. Mālik, namely the ʿUbayd b. Zayd, Umayya b. Zayd and Ḍubayʿa b. Zayd; Gil, "The Medinan opposition", 71. Note Gil's remark on p. 74: "As to [the fortress] al-Shunayf, there is a tradition saying that it belonged to the B. Ḍubayʿa, not to the B. ʿAmru b. ʿAwf . . . there must have been envy on the part of the B. Ḍubayʿa against the B. ʿAmr b. ʿAwf". But the Ḍubayʿa were part of the ʿAmr b. ʿAwf and there is no contradiction between the two statements concerning the fortress! (A. Sprenger, *Das Leben und die Lehre des Moḥammad*, Berlin 1869, III, 33, n. 2 correctly says that the builders were of the ʿAmr b. ʿAwf.) Incidentally, Gil vocalizes *aṭm*, read: *uṭum*, and the correct rendering is "fortress" or "tower-house", rather than "building". In his discussion on the builders' motives, Gil (p. 72) says that the builders wished "to compensate themselves for the fact that the Prophet had prayed in the Mosque of Qubāʾ, built by the B. ʿAmru b. ʿAwf. Thus, it was the envy on the part of the B. Ghanm b. ʿAwf that motivated them to build the mosque". He goes on to point out an inconsistency: one of the builders was himself of the B. ʿAmr b. ʿAwf.

[92] *Aghānī*, XIII, 120:10 (Zayd b. Umayya b. Zayd is erroneously written twice). See also Ibn Ḥazm, *Ansāb*, 333–34; Ibn al-Kalbī, *Jamhara*,

The Zayd functioned as one body in the legal sense: we deduce this from the fact that they, probably as a collective body, had clients: the ʿAjlān of the Balī were the clients of Zayd b. Mālik b. ʿAwf.[93]

Much of what we know about the Zayd concerns their quarters in Qubāʾ. As was always the case in pre-Islamic Medina, the fortresses were the most prominent element both in the landscape and in the literary evidence. The Zayd's fortresses were very near each other: Samhūdī says that the fourteen fortresses in Qubāʾ called al-Ṣayāṣī[94] were close enough for their inhabitants to

---

624–26, 626.

[93] Ibn Saʿd, III, 465: ... "the B. al-ʿAjlān b. Ḥāritha of Balī Quḍāʿa, all of whom are the clients of the B. Zayd b. Mālik b. ʿAwf", or "... the clients of all of the B. Zayd ..."; the former possibility seems to be supported by Ibn ʿAbd al-Barr's comment in the *Istīʿāb*, III, 924: *wa-B. l-ʿAjlān l-Balawiyyūna kulluhum ḥulafāʾ B. ʿAmr b. ʿAwf*; also, by this passage in Ibn al-Kalbī, *Nasab Maʿadd*, II, 711: *fa-walada Ḥāritha: al-ʿAjlān, baṭn, ḥalīfan li-B. Zayd b. Mālik* .... But then there is evidence of an ʿAjlānī who was a *ḥalīf* of another ʿAmr b. ʿAwf subdivision, namely, of the Jaḥjabā (Jazʾ b. ʿAbbās; Ibn Qudāma, *Istibṣār*, 317) and of ʿAjlānīs who were clients of another Aws subdivision: ʿAbda b. Mughīth of the ʿAjlān was the client of the Ẓafar (Nabīt); *Iṣāba*, IV, 391 (printed Muʿattib instead of Mughīth). Cf. Waq., I, 158–59 (Balawī clients of the Ẓafar who participated in Badr).

On the settlement of the ʿAjlān and other Balawī clans in Medina see Bakrī, I, 28. The entry in the *Iṣāba*, II, 454 on Ribʿī b. Abī Ribʿī (= Ribʿī b. Rāfiʿ) b. Yazīd [rather: Zayd, as in the other Companion dictionaries] b. Ḥāritha b. al-Jadd b. al-ʿAjlān, (etc.), of the ʿAjlān mentions that "they [i.e., the B. al-ʿAjlān] are the clients of the Zayd b. Mālik b. ʿAwf b. Mālik b. al-Aws; cf. *Istīʿāb*, II, 505; *Usd al-ghāba*, II, 162. When we are told that Murra b. al-Ḥārith b. ʿAdī b. al-Jadd b. al-ʿAjlān was the client of *Āl* ʿAmr b. ʿAwf (*Iṣāba*, VI, 77), and that Murra b. al-Ḥubāb b. ʿAdī b. al-Jadd b. al-ʿAjlān was the client of the ʿAmr b. ʿAwf (*Istīʿāb*, III, 1382), we have to assume that, in fact, the Zayd b. Mālik subdivision of the ʿAmr b. ʿAwf are meant, and not the ʿAmr b. ʿAwf in general. See also *Istīʿāb*, III, 923 f (ʿAbdallāh b. Salima al-ʿAjlānī, a client of the ʿAmr b. ʿAwf); Ibn Saʿd, IV, 377 (Judayy b. Murra b. Surāqa b. al-Ḥubāb b. ʿAdī b. al-Jadd b. al-ʿAjlān of the Balī, the clients of the ʿAmr b. ʿAwf). B. al-ʿAjlān, presumably our ʿAjlān, were the intendants (*sadana*) of the idol al-Saʿīda which was located in Uḥud and was worshipped by the Quḍāʿa, with the exception of the Wabara, and by the Azd; Ibn Ḥabīb, *Muḥabbar*, 316 f; Ibn Ḥazm, *Ansāb*, 493; Yaq., s.v. al-Saʿīda.

[94] Plural of *ṣīṣa*, "horn" of a bull or a cow; such horns were sometimes fixed on spears instead of iron heads; cf. Ibn al-Kalbī, *Nasab Maʿadd*, II, 545 (the first who replaced the heads made of bulls' horns with iron heads; cf. al-Ḥasan

"borrow fire" from one another.[95] These fourteen fortresses were located in the open area (*raḥba*), appropriately called Raḥbat B. Zayd.[96] To judge from the number of fortresses, the B. Zayd may well have been the strongest element in Qubā'.

Some of these fourteen Ṣayāṣī are known to us by name. Naturally, the historians of Medina address an Islamic audience of the first and second Islamic centuries when they mention the old sites with reference to their new functions or owners. The information, therefore, is at times a mixture of old and new.

Several of the fortresses belonged to the Ḍubay'a:

1. When the 'Amr b. 'Awf settled in Qubā', they built al-Shunayf fortress near the court of Abū Sufyān b. al-Ḥārith (of the Ḍubay'a) between Aḥjār al-Mirā' ("the stones of contention") and

b. Aḥmad al-Hamdānī, *al-Iklīl*, II, ed. Muḥammad b. 'Alī al-Akwa', Beirut 1407/1986, 236); it also means "anything with which one defends himself" and "a fortress". The name *al-ṣayāṣī* presumably relates to the shape of these fortresses.

[95] *Yata'āṭā ahluhā l-nīrān baynahum min qurbihā*; Samh., s.v. al-Ṣayāṣī, II, 1256; Lane, *Arabic-English Lexicon*, s.v. Concerning the "borrowing of fire" cf. A. Oppenheimer, in collaboration with B. Isaac and M. Lecker, *Babylonia Judaica in the Talmudic Period*, Wiesbaden 1983, s.v. Apamea, 29. Cf. also the description of the population density in Saba' before the disaster of Ma'rib happened, in 'Alī b. al-Ḥasan al-Khazrajī, *al-'Uqūd al-lu'lu'iyya fī ta'rīkh al-dawla al-rasūliyya*, ed. Muḥammad Basyūnī 'Asal, IV, Leiden-London 1913, 8 (*wa-kānū yata'āṭawna l-nīrān fīmā baynahum masīrata shahrayni fī shahrayni wa-qīla masīrata sittati ashhur fī mithlihā, wa-'llāhu a'lamu*). Fire and distance are related to each other in the alleged saying of the Prophet that Muslims and pagans should be far enough from one another "for their fires not to be able to see each other"; Ṭabarānī, *Kabīr*, II, 303; Ibn al-Athīr, *al-Nihāya fī gharīb al-ḥadīth wa-l-athar*, ed. Ṭāhir Aḥmad al-Zāwī and Maḥmūd Muḥammad al-Ṭanāḥī, Cairo 1385/1965, s.v. *r.'.y.*, II, 177 (*lā tarā'ā nārāhumā*). Al-Ṣīṣa was also the name of a specific fortress in Qubā' (below, 134). For the likening of *fitan* to *ṣayāṣī l-baqar* see, e.g., *TMD* ('Abdallāh b. Jābir), 217 f; I. Goldziher, "Neue Materialien zur Literatur des Überlieferungswesens bei den Muhammedanern", in *ZDMG* 50 (1896), 465–506, at 493. The peculiar *ṣayāṣī* in Qur'ān 33,26 ("And He brought down those of the People of the Book who supported them from their fortresses", etc.) are said by the commentators to refer to the fortresses (*ḥuṣūn*, *ḥuṣūn wa-āṭām*, also *quṣūr*) of the Jewish Qurayẓa (which were not, however, located in Qubā'); see, e.g., Ṭabarī, *Tafsīr*, XXI, 95, 98. The reference to Qurayẓa is puzzling; elsewhere only the fortresses of the Zayd are called Ṣayāṣī.

[96] Samh., I, 193.

Majlis Banī l-Mawālī (an Islamic place-name, and hence anachronistic in the context of the settlement of the ʿAmr b. ʿAwf).[97]

2. Al-Marāwiḥ fortress belonged to Thābit b. Abī al-Aqlaḥ (of the Ḍubayʿa) who was of the generation before the time of the Prophet: his son ʿĀṣim was a Companion.[98]

Other fortresses belonged to the ʿUbayd:

3. The Buʿbuʿ fortress was located in the (later) court of Abū Wadīʿa b. Khidhām and belonged to the ʿUbayd b. Zayd.[99]

4. The fortress of Kulthūm b. al-Hidm of the ʿUbayd b. Zayd (viz., its remains) was located in the (later) court of ʿAbdallāh b. Abī Aḥmad (b. Jaḥsh al-Asadī).[100]

---

[97] Samh., I, 193; Samh., s.v. II, 1246; *Maghānim*, s.v. 209. Cf. Wüstenfeld, *Medina*, 38 who has *aḥǵâr el-marâ*, translated as "Spiegelsteinen" (!). The site called Aḥjār al-Mirāʾ was the meeting-place of the Prophet and Gabriel; Mujāhid said that "they are Qubāʾ" (i.e., they are in Qubāʾ?); Samh., s.v., II, 1123. Mecca had a place of its own called Aḥjār al-Mirāʾ. Cf. perhaps the story on the blind Ibn ʿAbbās asking to be taken to *majlis al-mirāʾ* in Mecca, located between two of the Kaʿba gates, where people used to discuss questions of *jabr* and *qadar*; Muḥammad b. Yūsuf al-Janadī al-Kindī, *al-Sulūk fī ṭabaqāt al-ʿulamāʾ wa-l-mulūk*, ed. Muḥammad b. ʿAlī al-Akwaʿ al-Ḥiwālī, I, [Ṣanʿāʾ] 1403/1983, I, 110. Ṣufiyy al-Sibāb in Mecca was also called Aḥjār al-Mirāʾ; Bakrī, s.v. Ṣufiyy al-Sibāb, 838 (*kānat Quraysh tatamārā ʿindahā wa-huwa l-mawḍiʿ l-maʿrūf bi-aḥjāri l-mirāʾ*).

Majlis Ibn al-Mawlā (= Majlis Banī l-Mawālī) is mentioned in connection with Baḥraj (read: Baḥzaj? see below, 119n), a fortress built by the ʿAmr b. ʿAwf between Majlis Ibn al-Mawlā and the *ḥammām* in Qubāʾ which belonged to the ʿAzīz b. Mālik; *Maghānim*, s.v. Baḥraj. On the ʿAzīz see Ibn Ḥazm, *Ansāb*, 334. The above-mentioned Abū Sufyān b. al-Ḥārith, nicknamed *abū l-banāt*, was killed in the Battle of Uḥud; *Iṣāba*, VII, 182, 559. Three daughters of his appear in Ibn Saʿd, VIII, 347.

[98] *Iṣāba*, III, 569–70, Ibn Qudāma, *Istibṣār*, 284–87; *Usd al-ghāba*, III, 73–74; *Istīʿāb*, II, 779–81; Ibn Saʿd, III, 462–63.

[99] Samh., s.v. II, 1150; *Maghānim*, s.v. (printed: *wa-kāna mawḍiʿuhu fī dār Abī Wadīʿa b. Ḥidhām*; read: Khidhām); *ʿUmdat al-akhbār*, 241. Khidhām (b. Khālid) was one of the builders of the Ḍirār Mosque. He had a son called Wadīʿa (below, 113) and probably another called Abū Wadīʿa.

[100] Samh., I, 193. The passage refers to Kulthūm as one of the B. ʿUbayd b. Zayd b. Aẓlam, the brother of the B. ʿUbayd b. Zayd b. Mālik. This valuable remark may well preserve the name of a small tribal group incorporated into the ʿUbayd b. Zayd. On ʿAbdallāh b. Abī Aḥmad, see Ibn Saʿd, V, 62. In his report on the Prophet's stay after his Hijra with Kulthūm

One also expects to find fortresses in the Raḥbat B. Zayd belonging to the third component of the B. Zayd, the Umayya b. Zayd. However, evidence of this is still missing.[101]

BIOGRAPHICAL DETAILS ABOUT THE BUILDERS

The details on the builders collected in the following pages amount to a small sample of prosopographical evidence on early Islamic Medina.[102] The sources, and especially the biographical dictionaries, practically abound with solid information, often providing insights into family and other links between individuals.

The Ḍubayʿa

The major role in the Ḍirār incident was played by the Ḍubayʿa b. Zayd.[103]

1. Abū ʿĀmir ʿAbd ʿAmr[104] b. Ṣayfī b. al-Nuʿmān and his son Abū Ṣayfī (or Ṣayfī): Abū ʿĀmir al-Rāhib belonged to the Ḍubayʿa. He is always present in the background of the Ḍirār incident although he was not in Medina at the time of the incident itself. Abū ʿĀmir's court touched upon the Ḍirār Mosque (see below, 130).

---

b. al-Hidm, Mūsā b. ʿUqba adds that he stayed *in the court of Ibn Abī Aḥmad* (*fa-nazala ʿalā Kulthūm ... wa-kāna maskanuhu fī dāri bni Abī Aḥmad*); Bayhaqī, *Dalāʾil*, II, 500. Abū Aḥmad b. Jaḥsh al-Asadī was ʿAbdallāh b. Jaḥsh's brother; Ibn al-Kalbī, *Jamhara*, 186.

101 Presumably the fortresses which the Umayya received from the Jaḥjabā as blood-wit (above, 55 f) were not located in the Raḥba.

102 Cf. Crone, *Slaves on Horses*, 16.

103 As Gil realized. But Gil also tried to trace the Ḍubayʿa in later periods ("The Medinan opposition", 86, 92), in my opinion with less than spectacular success (the fact that different groups have the same name is a constant source of confusion): all of the Ḍubayʿa mentioned by him as active in Baṣra in the Umayyad and Abbasid periods are of another Ḍubayʿa, i.e., a branch of the Bakr b. Wāʾil tribe (Ḍubayʿa b. Qays b. Thaʿlaba b. ʿUkāba b. Ṣaʿb b. ʿAlī b. Bakr b. Wāʾil); see Ibn al-Athīr, *Lubāb*, s.v. al-Ḍubaʿī, II, 260; Ibn Ḥazm, *Ansāb*, 320–21.

104 For Companions of the Prophet named ʿAbd ʿAmr see *Iṣāba*, Index. ʿAbd ʿAmr b. Qunayʿ of the Bakr b. Wāʾil was renamed by the Prophet ʿAbdallāh; Ibn al-Kalbī, *Jamhara*, 537.

We know of two marriage links of Abū ʿĀmir al-Rāhib, both to women of the Aws. The mother of his daughter, al-Shamūs, was ʿAmīq bint al-Ḥārith of the Wāqif (Aws Allāh). Another wife, Salmā bint ʿĀmir of the Jaḥjabā (ʿAmr b. ʿAwf), bore him a daughter, Ḥabība.[105]

A son of Abū ʿĀmir whom some call Ṣayfī[106] while others call Abū Ṣayfī is mentioned in connection with the Ḍirār incident and Abū ʿĀmir's exile. An interpretation of Qur'ān 7,175[107] quotes the Anṣār as saying that the verse refers to "the son of the God-fearing, or the ascetic" (*ibn al-rāhib*) for whom (= the *rāhib*) the *Masjid al-shiqāq* was built.[108] The Qur'ān commentator, Ibn Zayd (above, 97n), explicitly states that Abū ʿĀmir had a son called Ṣayfī: Abū ʿĀmir, he says, fathered Ḥanẓala, who was "the one washed by the angels", Ṣayfī, and his brother.[109] These three sons, the commentator continues, were (viz., unlike their father) among the best Muslims.[110]

---

[105] Ibn Saʿd VIII, 345.

[106] Abū ʿĀmir's father was also called Ṣayfī; *Aghānī*, XV, 163:21.

[107] "And recite to them the tiding of him to whom We gave Our signs, but he cast them off, and Satan followed after him, and he became one of the perverts".

[108] The word *ibn* could, however, be superfluous; see Ibn Shabba, *Medina*, I, 55 where the word *ibn* is missing (...Ibn ʿAbbās: *huwa l-rāhibu lladhī banā* [!] *masjida l-shiqāq*); cf. Suyūṭī, *Durr*, III, 146:19 (*huwa bnu l-rāhibi lladhī buniya lahu masjidu l-shiqāq*). Another version of Ibn ʿAbbās' interpretation has: Ṣayfī b. al-Rāhib; *Durr, loc. cit.* Saʿīd b. al-Musayyab has: Abū ʿĀmir b. Ṣayfī (i.e., Abū ʿĀmir himself), which is followed by the story of Abū ʿĀmir's dispute with the Prophet over the true *ḥanīfiyya*; Qurṭubī, *al-Jāmiʿ li-aḥkām al-qur'ān*, VII, 320.

[109] *Wa-akhīhi*, while one expects here: *wa-akhīhimā*; read: *wa-Zayd*? We know that Abū ʿĀmir had a son called Zayd: Hind bint Zayd b. Abī ʿĀmir al-Rāhib married ʿAbd al-Raḥmān b. Saʿd b. Zurāra; Ibn Saʿd, *Qism mutammim*, 286 (the printed pedigree is wrong, "b. ʿAbdallāh b. ʿAbd al-Raḥmān" is superfluous). This was a marriage between the granddaughter of one *munāfiq* and the son of another; on Saʿd b. Zurāra see Waq., III, 1009; Ibn Qudāma, *Istibṣār*, 59 (*fī islāmihi shakk*). The unnamed brother could also be ʿĀmir (Abū ʿĀmir's first-born). On ʿĀmir b. Abī ʿĀmir al-Rāhib see Ibn Saʿd, VIII, 346. Ṣayfī b. al-Rāhib is also mentioned by Muqātil; below, 108.

[110] Quoted in Ṭabarī, *Tafsīr*, XI, 20:10. A cautionary note would be in place here. Ṣayfī was not only the name of Abū ʿĀmir's father, but also that of another of the Prophet's leading adversaries, Abū Qays Ṣayfī b. al-Aslat of the Aws Allāh. To complicate matters even further, the name of Abū

Muqātil b. Ḥayyān has a report about "Abū Ṣayfī al-Rāhib" (read probably: Abū Ṣayfī [b.] al-Rāhib) who left Medina and went to Mecca:

> Suʿayda, whose pedigree was not reported, the wife of Abū Ṣayfī al-Rāhib. She was of the Anṣār. Abū Ṣayfī left Medina, having broken off from her family in enmity (*mughāḍiban li-ahlihā*) when they embraced Islam. He stayed in Mecca [i.e., with his wife] for a while (*ḥīnan*), then his wife Suʿayda set out for Medina in a Hijra [she was in fact returning there] during the truce (*hudna*) [i.e., the truce of Ḥudaybiyya]. They [the Meccans] asked the Messenger of God (*ṣ*) to return her to them, since they stipulated [at Ḥudaybiyya] that he would give them back those of them who would go to him. But he said: "The stipulation referred to men, not to women". And God revealed the *āyat al-imtiḥān*. This was mentioned by Muqātil b. Ḥayyān in his *Tafsīr*.[111]

Suʿayda reportedly belonged to the Umayya b. Zayd (a brother-clan of the Ḍubayʿa).[112]

Qays' father ("al-Aslat" or "one whose nose was cut off", was a nickname), was ʿĀmir. Confusion and contamination of these names, Abū Qays Ṣayfī b. al-Aslat/b. ʿĀmir and Abū ʿĀmir ʿAbd ʿAmr b. Ṣayfī, was possible.

[111] *Iṣāba*, VII, 700 (commentary on Qur'ān 60,10, *āyat al-imtiḥān* or "the verse of testing"). See also *Usd al-ghāba*, V, 475 (where Abū Ṣayfī is described as *mushrik muqīm bi-Makka*). On Muqātil (d. ca. 150/767) see *GAS*, I, 36.

[112] Suʿayda bint Bashīr/Bushayr b. ʿUbayd b. ʿAmr b. ʿUbayd b. Umayya b. Zayd; she is said to have pledged her allegiance to the Prophet; Ibn Saʿd, VIII, 349. Ibn Ḥabīb, *Muḥabbar*, 418 has this pedigree: Suʿayda bint Rifāʿa b. ʿAmr b. ʿUbayd b. Umayya. Cf. M. Lecker, "The Anṣārī wives of ʿUmar b. al-Khaṭṭāb and his brother, Zayd" (forthcoming). Muqātil b. Sulaymān identifies the woman who went to the Prophet during the truce (*muwādaʿa*) as Subayʿa bint al-Ḥārith al-Aslamiyya and says that she was married to Ṣayfī b. al-Rāhib, one of the pagans of Mecca (!). Her husband came to divorce her and demanded that she be returned; Muqātil, *Tafsīr*, II, 193b. The identity of the man who was Subayʿa's husband after her flight from Mecca is disputed; see Ibn Saʿd, III, 408; VIII, 287; Ibn al-Ṭallāʿ, *Aqḍiyat rasūli llāhi*, ed. Muḥammad Ḍiyā' al-Raḥmān al-Aʿẓamī, Cairo–Beirut, 1398/1978, 667 f (Saʿd b. Khawla, a Muhājir who was a client [*ḥalīf*] or *mawlā* of Abū Ruhm

The report probably deals with a son of Abū ʿĀmir al-Rāhib called Abū Ṣayfī [b.] al-Rāhib. It is not certain that the son's name was Abū Ṣayfī because elsewhere, the "Abū" is missing. One report[113] calls him Ṣayfī b. al-Rāhib, while another account, a reference to the commentary by Muqātil b. Ḥayyān quoted above, has only Ṣayfī (without mention of his father).[114] Yet Abū Ṣayfī may still be preferable to Ṣayfī as the son's name because it is supported by an independent testimony according to which Abū ʿĀmir had a son called Abū Ṣayfī. The biography of Abū ʿĀmir's grandson, ʿAbdallāh b. Ḥanẓala b. Abī ʿĀmir, contains details about ʿAbdallāh's children. ʿAbdallāh's cousin, Asmāʾ bint *Abī Ṣayfī* b. Abī ʿĀmir b. Ṣayfī, gave birth to two of them. Now that we know Abū ʿĀmir had a son called Abū Ṣayfī[115] we may assume that this son is referred to in the report just quoted on Suʿayda and Abū Ṣayfī [b.] al-Rāhib. Not only did Abū ʿĀmir leave Medina and go to Mecca, but a son of his did the same accompanied by his wife.

The report on Abū Ṣayfī and his wife should be read in conjunction with other reports on one of the tactics employed by the Prophet in his struggle to convert Medina, and indeed the whole of Arabia, namely the prohibition of intermarriages between Muslims and non-Muslims. The cause of the dispute between Abū ʿĀmir's son and his wife's family was presumably this: when they embraced Islam, they were urged by the Prophet to demand a divorce.[116] Divorce (and the consequent control of the

b. ʿAbd al-ʿUzzā [the father of Abū Sabra b. Abī Ruhm] of the Qurashī clan ʿĀmir b. Luʾayy); Ibn Qudāma, *Istibṣār*, 299 (Abū l-Baddāḥ b. ʿĀṣim b. ʿAdī [this is obviously an error, he was not a Companion; on him, see below, 136]).

[113] In which the wife in question is called Subayʿa bint al-Ḥārith al-Aslamiyya; see the preceding note.

[114] *Fatḥ al-bārī*, V, 257:19. He is called Ṣayfī in another commentary as well; Ṭabarī, *Tafsīr*, XI, 20:12; above, 107n.

[115] Ibn Saʿd, V, 65.

[116] The wife of Thābit b. al-Daḥdāḥ fled from her pagan husband to the Prophet who gave her in marriage to another man; below, 123. Cf. the prohibition, later abrogated, of inheritance between the Muhājirūn and the *aʿrāb*, glossed here as *al-tārikīna li-l-hijra*; Abū ʿUbayd al-Qāsim b. Sallām, *al-Nāsikh wa-l-mansūkh fī l-qurʾān al-ʿazīz*, ed. Muḥammad b. Ṣāliḥ al-Mudayfir, Riyāḍ 1411/1990, 78 f.

children by the Muslim parent) was an effective weapon resorted to by the Prophet more than once.

In the context of Abū ʿĀmir's association with the Meccans mention should be made of Abū ʿĀmir's *mawlā*, Mīnā, who presumably left Medina and went to Mecca with his master. In order to gain information on this little-known figure, Ibn Saʿd, who included in his biographical dictionary an entry on Mīnā's son al-Ḥakam, had to rely on his own fieldwork.[117] Ibn Saʿd quoted in this entry Mīnā's descendants who lived in his own time. They said that Abū ʿĀmir had given Mīnā to Abū Sufyān b. Ḥarb, who in turn sold him to the Prophet's uncle, ʿAbbās. Later ʿAbbās manumitted him and his offspring consequently called themselves the *mawālī* of ʿAbbās (*wa-lahu baqiyya l-yawma yantamūna ilā walāʾi l-ʿAbbās*).[118]

Abū ʿĀmir's son, Ḥanẓala, was a righteous Muslim.[119] He was not the only young Medinan who rebelled against the authority of his father at the time. Ḥanẓala was killed in the Battle of Uḥud fighting on the Prophet's side, while his father fought against the Prophet.[120] Ḥanẓala's widow was ʿAbdallāh b. Ubayy's daughter,

[117] Ibn Saʿd, V, 311. Al-Ḥakam was a traditionist; see also *Usd al-ghāba*, II, 38–39; Ibn Qudāma, *Istibṣār*, 290; *Tahdh.*, II, 440, no. 767.

[118] This *walāʾ*-claim looks suspicious: it could have emerged after the Abbasids came to power, when such status had obvious benefits. Mīnā's descendants provided their ancestor with a military record, reporting that he participated in the Tabūk expedition; *Iṣāba*, II, 110, quoting Ibn Saʿd, has it that Abū Sufyān gave him to ʿAbbās. However, this does not conform with the text in Ibn Saʿd's *Ṭabaqāt* where we find that Abū Sufyān sold him to ʿAbbās. But then, perhaps we have independent evidence to corroborate the *walāʾ*-claim: *Mīnā mawlā ʿAbbās* is one of the many said to have built the pulpit in the Prophet's Mosque; *Iṣāba*, VI, 242. For other versions concerning the identity of ʿAbbās' *mawlā*, or slave, who made the pulpit, see Samh, II, 393, 395–96.

[119] In Ibn Ḥabīb, *Muḥabbar*, 238 Ḥanẓala is listed among "those who prohibited the drinking of wine, intoxication and prostitution" (... *wa-l-azlām*, "divining arrows", read: *wa-l-zinā*). But the text may be garbled (*Ḥanẓala al-rāhib* [!] *b. Abī ʿĀmir al-ghasīl, ghasīlu l-malāʾika*).

[120] Waq., I, 237. The corpses of the Muslims killed in Uḥud were mutilated by the pagans but for Ḥanẓala's; his father was then with Abū Sufyān; *Istīʿāb*, I, 272–73. Abū ʿĀmir's fighting against the Prophet in Uḥud is also mentioned in Ibn Qudāma, *Istibṣār*, 289; Rubin, "Ḥanīfiyya", 86.

Jamīla.[121] The widow gave birth to ʿAbdallāh b. Ḥanẓala who was killed in the Battle of the Ḥarra (63/683; among those killed was also a son of Jamīla from another marriage).[122]

2–5. Jāriya b. ʿĀmir b. Mujammiʿ b. al-ʿAṭṭāf b. Ḍubayʿa b. Zayd and his sons, Mujammiʿ (who was the *imām*), Zayd and Yazīd.[123]

"THE PIECES OF GOLD"

ʿĀmir b. Mujammiʿ b. al-ʿAṭṭāf b. Ḍubayʿa was killed by the Khaṭma and his death caused a war "between them" (presumably between the ʿAmr b. ʿAwf and the Khaṭma).[124] ʿĀmir's

---

[121] This intermarriage between the Aws and Khazraj was at the same time a link between two leading families of the Anṣār; *Usd al-ghāba*, V, 418; cf. Wellhausen, *Skizzen* IV, 62, n. 2.

[122] Ibn Saʿd, V, 65–68, 81; VIII, 382–83; Ibn Qudāma, *Istibṣār*, 289–90: *wa-kānati l-Anṣār bāyaʿathu yawmaʾidhin*. Note, however, that there is no unanimity about ʿAbdallāh's command. Elsewhere, the commander of the Anṣār at the Battle of the Ḥarra is said to have been Muḥammad b. ʿAmr b. Ḥazm of the Najjār who was also killed there; *Tahdh.*, IX, 370. Ibn Ḥajar, aware of this difference, suggests that Muḥammad led the Khazraj while ʿAbdallāh led the Aws. In any case, five decades after the Prophet's death, the Anṣār, or some of them, were led in battle by the grandson of both Abū ʿĀmir al-Rāhib and ʿAbdallāh b. Ubayy. See also EI^2, s.v. ʿAbd Allāh b. Ḥanẓala (Zettersteén-Pellat).

[123] Waq., III, 1047; Balādh., *Ansāb*, I, 276:15; Ibn Ḥabīb, *Muḥabbar*, 468 (Jāriya's father was not ʿAmr but ʿĀmir). The list of builders in Tab., III, 111 [I, 1705] includes only two of Jāriya's sons, Mujammiʿ and Zayd. Jāriya and his three sons, Zayd, Yazīd and Mujammiʿ, pledged their allegiance to the Prophet; Ibn al-Kalbī, *Nasab Maʿadd*, I, 366; *Jamhara*, 624 (*huwa wa-banūhu Zayd wa-Yazīd wa-Mujammiʿ*). Dāraquṭnī says (see Ibn Mākūlā, II, 4:11), having mentioned Jāriya [b. ʿĀmir] b. Mujammiʿ, that his two sons, Mujammiʿ and Yazīd, were righteous Companions of the Prophet (*lahumā ṣuḥba wa-ʾstiqāma maʿa l-nabī [ṣ]*). We also find it claimed (*op. cit.*, 5) that Zayd b. Jāriya set out to fight in the Battle of Uḥud but the Prophet found him to be too young. The source for the last-mentioned report is no other than Zayd himself and the report was transmitted by his descendants. Ibn Isḥāq includes Jāriya and his two sons, Zayd and Mujammiʿ, in the list of *munāfiqūn* under "B. Thaʿlaba b. ʿAmr b. ʿAwf"; see Ibn Hishām, II, 169. Gil, "The Medinan opposition", 73, n. 15 quotes Ibn Ḥazm, *Jawāmiʿ*, 75 for this puzzling pedigree. On the Kūfan Mujammiʿ b. Yaḥyā b. Yazīd b. Jāriya see Ibn Saʿd, VI, 368.

[124] Ibn al-Kalbī, *Nasab Maʿadd*, I, 366, 385; Ibn al-Kalbī, *Jamhara*, 624, 643.

son, Jāriya, and the latter's three sons have been mentioned in connection with the Ḍirār incident.[125]

The descendants of ʿĀmir b. Mujammiʿ form a special genealogical group within the Ḍubayʿa. Wāqidī "and others" said that the B. ʿĀmir (i.e., the descendants of ʿĀmir b. Mujammiʿ) were called "the pieces of gold" (*kisar al-dhahab*) in the Jāhiliyya because of their status of nobility in their clan (*li-sharafihim fī qawmihim*).[126]

There are indications, though, that the group called "pieces of gold" also included the rest of the Ḍubayʿa or even the B. Zayd b. Mālik as a whole. The story of the Battle of Uḥud contains a scene involving a woman of the Umayya b. Zayd, Sulāfa bint Saʿd b. Shuhayd, who was married to a Meccan.[127] Several sons of hers as well as her Meccan husband were killed in the Battle of Uḥud fighting against the Prophet. The man who killed one (or more) of her sons was ʿĀṣim b. Thābit b. Abī l-Aqlaḥ al-Anṣārī of the Ḍubayʿa (cf. above, 53n). As he was dealing the deadly blow to one of Sulāfa's sons, ʿĀṣim identified himself in the old Arabian manner as Ibn Abī al-Aqlaḥ. The fatally wounded son who conveyed this information to his mother was an unwitting witness: having been born in Mecca he had little knowledge of Anṣārī genealogies. However, the mother, whose alleged reaction we are interested in here, immediately recognized the enemy as a fellow tribesman. She remarked, *Aqlaḥī wa-'llāhi* (the name of the slayer's grandfather was Abū l-Aqlaḥ), which is glossed: *min rahṭī*, "from my own people". In another version, ʿĀṣim identified himself as *ibn kisra*, which is followed by this gloss: *kānū (sic) yuqālu lahum fī l-jāhiliyya banū kisar al-dhahab*. Sulāfa's reaction, according to this version, was: *iḥdā wa-'llāhi kisarī*,

---

[125] For a fourth son of Jāriya called Bukayr see Ibn Saʿd, *Qism mutammim*, 468; Ibn Saʿd, V, 85.

[126] Ibn Saʿd, IV, 372; Ibn Qudāma, *Istibṣār*, 291. For gold mentioned in a similar context cf. the phrase *fa-naḥnu sulālatu bayti l-dhahab* (in an alleged elegy by Muʿāwiya's mother Hind bint ʿUtba on her father); *TMD (Tarājim al-nisā')*, ed. Sukayna al-Shihābī, Damascus n. d., 444:4.

[127] Read "Shuhayd" instead of "Sahl" in Lecker, *The Banū Sulaym*, 76. Sulāfa's affiliation to the Umayya b. Zayd is inferred from the pedigree of her brother, ʿUmayr, who was a Companion; on him, see *Iṣāba*, IV, 718–19; *Usd al-ghāba*, IV, 143–44; *Istīʿāb*, III, 1215–17; Ibn Saʿd, IV, 374–75.

"By God, [he is] one of my *kisar*".[128] That day, the report goes on, Sulāfa vowed to drink wine from 'Āṣim b. Thābit's skull and promised a reward of one hundred camels for it.[129]

Now, it will be remembered that the slayer and the mother belonged to different clans of the Zayd b. Mālik: 'Āṣim was of the Ḍubay'a b. Zayd, though he was not a descendant of 'Āmir b. Mujammi', while Sulāfa belonged to the Umayya b. Zayd. The mother's declaration that the slayer was "one of her 'pieces of gold'" invites a definition of the "pieces" group which includes both the Ḍubay'a and the Umayya. Indeed, one such definition comes from Samhūdī: they were the Umayya, 'Ubayd and Ḍubay'a sons of Zayd b. Mālik b. 'Awf.[130] In other words, the "pieces of gold" were the Zayd b. Mālik as a whole.

6. Bijād b. 'Uthmān b. 'Āmir b. Mujammi' b. al-'Aṭṭāf:[131] his pedigree shows that he was a nephew of the above-mentioned Jāriya b. 'Āmir (and a cousin of Jāriya's sons). There was a marriage link between his family and that of another builder, as Bijād's daughter, Umāma, married Wadī'a, the son of Khidhām b. Khālid (of the 'Ubayd b. Zayd) and bore him a son, Thābit.[132]

7. Abū Ḥabība al-Adra' b. al-Az'ar b. Zayd b. al-'Aṭṭāf:his son, 'Abdallāh, was a Companion of the Prophet and participated in the Ḥudaybiyya expedition.[133] It is ironical, in view of the Ḍirār

[128] Muṣ'ab b. 'Abdallāh al-Zubayrī, *Nasab Quraysh*, ed. E. Lévi-Provençal, Cairo 1953, 252; Waq., I, 227–28, 356.

[129] She nearly fulfilled her vow; Waq., I, 356.

[130] Samh., I, 197.

[131] Gil, "The Medinan opposition", 79; Ibn Hishām, II, 168; Balādh., *Ansāb*, I, 275:13; Ibn Sa'd, IV, 373.

[132] See below, 129n. Bijād married (probably at different periods) two women from the Umayya b. Zayd (of the 'Amr b. 'Awf); see Ibn Sa'd, VIII, 348–49. On the meanings of the name Bijād see al-Aṣma'ī, *Ishtiqāq al-asmā'*, ed. Ramaḍān 'Abd al-Tawwāb and Ṣalāḥ al-Dīn al-Hādī, Cairo 1400/1980, 100; Ibn Durayd, *Ishtiqāq*, 343.

[133] Abū Ḥabība's uncle, Abū Mulayl b. al-Az'ar, a Badrī, was the one who said during the Battle of the Ditch: "Verily our houses are open and exposed" (Qur'ān 33,13); Ibn al-Kalbī, *Nasab Ma'add*, I, 366; *Jamhara*, 623f (for another version found in the same source, see below); *Iṣāba*, VII, 386 (quoting Ibn al-Kalbī; but note the difference: Ibn Ḥajar's phrasing *annahu mimman qāla*, etc. has no support in the two sources quoted above, which

incident, that this ʿAbdallāh reports on a practice of the Prophet in the Mosque of Qubāʾ. Asked about what he "attained" from the Prophet (*mā adrakta min rasūli llāhi*), he answered: "I saw him pray in the Mosque of Qubāʾ with his shoes on".[134] After the time of the Prophet, a granddaughter of Abū Ḥabība married Mujammiʿ b. Yazīd b. Jāriya.[135]

8. Nabtal b. al-Ḥārith b. Qays b. Zayd b. Ḍubayʿa or his son, ʿAbdallāh b. Nabtal: according to some, it was his son ʿAbdallāh who took part in the incident.[136] Nabtal b. al-Ḥārith was a *munāfiq*.[137]

---

have *wa-huwa lladhī qāla*, and *wa-huwa l-qāʾil*, respectively). Elsewhere, it was Muʿattib b. Qushayr who said it; Ibn Durayd, *Ishtiqāq*, 438. The common interpretations of this verse mention the Ḥāritha of the Aws and the Salima of the Khazraj as the culprits; see, e.g., Muqātil, *Tafsīr*, II, 88b (Ḥāritha, Salima); Ṭabarī, *Tafsīr*, XXI, 86 (Ḥāritha); Suyūṭī, *Durr*, V, 188 (Ḥāritha); Ibn al-Kalbī, *Jamhara*, 638 (*qāla Hishām* [i.e., Ibn al-Kalbī]: *fīhim nifāq wa-humu lladhīna qālu, inna buyūtanā ʿawra*; this presumably relates to the Ḥāritha as a whole).

[134] Ibn Saʿd, I, 480; *Iṣāba*, IV, 53–54 (Abū Ḥabība's name, or perhaps his nickname, was al-Adraʿ, "one whose father is free, or an Arab, and whose mother is a slave"; see Lane, *Arabic-English Lexicon*, s.v.). The report is transmitted by the fellow Ḍubayʿīs Mujammiʿ b. Yaʿqūb b. Jāriya < Muḥammad b. Ismāʿīl b. Mujammiʿ who was ʿAbdallāh's grandson on the mother's side. The Ḥadīth, equipped as it is with an unmistakable family-*isnād*, may have come into being in order to support ʿAbdallāh's claim to Companion status. On praying in one's shoes see M.J. Kister, "'Do not assimilate yourselves ...'", 335–49 and the Appendix to the article written by Menahem Kister, 356–68. Cf. the Ḥadīth of Mujammiʿ b. Jāriya on the *dajjāl*; Aḥmad, IV, 390 (*musnad al-Kūfiyyīna*).

[135] Gil, "The Medinan opposition", 72, n. 13; Ibn Saʿd, III, 471; Ibn Saʿd, V, 84. Another granddaughter of Abū Ḥabība, Umm Salama bint al-Nuʿmān b. Abī Ḥabība, married the grandson of Zayd b. Thābit, Ibrāhīm b. Yaḥyā b. Zayd b. Thābit; Ibn Saʿd, *Qism mutammim*, 286.

[136] Ibn Qudāma, *Istibṣār*, 292.

[137] Ibn al-Kalbī, *Jamhara*, 624. In Ibn al-Kalbī, *Nasab Maʿadd*, I, 367 he is called Nabtal b. Qays (his father's name having been omitted); cf. *Iṣāba*, VI, 418. There is some difficulty regarding his identity. A Nabtal b. al-Ḥārith of the ʿAmr b. ʿAwf was killed in the Battle of Buʿāth shortly before Islam at the hands of Asʿad b. Zurāra; Samh., I, 249. We also find in the list of *munāfiqūn* belonging to the Lawdhān (a subdivision of the ʿAmr b. ʿAwf) a Nabtal b. al-Ḥārith; Ibn Hishām, II, 168. (On the Lawdhān see Ibn Ḥazm, *Ansāb*, 337; Ibn al-Kalbī, *Jamhara*, 622; Samh., I, 195.) The assumption that there were three Nabtal b. al-Ḥārith among the ʿAmr b. ʿAwf seems

The following humorous anecdote indicates that ʿAbdallāh b. Nabtal (not his father) was one of the builders of the Ḍirār Mosque. It is yet another insight into the environment in which the *sīra* emerged during the first Islamic century. It shows that the history of the individuals whom the Islamic literature calls *munāfiqūn* continued to be an acute problem for their descendants. For those whose fathers were on the wrong side and opposed the Prophet, this history was not a remote field of scholarship but a blot on the family's reputation. Islamic apologetics reflect the tension between the image of the ideal Companion and the embarrassing attitude of some fathers at the time of the Prophet.

In the humorous anecdote, the actors are a grandson of ʿAbdallāh b. Nabtal whose name is not specified; Khārija, the son of the Companion Zayd b. Thābit; and a Persian *mawlā*, ʿAbdallāh al-Qarrāẓ who makes a living by selling *qaraẓ*-leaves used for tanning hides. The place is Medina and the time a few decades after the time of the Prophet. Khārija uses to give (or sell) the people cool water mixed with honey. ʿAbdallāh al-Qarrāẓ uses to visit him. He is a Persian taken captive in the days of ʿUmar b. al-Khaṭṭāb. When the Persian *mawlā* comes one day, he finds there a descendant of ʿAbdallāh b. Nabtal who begins mocking him. The Persian is ugly, he has a big head and long ears. The following dialogue takes place:

> Persian: "Who are you, young man?"
> Young man: "A man of the Anṣār".
> Persian: "Welcome to the Anṣār; exactly of what clan?"
> Young man: "I am so-and-so, son of al-Ḥārith b. ʿAbdallāh b. Nabtal".
> Persian: "But your grandfather was not one of the Anṣār [or "helpers"; *ammā jadduka fa-lam yanṣur*]. Do you know the Qur'ān verse revealed concerning him? Don't you know what it [i.e., the verse] did to

far-fetched because the name Nabtal is rare.

> him? Do you think it disgraced him? By God, it did disgrace him".[138]

In this fine literary piece the harassed ugly Persian *mawlā* exchanges roles with the nasty Anṣārī. The *mawlā*'s impressive command of Anṣārī genealogy and *asbāb al-nuzūl* stands in sharp contrast to his appearance.[139] Perhaps this encounter never occurred. But, whoever may have fabricated it, took for granted as his starting point, that the grandson of ʿAbdallāh b. Nabtal could have been embarrassed by a reference to his grandfather's attitude at the Prophet's time.[140]

To end this discussion on Nabtal and his son, yet another case of a family link between the builders of the Ḍirār Mosque should be added. A while after the time of the Prophet, ʿAbdallāh's daughter, Lubnā, married ʿUbaydallāh b. Mujammiʿ b. Jāriya who was later killed in the Battle of the Ḥarra.[141]

The ʿUbayd

9. Khidhām b. Khālid:[142] the Ḍirār Mosque was located in Khidhām's court (see below). Some wrongly called him Khidhām b. Wadīʿa. The confusion was probably caused by the fact that Khidhām had a son named Wadīʿa.[143]

---

[138] Balādh., *Ansāb*, I, 275–76 (the last sentence is not smooth: *a-mā tadrī mā ṣanaʿat*—printed *ṣanaʿta*—*bihi tarāhu* [*sic*] *faḍaḥathu, wa-'llāhi wa-hiya l-fāḍiḥa*). Sura 9 is called *al-fāḍiḥa*; see, e.g., Suyūṭī, *Durr*, III, 208:24. The Persian refers to Qur'ān 9,61. On Khārija see Ibn Saʿd, V, 262.

[139] Cf. the angry Hārūn al-Rashīd insulting a Qurashī for having to consult a Persian about his own genealogy; Goldziher, *Muslim Studies*, I, 176 = *Aghānī*, VI, 69. Cf. J. Sadan, "The Epistle on Ugliness by Güzelhisari", in *al-Karmil: Studies in Arabic Language and Literature*, 9 (1988), 7–33, at 17–19 (in Arabic).

[140] See the scene where ʿAbdallāh is mending a pipe on the roof of the Ḍirār Mosque; below, 142.

[141] Ibn Saʿd, V, 260 (another son of Mujammiʿ, Yaḥyā, was also killed in the same battle).

[142] Ibn Qudāma, *Istibṣār*, 321:-3.

[143] Ibn Saʿd, IV, 373 (Wadīʿa b. Khidhām was one of the *munāfiqūn*). After his Hijra, ʿUthmān b. ʿAffān stayed with Khidhām b. Wadīʿa whom some called Khidhām b. Khālid; Ibn Qudāma, *Istibṣār*, 330. On Wadīʿa see also Ibn Ḥazm, *Ansāb*, 334:10 ("of the people of the Ḍirār Mosque"). Gil, "The

Again, we have here a marriage link between the families involved in the Ḍirār incident. Sometime after the Battle of Uḥud, and against his will, Khidhām b. Khālid became the father-in-law of Abū Lubāba (on whom, see below). Khidhām's daughter, Khansā', had been married to Anas (or Unays) b. Qatāda of the 'Ubayd b. Zayd (i.e., a member of her own clan), who was later killed in the Battle of Uḥud. Her father then married her off to a man of the Muzayna whom she disliked. So she went to the Prophet who abrogated the marriage and gave her away in marriage to Abū Lubāba. She bore the latter a son, al-Sā'ib.[144] The scandal happened among the Zayd b. Mālik: the woman rebelled against her father, placing herself under the Prophet's guardianship.

The Umayya

10. Abū Lubāba: although his name is not on the list of builders, he nevertheless merits a mention. An apologetic tone is evident in the following vague remark on Abū Lubāba's role in the Ḍirār

Medinan opposition", 78 mentions that while Khidhām is usually said to have been of the 'Ubayd b. Zayd, some versions relate him to the 'Amr b. 'Awf. But there is no contradiction here: the 'Ubayd were a subdivision of the 'Amr b. 'Awf. See the pedigree of Khidhām in Ibn Sa'd, V, 260: Khidhām b. Khālid b. Tha'laba b. Zayd b. 'Ubayd b. Zayd, etc.

[144] Gil, "The Medinan opposition", 78–79 and the sources quoted there; *Iṣāba*, I, 137–38, and VII, 611–12; *Usd al-ghāba*, I, 113, 126, 135 (his wife is wrongly called here Khansā' al-Asadiyya, which misled Watt, see his *Medina*, 385; Watt observed that "personal matters about which we are not informed were also involved"); Ibn Sa'd, III, 464; *Istī'āb*, IV, 1826 (who rejects, presumably correctly, the claim that she was then a virgin); also see Ibn Qudāma, *Istibṣār*, 330–31. According to one version, her future husband was to be of the 'Awf (b. al-Khazraj?); Ibn Sa'd, III, 464; Ibn Qudāma, *Istibṣār*, 294; Ibn Sa'd, III, 457 (who calls the woman in question Zaynab bint Khidhām b. Khālid). For a report on the Qurayẓa going back to Abū Lubāba > his son, al-Sā'ib, see Waq., II, 506:7. Gil suggests that Abū Lubāba was a close relative of her former husband Unays b. Qatāda, since she refers to him as *'amm waladī*; see, e.g., Ibn Sa'd, VIII, 457. However, this is doubtful: Unays was of the 'Ubayd b. Zayd, while Abū Lubāba was of their brother-clan, the Umayya b. Zayd. The expression *'amm waladī* should be interpreted as a statement that he, unlike the husband chosen for her by her father, was a fellow member of the Zayd b. Mālik.

incident. Our source goes out of his way to emphasize that he was not a *munāfiq* but an innocent helper:

> Abū Lubāba b. ʿAbd al-Mundhir helped them in it with timber. He was not accused of *nifāq* (*wa-kāna ghayra maghmūṣin ʿalayhi fī l-nifāq*) but used to do things that caused dissatisfaction (*wa-lakinnahu qad kāna yafʿalu umūran tukrahu lahu*). [The Prophet is not specifically mentioned, but it is no doubt his dissatisfaction that our source has in mind.] When the mosque was destroyed, Abū Lubāba took that timber which was his and built with it a house. The house he built was on its side [i.e., on the side of the destroyed mosque].[145]

The apologetic comments ("he was not accused of *nifāq*", etc.) do not seem to belong in this report; perhaps they were added in the margin of the original account and later incorporated into the text by a scribe. The comments were made by someone friendly to Abū Lubāba who was concerned about the possible damage to his reputation. This source, therefore, took special pains to explain that his misdemeanours fell short of making him a full-fledged *munāfiq*.[146]

[145] Waq., III, 1047; Gil, "The Medinan opposition", 71–72. Watt adopts the apologetic formulation (*Medina*, 190): "Abū Lubābah had made a gift for the mosque but was clear of the intrigues". Note that in this report the mosque was destroyed (*fa-lammā hudima*), not burnt down. Cf. a similar apologetic remark made concerning Kaʿb b. Mālik's refusal to set out to Tabūk: he was *rajul ṣidq ghayr maṭʿūn ʿalayhi*. The reason Kaʿb stayed behind, we are told, was weariness; Ṭabrisī, *Tafsīr*, X, 136. One who was accused in connection with his faith was al-Ḥārith b. Hishām of the Makhzūm, about whom it is said: *wa-kāna maghmūṣan ʿalayhi fī islāmihi*; Balādh., *Ansāb*, I, 363. Elsewhere we are told that he became a good Muslim when Mecca was conquered (*thumma ḥasuna islāmuhu*; *Iṣāba*, I, 607). This should come as no surprise because one expects his family members or other Makhzūmīs to say kind things about him.

[146] Cf. the elusive language used concerning a *munāfiq* of the Najjār (Khazraj), Qays b. Qahd: *wa-lam yakun Qays bi-l-maḥmūd fī aṣḥābi l-nabī (ṣ)*; *Usd al-ghāba*, IV, 224:5.

The Ḥanash

11. ʿAbbād b. Ḥunayf: his role in Islamic history was completely different to that of his two brothers, Sahl and ʿUthmān, who were both governors in the early Islamic state.[147]

Being of the Ḥanash, ʿAbbād, and probably Baḥzaj as well (see below), are the odd ones out in the list of builders. The Ḥanash, while belonging to the ʿAmr b. ʿAwf, were not of the Zayd b. Mālik (whose eponym, Zayd, was Ḥanash's nephew). However, the evidence linking the Ḥanash, or part of them, to the Zayd suffices to account for ʿAbbād's role in the Ḍirār incident.

The B. Ḥanash were "of the people of the mosque, i.e., the Mosque of Qubāʾ" (*wa-hum min ahli l-masjid, yaʿnī masjid Qubāʾ*).[148] This obscure statement, which is not made in reference to other subdivisions of the ʿAmr b. ʿAwf, appears in Ibn Saʿd's *Ṭabaqāt* at the beginning of the entry on ʿAbbād b. Ḥunayf's brother, Sahl. Its context is presumably the internal divisions of the ʿAmr b. ʿAwf. Part of them, that is to say, the B. Zayd b. Mālik, were "of the people of the mosque" by virtue of its location: simply, it was in their territory. The Ḥanash were "of the people of the mosque" because of their incorporation into a

[147] ʿAbbād and his brothers should not be linked with the *munāfiq* Saʿd b. Ḥunayf. One source (Balādh., *Ansāb*, I, 284) lists Saʿd among the Naḍīr and remarks that he "sought shelter in Islam" (i.e., converted outwardly, as a *munāfiq*) while other sources (Ibn Hishām, II, 161; Waq., III, 1059) say that he was of the Qaynuqāʿ. For an explicit statement that Sahl, ʿUthmān and ʿAbbād were brothers, see Ibn al-Kalbī, *Nasab Maʿadd*, I, 372 f. Cf. Ibn al-Kalbī, *Jamhara*, 630. For a marriage of ʿAbbād's granddaughter, Mandūs bint Ḥakīm, to ʿUthmān's grandson, ʿAbd al-ʿAzīz b. ʿAbdallāh b. ʿUthmān, see Ibn Saʿd, *Qism mutammim*, 467 (instead of Baḥraj, read: Baḥzaj); their great-grandson was called al-Ḥunayfī (after the ancestor Ḥunayf). Ibn Mākūlā, II, 559 remarks about ʿAbbād that "he is said to be the brother of Sahl and ʿUthmān". This comment reveals a certain awkwardness concerning the family relationship between the two righteous brothers and ʿAbbād, the family's black sheep. Ibn Mākūlā mentions two grandsons of ʿAbbād, ʿUthmān and Ḥakīm, sons of Ḥakīm b. ʿAbbād b. Ḥunayf. Ibn Saʿd, *Qism mutammim*, 298 f has entries on both. Two sons and one grandson of ʿUthmān, and a son of ʿAbbād, were killed in the Battle of the Ḥarra; Khalīfa, *Taʾrīkh*, I, 304.

[148] Ibn Saʿd, III, 471.

subdivision of the Zayd, i.e., the Ḍubay'a. At an unknown date, presumably before Islam, the Ḥanash "entered" the Ḍubay'a (i.e., became their clients, perhaps moving into their quarters; no adaptation of their genealogy is mentioned).[149]

The richness of genealogical detail allows us to investigate even further the link between the Ḥanash and the Zayd. The mother of Sahl b. Ḥunayf (and presumably of his brothers, 'Uthmān and 'Abbād; in the context of the Ḍirār Mosque we are mainly concerned with 'Abbād), was of the Aws Allāh.[150] After having been married to Sahl's father, who was of course of the Ḥanash, she divorced him and married no other than Abū Ḥabība b. al-Az'ar, who has just been mentioned as one of the builders (above, 113). As a result, Sahl (and presumably his brothers as well) had half-brothers belonging to the Ḍubay'a, namely 'Abdallāh and al-Nu'mān, the sons of Abū Ḥabība b. al-Az'ar.[151]

Having noted the marriage of Sahl's mother to Abū Ḥabība, we can now turn to the following curious coincidence: when As'ad b. Zurāra, the *naqīb* of the Najjār (Khazraj) died, the Prophet declared himself the *naqīb* of the Najjār. He also became the guardian of As'ad's daughters.[152] Finding a suitable match for the girls was naturally a major concern for the guardian and the Prophet gave one daughter, Ḥabība, to Sahl b. Ḥunayf.[153] He gave another daughter of As'ad, Kabsha, to no other than Sahl's half-brother, 'Abdallāh b. Abī Ḥabība.[154]

[149] Ibn Ḥazm, *Ansāb*, 332:–2: *dakhala B. Ḥanash fī B. Ḍubay'a b. Zayd*. Ibn al-Kalbī, *Jamhara*, 622 says that the Ḥanash were tribal groups incorporated into the Ḍubay'a (*buṭūn fī B. Ḍubay'a b. Zayd*). This incorporation may be the reason for Sahl b. Ḥunayf's inclusion among the Ḍubay'a in the list of Badrīs; Waq., I, 159.

[150] She was of the Ja'ādira and, more precisely, of the Umayya b. Zayd b. Qays b. 'Āmira b. Murra.

[151] Ibn Sa'd, III, 471. (For another marriage link between the Ḥanash and the Ja'ādira, or more precisely, the Wā'il b. Zayd, see Ibn Sa'd, VIII, 352.)

[152] Ibn Hishām, II, 154; Ibn Qudāma, *Istibṣār*, 58:–2.

[153] She bore him Abū Umāma As'ad b. Sahl; Balādh., *Ansāb*, I, 243:14; Ibn Sa'd, III, 471. Sahl's marriage to the daughter of the late *naqīb* of the Najjār may have paved his way to positions of authority in the early Islamic state (below, 123); see Ibn Sa'd, VIII, 439–40.

[154] Ibn Sa'd, III, 440.

So, considering Ḥanash's incorporation into the Ḍubayʿa, ʿAbbād's inclusion in the list of builders is accounted for.

12. Baḥzaj:[155] he is a mysterious figure. Some biographical details on him are found in the following report (by Ibn ʿAbbās):

> When the Messenger of God (*ṣ*) built the Mosque of Qubā', people of the Anṣār, among them Baḥzaj,[156] the grandfather [or ancestor] of ʿAbdallāh b. Ḥunayf,[157] together with Wadīʿa b. Khidhām[158] and Mujammiʿ b. Jāriya al-Anṣārī, went out and built *Masjid al-nifāq*. The Messenger of God said to Baḥzaj: "Woe unto thee, Baḥzaj, what did you wish to gain by what I see?" [*waylaka yā Yakhdaj*(!) *mā aradta ilā mā arā*; the alleged scolding took place at the site of the accursed mosque, while the Prophet was looking at it]. Baḥzaj replied: "By God, I only meant to do good" (*mā aradtu illā l-ḥusnā*).[159]

[155] This is a nickname. The *Lisān al-ʿarab*, s.v., quotes this interpretation, striking a note of skepticism (*wa-'llāhu aʿlamu*, "and God knows best"): said about a man, it means "short with a large belly". A big belly gave another eponym of a Medinan clan his nickname: al-Ḥublā, "the pregnant woman"; Ibn Ḥazm, *Ansāb*, 354:–3 (*luqqiba bi-dhālika li-ʿiẓam baṭnihi*).

[156] Printed: Bakhdaj!

[157] This remark was made by the two commentators mentioned below (or by a scribe), not by Ibn ʿAbbās.

[158] Printed: Ḥizām!

[159] Gil, "The Medinan opposition", 79 = Suyūṭī, *Durr*, III, 276:18, quoting the commentaries of Ibn Abī Ḥātim and Ibn Mardawayh; see *GAS*, I, 179 and 225, respectively. Also Ṭabarī, *Tafsīr*, XI, 19:10. Gil says that according to Suyūṭī, Baḥzaj's father is ʿUthmān. But I could not find this in the *Durr* (which seems to be the source referred to by Gil). Gil's summary of this dialogue is inaccurate. He says: "He once was asked by the Prophet what he thought about his views; he answered treacherously that he fully agreed with them". Cf. a similar expression in Tab., V, 168 [I, 12]: *mā aradta ilā mā ṣanaʿta*. Gil (*loc. cit.*, n. 30) refers to Ibn al-Najjār (*Durra*, 382), saying that this source calls him Makhdaj b. ʿUthmān, "which means that he was Bijād's brother". In fact, Ibn al-Najjār includes in the participants' list Maḥdaj (read: Baḥzaj; his father's name is not mentioned!) and Bijād b. ʿUthmān. (True, the *Sīra Shāmiyya*, V, 676, quoting Ibn Isḥāq, lists Baḥzaj *b. ʿUthmān* of the Ḍubayʿa among the builders of the Ḍirār Mosque.)

There are a few indications that Baḥzaj was of the Ḥanash. His name on the builders' list is followed by this remark: *wa-huwa ilā B. Ḍubay'a*, i.e., he was a client of the Ḍubay'a.[160] As we have seen, the Ḥanash were incorporated into the Ḍubay'a as clients. This explains why in Ibn Isḥāq's list of *munāfiqūn*, towards the end of the names of those who belonged to the Ḍubay'a, was 'Abbād b. Ḥunayf (of the Ḥanash), followed immediately by our Baḥzaj.[161] That Baḥzaj is a Ḥanashī can also be deduced from the occurrence of this rare name in the pedigree of the Ḥanash.[162] In short, there were two Ḥanashīs involved in the Ḍirār incident.[163]

The Ḥanash conclude this short prosopographical discussion on the builders of the Ḍirār Mosque. The final notes of this section concern the client status of the Ḥanash with regard to the position held by some of them in the nascent Islamic state. This presumably small and insignificant client group rose to considerable prominence under the Prophet and the early caliphs. There can be no doubt that on the eve of Islam their masters, the Ḍubay'a,

---

[160] E.g., Tab., III, 111 [I, 1705].

[161] Ibn Hishām, II, 169.

[162] Gil, "The Medinan opposition", 79 suggests to replace "Baḥzaj/'Amr, son of Ḥanash", by "Baḥzaj b. Khansā' bint Khidhām b. Khālid" in order to get as a result "Baḥzaj/'Amr, son of Khansā' and grandson of Khidhām b. Khālid". He says: "We have just *seen* [the italics are mine—M.L.] that his real (or additional) name was 'Amru, and that he was the grandson of Khidhām b. Khālid and the son of Khansā'". This reconstruction seems to me impossible. Our Baḥzaj could not have been identical with Baḥzaj/'Amr b. Ḥanash who was the son of Ḥanash's eponym, because Baḥzaj/'Amr lived seven generations before the Prophet's time; Ibn Ḥazm, *Ansāb*, 336. Incidentally, it is not certain that Baḥzaj's name was 'Amr; the pedigree of a woman belonging to the Ḥanash (al-Furay'a, or Qurayba, bint Qays; Ibn Sa'd, VIII, 352) ends with "... b. 'Amr b. Jusham, who was the one called Baḥzaj, b. Ḥanash"; in other words, another name, Jusham/Baḥzaj, appears between 'Amr and Ḥanash. On the name cf. M. Marín, "Le nom *Ḥanaš* dans l'onomastique arabe", in *Cahiers d'onomastique arabe 1982–1984*, 51–55, at 52, no. 7.

[163] "Baḥraj", as a name of a fortress in Qubā' (above, 105n), should perhaps be read "Baḥzaj", but this is not certain: it belonged to the 'Azīz b. Mālik subdivision of the 'Amr b. 'Awf, while our Baḥzaj was of the Ḥanash. (However, it could have become the property of the 'Azīz after the presumed shift of the Ḥanash to the quarters of the Ḍubay'a.)

were stronger and more prestigious; yet the Ḥanashīs, Sahl b. Ḥunayf and his brother 'Uthmān were given offices of authority. Sahl, who took part in the Battle of Badr,[164] and his brother, 'Uthmān (but not their brother, 'Abbād, who was a *munāfiq* and hence lacked Islamic credentials), were high officials in the Islamic state. As we have seen, Sahl received in marriage from the Prophet the daughter of the deceased *naqīb* of the Khazraj, As'ad b. Zurāra. There are further reliable indications that the Prophet favoured him. He also gave him in marriage Umayma bint Bishr of the Umayya b. Zayd. She had been married to Thābit b. al-Daḥdāḥ and "fled from him to the Prophet" (i.e., making him her guardian), when her husband was still a pagan. She bore Sahl a son, 'Abdallāh.[165] Only two Anṣār, one of whom was Sahl, were among those who received a share in the estates of the expelled Naḍīr, the rest being of the Muhājirūn. "The two were poor" (*kānā faqīrayni/muḥtājayni*), our source explains.[166]

The leading families of the Anṣār preserved their power and prestige among the Anṣār (cf. above, 111n). Yet the new social and political order established by Islam created opportunities for qualified, less prestigious members of Medinan society to rise to prominence. They had to acquire the necessary Islamic credentials in the battlefield, display unwavering loyalty to the Prophet and, at a later period, convince the Qurashī sovereigns that they did not challenge their superiority (i.e., that they were not "subversive elements"). The Caliph 'Umar b. al-Khaṭṭāb put 'Uthmān b. Ḥunayf in charge of the measurement of land in the recently-conquered Sawād of Iraq and the collection of land and poll taxes (*misāḥata l-arḍīna wa-jibāyatahā wa-ḍarba l-kharāji wa-l-jizyati 'alā ahlihā*).[167] Both he and his brother, Sahl, served in 'Alī b. Abī Ṭālib's administration: 'Uthmān was 'Alī's governor in

[164] Ibn Sa'd, III, 471–73 (471:3, instead of 'Amr b. al-Ḥārith, read: 'Amr b. Ḥanash).

[165] Ibn Qudāma, *Istibṣār*, 282–83. Note that the list of Sahl's children in Ibn Sa'd, III, 471 does not include 'Abdallāh; however, one of the versions concerning Sahl's *kunya* is Abū 'Abdallāh.

[166] Ibn Sa'd, III, 472; Waq., I, 379–80. The orchard of Sahl and the other Anṣārī, Abū Dujāna, was called *māl Ibn Kharasha* (Kharasha being Abū Dujāna's father or grandfather; *Iṣāba*, VII, 119).

[167] Ibn Qudāma, *Istibṣār*, 321.

Baṣra,[168] while Sahl was 'Alī's governor in Medina,[169] and later in Fārs.[170]

When the Caliph 'Uthmān was prevented from leading the prayer, Sahl's son, Abū Umāma As'ad b. Sahl b. Ḥunayf,[171] was chosen to lead the prayer (in the Prophet's Mosque).[172]

The position of Sahl and 'Uthmān at the time of the "righteous caliphs" is noteworthy when we consider the client status of the Ḥanash. Their legal inferiority (cf. below, 137) may have made them more willing to support the new religion and, more significantly, rendered them less threatening and hence more appealing in the eyes of the Prophet and the later Qurashī rulers.

The enigma of Ghanm b. 'Awf and Sālim b. 'Awf

Having looked at the lists of participants in the Ḍirār incident we are now in a position to investigate the enigma of two groups referred to in connection with this event. Sa'īd b. Jubayr (above, 76) mentions the Ghanm b. 'Awf as the builders. These Ghanm, together with a seeming brother-clan called Sālim b. 'Awf, appear in a report from an unspecified source relating that people of the Ghanm b. 'Awf and the Sālim b. 'Awf "among whom there was *nifāq*" envied *their fellow-tribesmen* (*qawmahum*), the 'Amr b. 'Awf. *Abū 'Āmir al-Rāhib*, whom the Prophet called *al-fāsiq* ("the sinful, immoral"), *was one of them.*[173]

---

[168] *Istī'āb*, III, 1033; Khalīfa, *Ta'rīkh*, I, 199, 232.

[169] Khalīfa, *Ta'rīkh*, I, 199.

[170] Tab., V, 137 [I, 3449]; Khalīfa, *Ta'rīkh*, I, 216.

[171] On his mother's side he was a grandson of the Companion As'ad b. Zurāra; above, 120n.

[172] Ibn Qudāma, *Istibṣār*, 321; *TMD, Tahdh.*, III, 9:4; Ibn Shabba, *Medina*, IV, 1217–19 (according to one version, Caliph 'Uthmān ordered that Abū Umāma or the latter's father, Sahl, should replace him; indeed, according to one report from 'Urwa b. al-Zubayr, Sahl led the Friday-prayer).

[173] Samh., II, 817. Gil, "The Medinan opposition", 73, n. 15 quotes from Muḥammad b. Yūsuf Abū Ḥayyān, *al-Tafsīr al-kabīr al-musammā bi-l-baḥr al-muḥīṭ*, Cairo 1328/1910, V, 97–98 that the builders were of the B. Ghanm b. 'Awf and B. Sālim b. 'Awf (who were the cousins of the 'Amr b. 'Awf). Diyārbakrī, *Khamīs*, II, 130:13 says that the brothers of the 'Amr b. 'Awf who envied them were the Ghanm b. 'Awf b. Ghanm, but the second Ghanm is a dittography. There is a perfect parallel for these two groups among the Khazraj subdivision called 'Awf b. al-Khazraj: there was, for example, a

To be sure, the names Ghanm, ʿAwf and Sālim are rather common in Anṣārī genealogies; but a plausible identification must be suggested within the lines already drawn above on the basis of the available evidence. There can be no doubt that our investigation must be limited to the ʿAmr b. ʿAwf because all the builders came from their ranks. The possibility that the mosque was put up by a group not living in Qubāʾ should be ruled out: everything we have learnt about so far, and will learn of later in this chapter, suggests that the Ḍirār incident was a local matter, involving the inhabitants of Qubāʾ. It concerned a specific area of Qubāʾ where both rival mosques, the Mosque of Qubāʾ and the Mosque of Ḍirār, were located. The assumption put forward by F. Buhl, and more recently M. Gil, that the builders of the Ḍirār Mosque were of the Khazraj, cannot be accepted.[174]

court (*dār*) belonging to the B. Sālim and B. Ghanm b. ʿAwf (below, 126n). But the mention of Abū ʿĀmir and the builders' identity discussed above rule out the Khazrajī option. The Sālim mentioned by Muqātil in connection with the Ḍirār are in fact the B. al-Salm; above, 91.

[174] See Buhl, *Leben*, 329: the B. Sālim b. ʿAwf who built the Ḍirār Mosque were of the Khazraj. See esp. Gil, "The Medinan opposition", 72, 87; *idem*, "The creed of Abū ʿĀmir", 45. Incidentally, the nickname Qawāqil(a) does not mean "hospitable people" (Gil refers to Ṭabarī, II, 355 [I, 1212], but there is no interpretation of Qawāqil[a] there). It conveys, as can be seen from some of the interpretations adduced by Gil himself, the concept of unlimited protection: a strong and prestigious clan grants protection beyond the confines of its own court; see, e.g., Waq., I, 167: *innamā summiya Qawqalan liannahu kāna idhā stajāra bihi rajulun qāla lahu: qawqil bi-aʿlā Yathrib wa-asfalihā fa-anta āmin, fa-summiya l-Qawqal*; Ibn Saʿd, III, 548: *wa-kāna Qawqal lahu ʿizz, wa-kāna yaqūlu li-l-khāʾif idhā jāʾahu: qawqil ḥaythu shiʾta fa-innaka āmin*; Ibn al-Kalbī, *Nasab Maʿadd*, I, 414: *summiya Qawqal lianna l-rajul kāna idhā nazala l-Madīna qīla lahu: qawqil ḥaythu shiʾta, maʿnāhu nzil ḥaythu shiʾta*; also Samh., I, 200:1: *summū bi-dhālika li-annahum kānū idhā ajārū jāran qālū* [printed: *qāla*!] *lahu: qawqil ḥaythu shiʾta*. See correctly in Serjeant, "Meccan trade", 483b: "when a man took protection (*istajāra*) with them they gave him an arrow and said: 'Move about in Yathrib where you wish'" (Ibn Hishām, II, 74: *kānū idhā stajāra bihimi l-rajul dafaʿū lahu sahman wa-qālū lahu: qawqil bihi bi-Yathrib ḥaythu shiʾta*; Ibn Hishām adds: *al-qawqala ḍarb mina l-mashy*). Cf. Fraenkel, "Das Schutzrecht der Araber", 294–96. Cf. a similar background of the tribal appellative al-Jaʿādir(a) (cf. above, 34): when they granted someone protection they said: "*jaʿdir*, i.e., go, wherever you want, there is no fear for you" (*jaʿdir ḥaythu shiʾta, ayi dhhab ḥaythu shiʾta fa-lā baʾsa ʿalayka*); Samh., I, 197.

While no satisfactory solution concerning the identity of these enigmatic groups can be reached, further discussion of previous research is in place here. Part of Gil's evidence is irrelevant to the Ḍirār incident. As is well-known, tribal genealogies in general are often treacherous and misleading.[175] Gil admits (p. 87) that "no names of specific persons of the Khazraj clans have been preserved to show us what their role was in the building of the mosque".[176] Yet he concludes (p. 91) that in the year 630 there was an "internal struggle" in which "the chief rivals were groups whose cores were two larger clans, the Zayd of Aws and the ʿAwf of Khazraj. A special position in the outstanding events of the period was held by the two sub-clans, apparently among the most noble and prestigious in Medina, the Ḍubayʿa and the Qawāqila".[177] Again, the assumed involvement of the Khazraj cannot be upheld because it contradicts all the available evidence on the identity of the participants in the Ḍirār incident.

It is true that "Ghanm b. ʿAwf" and "Sālim b. ʿAwf" can be found among the ʿAwf b. al-Khazraj whose court was close to Qubāʾ.[178] No other subdivision of the Khazraj lived in such

---

[175] Gil, 87, n. 53 refers to Ibn Saʿd, III, 422: the Ghanm live near the *masjid* (*wa-hum jīrān al-masjid*). However, these Ghanm, while being of the Khazraj, are not those whom Gil has in mind; they were not of the ʿAwf b. al-Khazraj but of the Najjār. Hence the mosque near which they lived was the Prophet's Mosque. Quite remarkably, Gil quotes Masʿūdī, *Tanbīh*, 272:11 who says that the Ḍirār Mosque was located in the court of the Sālim (read: Salm!) b. ʿAwf *mina l-Aws* (through what must have been a printing error, the last two words are missing from Gil's note).

[176] However, he refers in this context to Abū Khaythama, one of those who stayed behind when the expedition of Tabūk set out, who was of the Sālim. But his name and clan's name are much disputed and he is not linked to the Ḍirār incident but to the expedition of Tabūk.

[177] See also Watt's suggestions (*Medina*, 167) concerning three people called "Sālim". They seem to me unfounded: Wāqif was known as Mālik, not as Sālim, though he indeed had a brother called al-Salm (not Sālim); Ibn Ḥazm, *Ansāb*, 344; Ibn al-Kalbī, *Jamhara*, 644.

[178] Lecker, "On the markets of Medina", 135 f. The court (*dār*) of the B. Sālim and B. Ghanm b. ʿAwf b. ʿAmr b. ʿAwf b. al-Khazraj (between Qubāʾ and Medina) included a fortress called *uṭum al-Qawāqil* near al-ʿAṣaba, which belonged to the Sālim b. ʿAwf (i.e., to one of the two groups inhabiting the above-mentioned court); Samh., I, 199–200; cf. Wellhausen, *Skizzen* IV, 37, n. 1. It is also true that some Khazrajīs (of the Zurayq) who were the

propinquity to Qubā' and the nearby village of al-'Aṣaba.[179] It may also be added that a man who according to some belonged to these Sālim b. 'Awf, Mālik b. al-Dukhshum, allegedly scurried (together with a client of the 'Amr b. 'Awf) from his own house to the Ḍirār Mosque, carrying a burning palm-branch (which suggests that the two places were at the most a few hundred meters apart).[180] But this is not decisive and we still have no real evidence of Khazrajī involvement in the building of the Ḍirār Mosque. Some five centuries ago, the outstanding critical and penetrating historian of Medina, Samhūdī, well aware of this difficulty, noted that Abū 'Āmir was of the Ḍubay'a, of the Aws, while the Ghanm b. 'Awf and the Sālim b. 'Awf were of the Khazraj, and were not in Qubā'. This, he cautiously reasoned, should be examined.[181] So the conclusion remains that the Ḍirār incident was strictly a Qubā' affair and involved the 'Amr b. 'Awf and their clients.

At this point, some comments about the destruction of the mosque are called for. To begin with, we shall deal with the man who scurried with a burning palm-branch. The common version concerning his origin makes him a member of the 'Awf of the Khazraj:

---

clients of the 'Amr b. 'Awf lived in Qubā'; see above, 50. But they are not linked to the Ḍirār incident.

179 The inhabitants of al-'Aṣaba, the Jaḥjabā, once ambushed a Najjārī married to a woman of the Sālim b. 'Awf. He was rescued by the Qawāqil; *Aghānī*, XIII, 123:20; Wellhausen, *Skizzen* IV, 42–43. The mothers of Uḥayḥa b. al-Julāḥ (Jaḥjabā) and Mālik b. al-'Ajlān (Qawāqila) were sisters; Watt, *Medina*, 156 (I could not find the source of this statement). Cf. Ḥassān, *Dīwān*, II, 37, 41: Mālik's mother was of the 'Amr b. 'Awf.

180 A Shī'ite *tafsīr* specifically mentions the court of the Sālim (read: al-Salm?) as the site of the mosque proposed by the *munāfiqūn*; al-Qummī (3rd/9th–4th/10th century), *Tafsīr*, ed. Ṭayyib al-Mūsawī al-Jazā'irī, Najaf 1386/1966, I, 305: *yā rasūla llāhi, a-ta'dhanu lanā an nabniya masjidan fī B. Sālim li-l-'alīl wa-l-laylati l-maṭīra wa-l-shaykhi l-fānī?* Also *Biḥār al-anwār*, XXI, 255 (quoting al-Qummī). The same source tells how the above-mentioned Mālik b. al-Dukhshum asked his partner (here called 'Āmir b. 'Adī, read: 'Āṣim b. 'Adī) to wait for him until he fetched a torch from his house: *intaẓirnī ḥattā ukhrija nāran min manzilī fa-dakhala fa-jā'a bi-nār wa-ash'ala fī sa'afi l-nakhl thumma ash'alahu fī l-masjid fa-tafarraqū*; Qummī, *loc. cit.*

181 See Samh., II, 817.

he was Mālik b. al-Dukhshum or b. al-Dukhayshin of the ʿAwf b. al-Khazraj. But according to others he was of the ʿAmr b. ʿAwf.[182] Yet others said that he was of the Khuzāʿa.[183]

As a front-line warrior of Islam, Mālik is quite a dubious character. He was accused by a member of his clan, in the latter's house, of being a *munāfiq*.[184] Mālik, we are told, was a *munāfiq*, even a prominent one, who did not love God and His Messenger.[185] His marriage at some stage to Jamīla, the daughter of the Prophet's adversary ʿAbdallāh b. Ubayy,[186] could not have contributed to his reputation. Considering all this, Mālik's role in the Ḍirār incident, if at all historical, could be an act of expiation. But it seems more likely that the report on his part in the incident is "literary expiation", in other words, it belongs to the realm of apologetics. If this is correct, then the report had to originate with one of his descendants or fellow tribesmen.[187]

The above discussion admittedly leaves us with no satisfactory identification of the Ghanm and Sālim whom some mention as the builders of the Ḍirār Mosque. There are two possibilities. Either our information on the ʿAmr b. ʿAwf genealogy is incomplete, or these groups were invented in a clumsy ploy to divert the blame from the real builders. The first possibility is un-

[182] Ṭabrisī, *Tafsīr*, X, 143:–5; *Biḥār al-anwār*, XXI, 254. Similarly, Zurqānī, III, 80:14 calls him al-Awsī. Also the *Iṣāba*, V, 721 calls him al-Awsī, adding that his pedigree was disputed. The report on his exploit (which is a fragment of a longer report) exists in two versions: Mālik with another man, and Mālik with others; see, e.g., Samh., II, 816. At first glance, it seems that the text in Waq., III, 1046 suggests that the mosque which was burnt down was that of the Sālim who were, according to some, Mālik's clan. But the word *masjid* is clearly a dittography; cf. Ibn Hishām, IV, 174.

[183] Qummī, *Tafsīr*, I, 305 (printed Mālik b. al-D.j.sh.m.).

[184] See, e.g., *Usd al-ghāba*, IV, 278.

[185] *Fatḥ al-bārī*, I, 435:22; Ṭabarānī, *Kabīr*, XVIII, 25 f (see, e.g., p. 26: *kahfu l-munāfiqīna wa-maʾwāhum*); Ibn Qudāma, *Istibṣār*, 192.

[186] Ibn Saʿd, III, 549. He was her third husband (she had four); Ibn Saʿd, VIII, 382–83. Their daughter, al-Furayʿa, married Hilāl b. Umayya of the Wāqif; Ibn Saʿd, VIII, 380. (Hilāl was also married to Mulayka bint ʿAbdallāh b. Ubayy; Ibn Saʿd, VIII, 383.)

[187] Cf. the curious claim made by some that Waḥshī, who slew the Prophet's uncle, Ḥamza, in the Battle of Uḥud, was one of those who killed Musaylima in the Battle of Yamāma; *Iṣāba*, VI, 601.

satisfactory. There are certainly lacunae in our data on Anṣārī genealogies, but having studied the list of builders in much detail, it may be confidently put that their precise tribal affiliation was *not* to a group called Ghanm b. ʿAwf or another called Sālim b. ʿAwf. This leaves us with the admittedly inconvenient latter alternative, namely that the groups were invented.[188]

The location of the Ḍirār Mosque

We now shift the focus from the individuals and clans to the geographical evidence. In view of the list of participants, there can be no doubt that the Ḍirār Mosque was in the territory of the Zayd b. Mālik. But the evidence permits us to go beyond this general statement.

Concerning the court in which the Ḍirār Mosque was located, there are two versions, both relating to members of the Zayd:

1. According to one version (Ibn Isḥāq, as well as one of the reports in Wāqidī), it was in the court of Khidhām b. Khālid (of the ʿUbayd b. Zayd): *wa-ukhrija min dār Khidhām b. Khālid*, i.e., he donated the land to build it.[189]

---

[188] Note that the Ghanm b. ʿAwf appear in the "friendliest" account as far as the culprits are concerned, i.e., Saʿīd b. Jubayr's. Ignorance of Anṣārī genealogies on Saʿid's part must be ruled out: Saʿīd, a *mawlā* of the Asad (who rebelled with Ibn al-Ashʿath and was executed by al-Ḥajjāj in 95/714) lived in Kūfa and had access to many Anṣārī informants. On him see *Tahdh.*, IV, 11–14; Dhahabī, *Nubalāʾ*, IV, 321–43; Ibn Saʿd, IV, 256–67. Ayyūb who transmits from Saʿīd is Ayyūb al-Sakhtiyānī. Saʿīd's Shīʿite sympathies are possibly alluded to in his remark that since the murder of Ḥusayn he would read the whole of the Qurʾān every other night unless he was on a journey or sick; Ibn Saʿd, VI, 259–60. Note in this context that one of the builders of the Ḍirār Mosque, Mujammiʿ b. Jāriya, and the grandson of another builder, Thābit b. Wadīʿa b. Khidhām (b. Khālid), settled in Kūfa ; Ibn Saʿd, VI, 52. On Thābit's son, Yazīd, see Ibn Saʿd, V, 260.

[189] The same phrase is also used in another context. Ibn al-Kalbī, *Nasab Maʿadd*, 144 reports that Ṭalq b. ʿAmr b. Hammām b. *Murra* of the Kinda built the mosque of *B. Murra* (viz., for the descendants of his great-grandfather Murra) in his court: *wa-huwa lladhī banā masjid B. Murra wa-akhrajahu min dārihi.*

2. As mentioned in another version (Wāqidī), it was in the court of Wadīʿa b. Thābit (of the Umayya b. Zayd).[190] The existence of two versions is confirmed by another source who says, while listing the *munāfiqūn* of the Aws: *wa-Khidhām b. Khālid, wa-huwa lladhī ukhrija masjidu l-ḍirār min dārihi, wa-yuqālu innā lladhī akhrajahu min dārihi Wadīʿa b. Thābit.*[191] Gil commented: "According to Ibn Hishām the mosque was built as an addition to the house of Khidhām b. Khālid, whereas Wāqidī says it was part of the house of Wadīʿa b. Thābit, adjacent to that of Abū ʿĀmir".[192] Before discussing these statements in some detail, it should be noted that it is better to render *dār* as "court".[193]

In fact, Wāqidī (pp. 1047, 1048) refers to the location of the Ḍirār Mosque three times:

1. In the somewhat vague expression *wa-kāna min dāri Wadīʿa b. Thābit, wa-dāru Abī ʿĀmir ilā janbihimā, fa-aḥraqūhumā maʿa-hu.* I.e., the court of Wadīʿa in which the Ḍirār Mosque was located, and the adjacent court of Abū ʿĀmir were burnt down, together with the Ḍirār Mosque.[194]

2. In the list of builders, the expression *wa-min dārihi ukhrija* follows the name of Khidhām b. Khālid. But the insertion of the

[190] Ibn Hishām, IV, 174; Waq., III, 1047. The editor's addition of "Khidhām b. Khālid" between square brackets is unwarranted since the text should read: *wa-Wadīʿa b. Thābit, wa-min dārihi ukhrija.*

[191] Balādh., *Ansāb*, I, 277.

[192] "The Medinan opposition", 71.

[193] See Kister, "The massacre of the Banū Qurayẓa", 74, n. 39. Also Wellhausen, *Skizzen* IV, 17–18: "Die kleinste politische Einheit war die Dâr. Das Wort wird öfters sehr irreführend mit Haus wiedergegeben, es bedeutet stets einen Komplex zusammengehöriger Wohnungen. Es ist Gehöft und Sippe zugleich". For *dār* as the smallest unit of the *khiṭṭa* in the garrison cities ("in the case of prominent individuals often a sizable estate [usually known as *ḳaṭīʿa*], otherwise a modest plot of land occupied by one or several families"), see *EI*^{2}, s.v. *Khiṭṭa*, 23a (P. Crone).

[194] The alternative reading, *wa-kāna min dāri ... wa-dāri ..., ilā janbihimā*, while possible ("and it was near the court of ... and the court of ..., on their side"; for *min* denoting distance cf. W. Wright, *A Grammar of the Arabic Language*, Cambridge 1955, II, 132), is less likely because we already know that according to one version, the mosque was in Wadīʿa's court.

name by the editor in this place is inappropriate (above, 130n) as it should come after Wadīʿa's name.

3. ʿĀṣim b. ʿAdī's report about the works on the roof of the mosque (below, 142) includes this expression: *wa-ukhrija min dār Khidhām b. Khālid* (followed immediately by: *wa-Wadīʿa b. Thābit fī hāʾulāʾi l-nafar*). In sum, Wāqidī has both versions concerning the court in which the Ḍirār Mosque was located.

The account on the burning down of the Ḍirār Mosque, though possibly apocryphal, shows in any case that the courts of Wadīʿa (Umayya b. Zayd) and, more significantly of Abū ʿĀmir al-Rāhib (Ḍubayʿa b. Zayd), were close to this mosque.[195]

It is rather tempting to prefer one of the versions about the location of the Ḍirār Mosque, i.e., the Khidhām version (*wa-ukhrija min dār Khidhām b. Khālid*) because of two further pieces of information: first, Abū Lubāba's above-mentioned marriage to Khidhām's daughter; and second, the fact that Abū Lubāba's house was built near the site of the Ḍirār Mosque.[196] Interpretations may vary, but the mere juxtaposition of these details demonstrates how the evidence can be put to work.

We follow the lead of the evidence concerning Abū Lubāba and his descendants to find out about the Jewish presence in Qubāʾ, probably in the very area where the Ḍirār Mosque was built. It is not clear exactly how this evidence should be associated with the incident — it will be remembered that Muqātil b. Sulaymān called Abū ʿĀmir al-Rāhib: *al-yahūdī* (above, 88); but it is important nevertheless.

---

[195] Gil, "The Medinan opposition", 78 wrongly identifies Wadīʿa b. Khidhām b. Khālid with Wadīʿa b. Thābit: the former was of the ʿUbayd b. Zayd and the latter of the Umayya b. Zayd. Wāqidī (III, 1047, 1048) does not say, as Gil believes, that the Ḍirār Mosque "was made from the house of Wadīʿa b. Thābit", he merely lists Wadīʿa b. Thābit as one of the builders. Referring to Ibn Hishām, III, 200 and Tab., II, 554 [I, 1452], Gil says that Wadīʿa b. Khidhām was a supporter and friend of the Jewish Naḍīr. But the Wadīʿa in that report was of the ʿAwf b. al-Khazraj and could not have been identical with our Wadīʿa b. Khidhām, who was of the Aws.

[196] Waq., III, 1047:7 (if I understand the text correctly). Perhaps the Prophet, who gave Khidhām's daughter in marriage to Abū Lubāba, also turned over to him part of his father-in-law's court.

The clue is provided by records concerning Abū Lubāba and his descendants. We have just seen that after the destruction of the Ḍirār Mosque, Abū Lubāba (a member of the Umayya b. Zayd) built a house near it. Skipping three generations, we find a court owned by Abū Lubāba's great-grandson (and before him presumably by Abū Lubāba's son and grandson) which must have had Abū Lubāba's property as its nucleus. We now take a closer look at the evidence concerning Abū Lubāba's offspring. Abū Lubāba's son, al-Sā'ib (who was the grandson of Khidhām b. Khālid), had a wife from among the Quḍā'a whose father was a client (*ḥalīf*) of the 'Amr b. 'Awf.[197] She bore al-Sā'ib a son, Ḥusayn, and a daughter, Mulayka.[198] Ḥusayn's son, Tawba, who was Abū Lubāba's great-grandson owned a spacious court in Qubā' on the site of the former fortress of Thābit b. Abī al-Aqlaḥ of the Ḍubay'a, that is, al-Marāwiḥ fortress.[199] By Tawba's time the fortress was presumably in ruins, and it is in fact reported that the ruins were located in Tawba's court. Obviously, the people of Medina remembered the fortresses and their locations long after the structures' disappearance from the landscape.

But we are concerned here with the ruins of another fortress included in Tawba's court. Ibn Zabāla, to whom we owe much of what we know on the Jews of Medina, reports:

> In Qubā' there was a Jew who had a fortress called 'Āṣim ("the defender") which was located in [what

[197] She must have been of the 'Ajlān of Balī (on whom, see below), since 'Ajlān appears in her pedigree.

[198] Ibn Sa'd, V, 78. "Bishr b. al-Sā'ib" in Samh., I, 194:2 is presumably a misprint; read: Bashīr b. al-Sā'ib. Note that according to some, Abū Lubāba's name was Bashīr (while others have the diminutive form, Bushayr); see Lecker, "The Anṣārī wives of 'Umar b. al-Khaṭṭāb and his brother, Zayd" (forthcoming). For entries on Ḥusayn b. al-Sā'ib see *Usd al-ghāba*, II, 17; *Iṣāba*, II, 211.

[199] *Maghānim*, s.v., 374 (where the text is corrupt, as was noticed by the editor himself); '*Umdat al-akhbār*, 357–58; Samh., s.v. al-Marāwiḥ, II, 1303; above, 105. Cf. the Wāqim fortress, which belonged to the descendants (*Āl*) of Abū Lubāba, above, 57. Tawba's brother, al-Ḥajjāj, is mentioned by Ibn Ḥazm, *Ansāb*, 334:3.

> later became] the court of Tawba b. Ḥusayn b. al-Sā'ib b. Abī Lubāba. In it [i.e., in the fortress] the well called Qubā' was located.

Samhūdī complements Ibn Zabāla's words with a passage from Zayn al-Dīn al-Marāghī (d. 816/1413), the author of a history of Medina entitled *Taḥqīq al-nuṣra fī talkhīṣ ma'ālim dār al-hijra.*[200] Samhūdī suggests that the copy of Ibn Zabāla's book which he himself used is defective:

> Qubā' was given its name after a well located in it, called Qubār.[201] But they considered the well's name a bad omen (*fa-taṭayyarū minhā*) [i.e., because of its association with *qabr*, "grave"] and called it Qubā', as was reported by Ibn Zabāla.[202]

The Jewish owner of the 'Āṣim fortress was al-Mu'tariḍ b. al-Ashwas, said to have been of the Naḍīr.[203] The same al-Mu'tariḍ

[200] *GAL*, I, 360.

[201] Printed: H.bār. However, we know from Samhūdī's comment later on the same page that al-Marāghī has: Q.tār, which Samhūdī amends to Qubār, relying on another source which quotes Ibn Zabāla. See also al-Marāghī, *Taḥqīq al-nuṣra*, MS Br. Lib. Or. 3615, 18a (where the reading appears to be: Q.thār). Q.tār does have some claim to authenticity because of the bad omen associated with it: *qatara*, said of subsistence, means: "it was barely sufficient" (Lane, *Arabic-English Lexicon*, s.v.), Qitra and Abū Qitra are nicknames of the devil; *Lisān al-'arab*, the end of s.v. Elsewhere there is yet another variant concerning the former name of Qubā'. Gil, "The creed of Abū 'Āmir", 29 prefers the reading Qubādh (= Abū Ḥātim al-Sijistānī, *al-Mu'ammarūna*, ed. 'Abd al-Mun'im 'Āmir, Cairo 1961 [bound with *al-Waṣāyā* by the same author], 91, quoting Ibn al-Kalbī). Interestingly, the *al-Mu'ammarūna* report explicitly refers to the former name of Qubā' as one used by the Jews, and to the latter, Qubā', as one used by the Anṣār (*kānati l-yahūd tusammī Qubā': Qubādh, bi-l-dhāl, fa-sammathā l-Anṣār Qubā'*). The name "Qubādh" could be referred to as evidence of Sassanian influence in pre-Islamic Medina, but the bad omen associated with the name according to Ibn Zabāla (see below) supports the reading Qubār.

[202] Samh., s.v. Qubā', II, 1284–85.

[203] Samh., I, 163:3; *Maghānim*, 331 quoting al-Zubayr (i.e., al-Zubayr b. Bakkār's *Akhbār al-Madīna*, *GAS*, I, 318); *'Umdat al-akhbār*, 341; Ibn Rusta, 61 (who quotes a report from Tawba b. al-Ḥasan [read: al-Ḥusayn] b. al-Sā'ib b. Abī Lubāba). In Wüstenfeld, *Medina*, 29 the name Tawba is

owned two more fortresses mentioned by Fīrūzābādī: al-Aʿnaq, located in the orchard (*māl*) called al-Bardaʿa, and Ṣīṣa, in the orchard of al-Samna (the reading of the last place-name, as is always the case with rare place-names, is uncertain). The three (probably adjacent) fortresses later became the property of one Salama b. Umayya of the ʿAmr b. ʿAwf.[204] The name Ṣīṣa clearly points to the Zayd b. Mālik who owned the fourteen fortresses called al-Ṣayāṣī in Raḥbat B. Zayd (above, 104).

In the 7th/13th century, Ibn al-Najjār wrote that the Ḍirār Mosque was close to that of Qubāʾ. It was large, had high walls and its stones were taken (i.e., to be used as building material). Its construction was sound.[205] But in the 8th/14th century, Jamāl al-Dīn al-Maṭarī[206] looked for the Ḍirār Mosque and found no trace of it around the Mosque of Qubāʾ or in any other place. Samhūdī (d. 911/1505) says that this is true for al-Maṭarī's time and for his own time. The description of the mosque by Ibn al-Najjār shows, Samhūdī adds, that it existed in this form in Ibn al-Najjār's time.[207]

---

garbled ("Buweima"). This ʿĀṣim fortress in Qubāʾ should not be confused with another fortress called ʿĀṣim located in the Sāfila; *Maghānim* and Samh., s.v. ʿĀṣim.

[204] *Maghānim*, 331. We were earlier told that the ʿĀṣim fortress was in Tawba's court; but there is no difficulty here since Salama presumably lived during a much later period (and might have been a descendant of Tawba).

[205] Samh., II, 818; Ibn al-Najjār (above, 98n), *Durra*, 382: *wa-hādhā l-masjid qarīb min masjid Qubāʾ wa-huwa kabīr wa-ḥīṭānuhu ʿāliya wa-tuʾkhadhu minhu l-ḥijāra wa-qad kāna bināʾuhu matīnan* (Samh. has: *malīḥan*!). Cf. the alleged instructions which Abū ʿĀmir sent from Syria to the *munāfiqūn* of his clan: they should build a mosque in opposition to the Mosque of Qubāʾ *and in order to humble it* (*muqāwamatan li-masjid Qubāʾ wa-taḥqīran lahu*), because he would arrive with an army to drive Muḥammad and his companions out of Medina. They built it and said: "Abū ʿĀmir will come and pray in it, and we shall [meanwhile] make it a place of worship"; Samh., II, 817 (this is an ingenious attempt at bridging the gap between the stronghold and mosque themes).

[206] D. 741/1340; al-Jāsir, *Muʾallafāt fī taʾrīkh al-Madīna*, 4, 465.

[207] As for the claim made by al-Maṭarī, that Ibn al-Najjār was wrong, Samhūdī quotes Majd al-Dīn al-Fīrūzābādī who says that from its existence at the time of Ibn al-Najjār it does not follow that it still stood (viz., that it could be located and identified—M.L.) in later times, and Ibn al-Najjār either quoted an earlier authority or saw it himself. As a possible source of Ibn

THE ROLE OF THE BALAWĪ CLIENTS

Besides the ʿAmr b. ʿAwf, Qubāʾ was inhabited by clients of other Anṣārī clans and, more significantly, by a large population of clients belonging to the Balī (a branch of the big tribal coalition of Quḍāʿa). Many, if not all of the Balawīs, converted to Judaism at some stage. Of the Balawī clans, only the ʿAjlān concern us in connection with the Ḍirār incident. They were the clients of the Zayd b. Mālik and it is not surprising that they were involved in the incident. None of the ʿAjlānīs participated in the building of the Ḍirār Mosque, but one of them helped to destroy it, while another later received the site on which it had been erected in order to put up a house for himself.

The *sīra* lists of participants in major battles and other events have not yet been subjected to detailed study. Such a study will have to gauge the differences between the early Islamic historians and show us whether, and to what extent, we can speak of a common list agreed upon by these historians. In any case, even in the present state of our knowledge we certainly cannot discard the testimony of the lists as sources of historical information.[208] The investigation of the Aws Allāh previously in this book (Ch. 2) has shown that they were absent from the major events of early Islam; hence, the lists which do not record them as participants do reflect historical fact. So, until further detailed research shows this approach to be wrong, the list of Badrīs should be considered as a general indicator of a clan's attitude to the Prophet in 2 A.H.

---

al-Najjār, al-Majd quotes a traveller of the 6th/12th century, al-Bashshārī, who said about the Ḍirār Mosque that the common people stoned it without being obliged to do so (*yataṭawwaʿu l-ʿawāmmu bi-hadmihi*). Yāqūt, al-Majd writes, quoted al-Bashshārī in his dictionary as did Ibn Jubayr in his *Riḥla*; Samh., II, 818–19; *Maghānim*, 325 (on al-Bashshārī see *loc. cit.*, n. 2); Yaq., s.v. Qubā, 302a.

[208] R. Sellheim, "Prophet, Chaliph und Geschichte: Die Muḥammad-Biographie des Ibn Isḥāq", in *Oriens* 18–19 (1965–66), 33–91, at 73–75, correctly includes the lists in what he terms the "Grundschicht" of the *sīra*. Cf. Crone, *Slaves on Horses*, 14. There are, of course, problems with lists; cf. M.J. Kister, "Notes on the papyrus account of the ʿAqaba meeting", in *Le Muséon* 76 (1963), 403–17, at 408, n. 22 = Balādh., *Ansāb*, I, 252–53.

In the present context we are mainly concerned with a comparison between the Zayd b. Mālik and their clients of the ʿAjlān. Wāqidī, for example, lists a total of fifteen warriors of the three subdivisions of the Zayd: nine of the Umayya b. Zayd, five of the Ḍubayʿa b. Zayd and one of the ʿUbayd b. Zayd. This is followed by seven warriors belonging to their clients (*wa-min ḥulafāʾihim*). With the exception of one (Sālim, *mawlā* Thubayta bint Yaʿār), these clients were of the ʿAjlān. In sum, in Badr we find fifteen warriors of the Zayd and six of their clients, the ʿAjlān.[209]

We owe our knowledge of the ʿAjlānīs in Badr to a member of the ʿAjlān themselves: Wāqidī concludes the list of Badrīs with an *isnād* going back to the ʿAjlānī Abū l-Baddāḥ who was the son of the Companion ʿĀṣim b. ʿAdī (see below, 138). Abū l-Baddāḥ is certainly the source of the list of clients who fought in Badr (most of whom were of his own clan), but he might also have been the source of the list of the Zayd.[210] Abū l-Baddāḥ was a tribal informant who collected and transmitted (or "specialized in") reports on the history of his clan.[211]

The number of ʿAjlānīs in Badr is impressive and seems to show that already in 2 A.H. the Prophet had a considerable following among them. It can be compared to the contribution of the Jaḥjabā of the ʿAmr b. ʿAwf who sent only one warrior to Badr, together with another warrior who belonged to their Balawī

---

[209] Ibn Qudāma, *Istibṣār*, 297 says that Maʿn b. ʿAdī al-Balawī was a *ḥalīf* of the ʿUbayd. He is presumably misled by the list of Badrīs which creates this impression by listing the ʿAjlān immediately after the ʿUbayd (see, e.g., Ibn Hishām, II, 345); in fact, the ʿAjlān were the clients of the Zayd b. Mālik as a whole; see above, 103.

[210] The list in Ibn Hishām, II, 345–46 is almost identical with Wāqidī's (Sālim is not mentioned). Ibn Saʿd, III, 465–68 concludes with the ʿAjlānī Badrīs the section on the Zayd who participated in Badr. For the genealogy of the ʿAjlān, see Ibn Ḥazm, *Ansāb*, 443:5; Ibn al-Kalbī, *Nasab Maʿadd*, II, 711.

[211] Another tribal informant among the ʿAjlān was a descendant of ʿAbdallāh b. Salima, a Companion who participated in Badr and was killed in Uḥud: Muḥammad b. ʿAbd al-Raḥmān al-ʿAjlānī "had stories which he related on the affairs of the people" (*wa-kānat ʿindahu aḥādīth yarwīhā min umūri l-nās*). Ibn al-Kalbī and others met him and transmitted from him; Ibn Saʿd, III, 468. Another ʿAjlānī, ʿAbd al-Raḥmān b. ʿAmr (Muḥammad's father?) is Ibn Zabāla's source for a report on the origin of the name Qubāʾ; see Samh., II, 1285. On Qubāʾ/Qubār cf. above, 133.

clients, the Unayf.[212] The testimony of the lists of *munāfiqūn* is rather telling: we find in them many of the ʿAmr b. ʿAwf[213] but none of the ʿAjlān or indeed any other Balawī clan inhabiting Qubāʾ.

ON THE STATUS OF CLIENTS

Before discussing the role of the ʿAjlān in the Ḍirār incident, a comment should be made on the status of clients in the tribal society of Medina. In most aspects of daily life one could not tell a client from a clan member. Economically, the clients of the Balī could have been as prosperous as the Aws and Khazraj or even more; after all, they had been in Medina before the Aws and Khazraj arrived.[214] We even find a marriage with a leading family of the Anṣār, which indicates that socially they were not held to be inferior.[215]

A client could play an influential role in the politics of pre-Islamic Medina. We have evidence relating to ʿĀṣim b. ʿAdī, the leader (*sayyid*) of the ʿAjlān[216] who was a client of the Zayd b. Mālik.[217] His name is linked to a poorly-documented expulsion of sections of the Aws from Medina in the pre-Islamic period since he was instrumental in the conclusion of a treaty between the expelled Aws and the Muzayna. The details of this event are found in the interpretation of a place-name reportedly called after ʿĀṣim:

---

[212] Waq., I, 160–61.

[213] See, e.g., Ibn Hishām, II, 166–70; Ibn Ḥabīb, *Muḥabbar*, 467–69.

[214] Abū al-Daḥdāḥ, a client of the Anṣār (probably of the ʿAmr b. ʿAwf: Abū Lubāba was his nephew [*ibn ukhtihi*]; Ibn Qudāma, *Istibṣār*, 339) owned two groves, one in the ʿĀliya and the other in the Sāfila; one of these groves included six hundred palm-trees; Qurṭubī, *al-Jāmiʿ li-aḥkām al-qurʾān*, III, 238:7.

[215] The Aws Allāh leader, Abū Qays b. al-Aslat, married Kabsha or Kubaysha bint Maʿn b. ʿĀṣim al-Anṣāriyya; *Iṣāba*, VIII, 92. She was his wife until he died and a son of Abū Qays (from another woman) wished to marry her; Ibn Qudāma, *Istibṣār*, 332 (she is called here Kabsha bint ʿĀṣim al-Awsiyya; the ambiguity concerning her name is a result of a confusion between the two brothers Maʿn b. ʿAdī and ʿĀṣim b. ʿAdī). Cf. W. Robertson Smith, *Kinship & Marriage in Early Arabia*², London 1907, 109n.

[216] *Iṣāba*, III, 572.

[217] See his pedigree in *Usd al-ghāba*, III, 75.

> Dhū ʿĀṣim is one of the wadis of al-ʿAqīq [south-west of Medina]. It was given this name because when the Aws were expelled from Medina and stayed in the Naqīʿ [i.e., the upper, southern part of the ʿAqīq Valley], they concluded a treaty with the Muzayna. The man who concluded the treaty between the two parties [viz., mediated between them] was ʿĀṣim b. ʿAdī b. al-ʿAjlān, and the branch of the valley (*shuʿba*) where the treaty was concluded was called Shuʿbat ʿĀṣim after him.[218]

Yet, in one crucial aspect, the pre-Islamic Balawī client was inferior to the fully-accredited member of the clan: he could not grant security which was binding for the fully-accredited members.[219] This serious legal restriction placed the client in an underprivileged position. The tribal society was sensitive to such differences and did not allow this clearly defined distinction between fully-accredited members and clients to be blurred. The most telling testimony that the distinction was preserved, and became a burden, is derived from the genealogical literature, namely from the evidence of the attempts by some Balawīs to fake an Anṣārī pedigree for themselves or their ancestors (above, 65).

As we have seen, ʿĀṣim b. ʿAdī was an important figure in Medinan society already before Islam. He preserved this status, and possibly became more prosperous, at the time of the Prophet. He is not said to have fought in Badr: there were obviously limits, so to speak, as to what his son, Abū l-Baddāḥ, a specialist in the history of the clan, could do for his father's Islamic reputation. Yet something could be done: we are told that when the Prophet was on his way to Badr, he sent ʿĀṣim (i.e., the text implies that ʿĀṣim was with him on the way to Badr) back to Medina to the (people of the) Ḍirār Mosque (!) "because of something [i.e., something suspicious, a plot] which had become known to

[218] Samh., s.v. ʿĀṣim, II, 1260–61.

[219] Cf. Fraenkel, "Das Schutzrecht der Araber", 296: "Ein Einzelner kann durch seine Schutzgewährung den ganzen Stamm binden; doch hat der Beisasse (Ḥalīf) im Gegensatze zu dem mächtigeren Hauptstamme dazu kein Recht".

him about them".[220] Another source replaces the Ḍirār Mosque with a less problematic expression: when the Prophet wanted to set out for Badr, he put 'Āṣim in charge of Qubā' and the people of the 'Āliya "because of something that became known to him about them" (*khallafa 'Āṣim b. 'Adī 'alā Qubā' wa-ahli l-'Āliya li-shay' balaghahu 'anhum*). 'Āṣim reportedly received his share in the spoils of Badr[221] (this is a way of saying that the Prophet recognized him as a Badrī with full rights, although he had not been on the battlefield). Both versions have no historical value. Returning from the way to the battlefield, or staying behind under the Prophet's instructions, are common themes or *topoi* in the *sīra*, sometimes combined with the mention of spoils.[222] Thus, 'Āṣim could claim the status of Badrī without having to be listed as a warrior; he wanted to fight but had to remain behind to carry out an important task.

A more detailed report names three persons who were on duty in Medina at that time: Abū Lubāba (of the Umayya b. Zayd) was in charge of Medina, 'Āṣim b. 'Adī was in charge of Qubā' and the people of the 'Āliya, and al-Ḥārith b. Ḥāṭib (yet another member of the Umayya b. Zayd) was given an unspecified job in connection with the 'Amr b. 'Awf (*amarahu bi-amrihi fī B. 'Amr b. 'Awf*).[223] This report, which reveals an evident ambiguity and overlapping in their alleged areas of authority, is not historical. It is a secondary product, created by the combination of three independent and unsynchronized reports of tribal historiography. Nonetheless, it is valuable for what it teaches us on the creative ways of tribal historiography.

Unsurprisingly, the appointment of 'Āṣim in charge of Qubā' and the people of the 'Āliya was reported by 'Āṣim's son, Abū

220 Waq., I, 159–60. Regarding the mention of the Ḍirār Mosque in a report relating to 2 A.H. cf. above, 82.

221 Ibn Sa'd, III, 466. Ibn Qudāma, *Istibṣār*, 298 has both versions. Cf. Watt, *Medina*, 236 ("During the Badr expedition there was another deputy in the suburb of Qubā', perhaps because this district was still mainly non-Muslim").

222 For example, it was claimed that on the way to Badr, Khawwāt b. Jubayr of the 'Amr b. 'Awf suffered from a leg injury and had to be sent back; *Iṣāba*, II, 346.

223 Waq., I, 101; Ibn Sa'd, III, 457, 461.

Baddāḥ , who in his turn quoted 'Āṣim himself.[224] This spurious report conveys the notion that 'Āṣim could be relied on even when his loyalty to the 'Amr b. 'Awf, whose client he was, conflicted with his loyalty to the Prophet; or, indeed, this was so especially when such a conflict arose. Seen in this light, the reference to the Ḍirār Mosque in connection with 'Āṣim's obscure assignment at the time of Badr (anachronistic or not) is meaningful: in the Ḍirār incident, as we shall see, the 'Ajlān supported the Prophet against the most influential families of the 'Amr b. 'Awf.

After the conquest of Khaybar, 'Āṣim was in charge of a share of its produce allotted to one hundred warriors.[225] His pregnant wife was among the Muslim women who attended that expedition and in Khaybar she reportedly gave birth to a daughter named Sahla.[226] 'Āṣim is said to have helped in supplying food for the warriors in the expedition of Tabūk (providing seventy, ninety or a hundred camel-loads of dates).[227] 'Āṣim, then, seems to have offered the Prophet unconditional support and the same would have been true of his brother, Ma'n. Ma'n's role in the early Islamic period was less prominent than his brother's. Ma'n participated in the great 'Aqaba meeting and in the main battles of the Prophet, and was killed fighting against Musaylima in Yamāma.[228]

We return now to the role of the 'Ajlān in the Ḍirār incident. Wāqidī mentions 'Āṣim b. 'Adī and Mālik b. al-Dukhshum

---

[224] *Iṣāba*, III, 572–73 (printed: Qaddāḥ!); Ibn Sa'd, III, 466. On Abū l-Baddāḥ see, e.g., Waq., III, 1110 (his Ḥadīth was transmitted by Abū Bakr [b. Muḥammad b. 'Amr] b. Ḥazm); *Iṣāba*, III, 573; Dhahabī, *Nubalā'*, I, 321; Ibn Sa'd, V, 261 (he died in 117/735 aged 84). Some claimed that Abū l-Baddāḥ was a Companion, but Ibn Ḥajar refutes this claim with convincing arguments; *Iṣāba*, VII, 48–49; Ibn Qudāma, *Istibṣār*, 299; also Ibn Sa'd, III, 461.

[225] Waq., II, 689, 718, 719; Ibn Hishām, III, 364, 365.

[226] Waq., II, 685. 'Āṣim was considered a desirable match. His daughter, Sahla, married, presumably around 20 A.H., 'Abd al-Raḥmān b. 'Awf, for whom she bore four children; Ibn Sa'd, III, 127; *Iṣāba*, III, 573. Sahla reported that the Prophet gave her a share in the spoils of Khaybar; Ibn Qudāma, *Istibṣār*, 299.

[227] Waq., III, 991; Ibn Hishām, III, 196; Suyūṭī, *Durr*, III, 264:2 (commentary on Qur'ān 9,79).

[228] *Iṣāba*, VI, 191.

(above, 127) as those who carried out the Prophet's order to destroy the Ḍirār Mosque. Ibn Isḥāq has: Mālik b. al-Dukhshum and Maʿn b. ʿAdī or his brother, ʿĀṣim.[229]

The identity of those who reportedly set the mosque ablaze is uncertain.[230] The site had been offered by the Prophet to ʿĀṣim b. ʿAdī as a court. But the pious ʿĀṣim said that he would not take as a court a mosque about which those Qur'ān verses were revealed, so he suggested that the Prophet grant it to a fellow ʿAjlānī, Thābit b. Aqram, who had no house (hence he could not afford to be too selective), and the Prophet consented.[231]

---

[229] Note that Ibn Isḥāq's *Maghāzī* had: Mālik (b. al-Dukhshum) and Maʿn b. ʿAdī; see *Fatḥ al-bārī*, I, 435:–6. Qurṭubī, *al-Jāmiʿ li-aḥkām al-qur'ān*, VIII, 253:–4, probably accumulating names from two or more reports, lists Mālik b. al-Dukhshum, Maʿn b. ʿAdī, ʿĀmir b. al-Sakan and Waḥshī. Elsewhere we find yet another name: Suwayd b. ʿAyyāsh al-Anṣārī was one of those sent to destroy the Ḍirār Mosque; *Iṣāba*, III, 227.

[230] Neither is it certain that it was burnt down at all. On the timber rescued from it see above, 118.

[231] Waq., III, 1047; Ibn Qudāma, *Istibṣār*, 300. The grant could be a reward for the ʿAjlāns' role in the incident. The people of Qubā' considered the place haunted: no child (or: no child of Thābit b. Aqram) was born in that house, no pigeon ever stopped there and no chicken ever hatched its eggs in it; *Sīra Shāmiyya*, V, 677; Waq., III, 1047. The former source shows that the house of Thābit, not the house of Abū Lubāba, is meant here: *fa-lam yūlad* [Waq. adds: *lahu*] *fī dhālika l-bayt mawlūd qaṭṭu wa-lam yanʿaq* [Waq.'s *wa-lam yaqif* is better, albeit looking like a *lectio facilior*, because *naʿaqa* is said of a raven, not a pigeon] *fīhi ḥamām qaṭṭu wa-lam taḥḍun fīhi dajāja qaṭṭu*. Wāqidī rather indiscriminately interpolates into a text dealing with Thābit b. Aqram's court another text, dealing with Abū Lubāba. How this can happen is not clear to me (it could be the work of a scribe). This practice of Wāqidī misled Gil, "The Medinan opposition", 71–72 to believe, that the house of Abū Lubāba is meant: "but there was a curse upon that house [= Abū Lubāba's house — M.L.] so that, e.g., there was never a child born in it". I estimate that there are practically hundreds of such problems with the present edition of Wāqidī. A new edition, based on parallel texts, will be a major contribution to Islamic scholarship.

The persistent curse is further evidence of the evil deeds of the *munāfiqūn*. The *Sīra Shāmiyya*, V, 677 quotes from Saʿīd b. Jubayr via Ibn al-Mundhir (d. ca. 318/930; probably from his *Tafsīr*; see *GAS*, I, 495–96), and from others, what might be a fragment of Saʿīd's account on the Ḍirār incident (above, 76): a hole was dug in the Ḍirār Mosque and smoke came out of it. (Smoke issuing from the mosque is also mentioned by Jābir b. ʿAbdallāh; *Biḥār al-anwār*, XXI, 254.) The place was a dunghill in the Abbasid period;

On the basis of the available information (some vital details may still be missing) it would seem that this grant of land was of symbolic importance: the place of worship of some of the strongest people in Qubā' was given to their homeless client. The humiliation of the *munāfiqūn* was complete.

An autobiographical report by 'Āṣim describing how he set the mosque ablaze is remarkably jocular and light-hearted:

> I do not forget their gazes directed at us (*mā ansā tasharrufahum ilaynā*) as if their ears were wolves' ears. We burnt it down until it was reduced to ashes. The one of them who remained in it was Zayd b. Jāriya b. 'Āmir [who persisted] until his buttocks were scorched. We destroyed it until we reduced it to rubble and they [i.e., the worshippers] dispersed.[232]

In what appears to be another fragment of the same auotobiographical report (*wa-kāna 'Āṣim b. 'Adī yukhbiru yaqūlu*), 'Āṣim b. 'Adī describes in first person a scene in Medina just before the expedition to Tabūk. The actors are 'Āṣim himself and two men, 'Abdallāh b. Nabtal[233] and Tha'laba b. Ḥāṭib who have just finished mending a pipe (a gutter) on the roof of the Ḍirār Mosque (*wa-humā yuṣliḥāni mīzāban, qad faraghā minhu*).

The two workers shouted from the roof to 'Āṣim, who was standing near the mosque: "'Āṣim, the Messenger of God has promised us to pray in it when he comes back". 'Āṣim does not

Ṭabarī, *Tafsīr*, XI, 25:18. The Shī'ite *tafsīr* of al-'Ayyāshī (3rd/9th century) includes a report on the impurity associated with the site of the demolished Ḍirār Mosque. *Masjid al-nifāq* (i.e, the ruined Ḍirār Mosque) was on the Prophet's way to the Mosque of Qubā'. It used to be sprinkled with water and ground leaves of the lote (*sidr*) tree. When the Prophet passed there, he would lift hi clothes and step on a stone on the side of the road. He passed by at a quick pace and disliked having his clothes contaminated by it; al-'Ayyāshī, quoted in *Biḥār al-anwār*, XXI, 256. On al-'Ayyāshī see *EI*², s.v. (B. Lewis).

232 Waq., III, 1046, 1047.

233 Above, 114. 'Abdallāh was one of "those who remained behind", viz., refused to participate in the Tabūk expedition; Ṭabarī, *Tafsīr*, X, 102:10 (quoting Mujāhid, commentary on Qur'ān 9,47); 104:5 (Ibn Isḥāq, commentary on 9,48).

tell us what he said to the builders, but shares with us what he said to himself:

> I said to myself: "By God, everyone of those who built this mosque is a *munāfiq* known as such. It was erected by Abū Ḥabība b. al-Azʿar, and was built in the court of Khidhām b. Khālid, and Wadīʿa b. Thābit was among those people. Whereas the mosque that was built by the Prophet with his own hand, while he was laying its foundation (?), Gabriel directed him towards the Kaʿba" [i.e., to show him the precise *qibla*].[234]

ʿĀṣim concludes his autobiographical story saying: "By God, by the time we returned from our journey [i.e., from the Tabūk expedition], Qur'ān verses had been revealed condemning it [= the Ḍirār Mosque] and its people who collected donations for building it and helped in it".

ʿĀṣim's report is a crude product (perhaps intentionally so); the style shows it to be an unedited and unrefined account. The

[234] Waq., III, 1048: *wa-l-masjidu lladhī banā rasūlu llāhi (ṣ) bi-yadihi yu'asssisuhu Jibrīl ʿalayhi l-salām ya'ummu bihi l-bayta*; the text is not smooth but the purport is clear and can also be drawn from other sources. See Suyūti, *Ḥujaj mubīna*, 53 < al-Zubayr b. Bakkār's *Akhbār al-Madīna* < Muḥammad b. al-Ḥasan (= Ibn Zabāla) < Sulaymān b. Dāwūd b. Qays < his father. Dāwūd (= probably al-Farrā', a *mawlā* of Quraysh who died in Medina at the time of al-Manṣūr; Ibn Saʿd, *Qism mutammim*, 404) said *annahu balaghahu anna l-nabiyya (ṣ) waḍaʿa asāsa l-masjid ḥīna waḍaʿahu wa-Jibrīlu qā'im yanẓuru ilā l-Kaʿba qad kushifa mā baynahu wa-baynahā*. (Cf. Jibrīl "showing" the Prophet the pre-Islamic battle of Dhū Qār; Suyūṭī, *Khaṣā'iṣ*, I, 454.) However, the Ḥadīth just quoted from Suyūṭī deals with the Prophet's Mosque. More to the point is a similar Ḥadīth relating to the Mosque of Qubā'. Its source is a member of a family often mentioned in this chapter: al-Shamūs bint al-Nuʿmān b. ʿĀmir b. Mujammiʿ al-Anṣāriyya. The Ḥadīth exists in two slightly different versions. The concluding phrases are, respectively: *wa-Jibrīl (ṣ)* [*sic* !] *ya'ummu bihi l-Kaʿba*; and the Prophet's statement *inna Jibrīl ʿalayhi l-salām huwa ya'ummu l-Kaʿba*, followed by al-Shamūs' remark: *fa-kāna yuqālu innahu aqwamu masjidin qiblatan*; Ṭabarānī, *Kabīr*, XXIV, 317 f; Suyūṭī, *Ḥujaj mubīna*, 61 (quoting Ṭabarānī); cf. *Iṣāba*, VII, 731 f (note Ibn Ḥajar's wrestling with the mention of the Kaʿba as *qibla* where one expects to find Jerusalem).

contents are somewhat unorthodox, too: ʿĀṣim claims an advantage over the Prophet (!) in having prior knowldege of the true nature of the Ḍirār Mosque. The revealed verses only confirmed what had already been known to him. Finally, it should be observed that this lively scene was addressed to an audience appreciative of the satirical treatment given to the Prophet's enemies.[235]

In the context of the role played by the ʿAjlān we should concern ourselves with the sense of confrontation evident in ʿĀṣim's presentation,[236] between this rich and prestigious client and his masters, the Zayd b. Mālik. The same is conveyed by his alleged assignment at the time of Badr (as already mentioned, he was put in charge of Qubā' and the people of the ʿĀliya). I base the following preliminary and tentative historical reconstruction on this element of confrontation and the meagre evidence adduced above.

In Qubā' we meet a large client population, including the ʿAjlān. With the advent of Islam they did not stop being clients, but those of them who were loyal to the Prophet could expect to be rewarded. The ʿAjlān, several of whom fought in Badr and among whom there were no *munāfiqūn*, were more loyal to the Prophet than were their masters, the Zayd b. Mālik. This at least seems true in the case of the builders of the Ḍirār Mosque. In other words, the Prophet could rely on their support even when he acted against their masters.

The builders, who included some men of note, were of the ʿAmr b. ʿAwf, mainly of the Zayd b. Mālik subdivision called Ḍubayʿa. They were inspired by their leader Abū ʿĀmir al-Rāhib, who lived in exile in Syria. Even Saʿīd b. Jubayr's account, which is the "friendliest" from the builders' point of view, gives Abū ʿĀmir a background role.

[235] We also encounter the combination of fire and satire in the story of the *munāfiq* al-Ḍaḥḥāk b. Khalīfa, who broke a leg while jumping from the roof of a house which had been set ablaze; Ibn Hishām, IV, 160.

[236] I do not assume that the scene described above took place. However, with or without a proper *isnād* (*isnād*s were not that important in this type of report), I see no reason to assume that it was invented by anyone other than ʿĀṣim or his son.

Prior to his departure, Abū ʿĀmir, a military and spiritual leader, had been one of the strongest men in Medina and probably the most influential and revered leader in Qubāʾ.[237] After his departure to Mecca, Abū ʿĀmir fought against the Prophet in the Battle of Uḥud. In one scene during this battle we find him with fifty men of his people (*qawm*) who fought under his command.[238]

Thus, in 9 A.H. many in Qubāʾ who had embraced Islam were still opposed to the political authority of the Prophet. Members of the most important families of the ʿAmr b. ʿAwf and others perhaps entertained the hope that their exiled leader, Abū ʿĀmir, might return and regain his authority.[239]

---

[237] For his role in the Battle of Buʿāth see *Aghānī*, XV, 163:21, 165:13. In his combination of asceticism and military leadership, Abū ʿĀmir can be considered an early Arabian prototype of *zuhhād* the like of ʿAbdallāh b. al-Mubārak, on whom cf. EI^2, s.v. (J. Robson). Cf. also ʿAbdallāh b. al-Mubārak, *al-Jihād*, ed. Nazīh Ḥammād, Beirut 1391/1971.

[238] Waq., I, 223. Cf. Ibn Hishām, III, 71 (he left Medina with fifty young men of the Aws, or, according to some, with fifteen men). The Prophet's knees were injured when he fell into one of the trenches dug by Abū ʿĀmir to make the Muslims stumble; Waq., I, 244. And see *op. cit.*, 252:-3. In another report, Abū ʿĀmir and Abū Sufyān survey the battlefield of Uḥud; Waq., I, 236–37. Wellhausen, *Skizzen* IV, 16, 17 wrongly assumed that Abū ʿĀmir was of the Aws Allāh. In fact, he was of the ʿAmr b. ʿAwf. See also J. Fück, "The originality of the Arabian prophet", in M. Swartz (trans. and ed.), *Studies on Islam*, New York-Oxford 1981, 86–98, at 91, and n. 11 on p. 98 (="Die Originalität des arabischen Propheten", in *ZDMG* 90 [1936], 509–25, at 516) and Buhl, *Leben*, 206 (both follow Wellhausen).

[239] A very important text is found in ʿAbd al-Jabbār's *Tathbīt dalāʾil al-nubuwwa*, ed. ʿAbd al-Karīm ʿUthmān, Beirut 1966–68, II, 474–75 (referring to Qurʾān 9,107–110). Fragments of it can be found in other sources but the details here about Abū ʿĀmir's propaganda against the Prophet are unique. According to this report, it was Abū ʿĀmir himself who built the Ḍirār Mosque before his departure to Mecca, he and the *munāfiqūn* were encouraged in their opposition to the Prophet by the Jews: ...*thumma* [i.e., after his dispute with the Prophet over the *ḥanīfiyya*] *aqbala Abū ʿĀmir ʿalā qawmihi yanhāhum ʿani ttibāʿi rasūli llāhi (ṣ) wa-ʿan ṭāʿatihi wa-yajtahidu, wa-aʿlām rasūli llāhi (ṣ) tatazāyadu wa-taẓharu wa-yakthuru atbāʿuhu min qawm Abī ʿĀmir fa-yazdādu ghayẓan wa-'ttakhadha masjidan yajmaʿu ilayhi l-nāsa fa-yuḥādithuhum fa-yanhāhum mini ttibāʿi rasūli llāhi (ṣ) wa-yazʿumu annahu ʿalā l-ḥanīfiyya wa-anna dīnahu sa-yaẓharu wa-yaṣīru fī jamāʿa wa-ʿizz, fa-kāna yajtamiʿu ilayhi qawm mina l-munāfiqīna wa-yajlisu ilayhimi l-yahūd wa-yuqawwūna minhumu l-khilāfa ʿalā rasūli llāhi (ṣ)* .... After the Battle of Uḥud, Abū ʿĀmir travelled to Byzantium and insti-

The mosque known in Islamic sources as the Ḍirār Mosque was not only a gathering place for the supporters of Abū ʿĀmir, but also a symbol of their tribal autonomy and independence away from the Prophet's territorial basis in the Sāfila where his control was far stronger. By acting resolutely and at a propitious moment against this edifice, the Prophet, without any bloodshed, humiliated and reduced the prestige of some of the most important families in Qubā' whose members were associated with the erection of the Ḍirār Mosque.

---

gated the Emperor to fight against the Prophet: *thumma ṣāra Abū ʿĀmir ilā l-Rūm wa-laqiya Qayṣar malika l-Rūm bi-l-Shām fa-daʿāhu ilā qitāl rasūli llāhi (ṣ) wa-l-muslimīna wa-ḥarraḍahu ʿalā dhālika wa-hawwana amrahum ʿindahu bi-ḍuʿfihim wa-faqrihim wa-qillati ʿadadihim wa-kathrati ʿaduwwihim wa-khawwafahu l-ʿawāqib in huwa lam yafʿal dhālika bi-mā lā ya'manuhu min quwwati l-islām. Thumma inna Abā ʿĀmir māta bi-l-Shām ṭarīdan gharīban waḥīdan kamā daʿā rasūlu llāhi (ṣ), wa-hādhā ayḍan min aʿlāmihi fī ijābati daʿwatihi.*

CONCLUDING REMARKS

Scholars studying the history of Islam can now benefit from a growing repository of Arabic texts which have never been employed in historical research. Both the development of modern scholarship in Islamic countries and the progress achieved in printing technologies assure us of a constant flow of Arabic texts for years to come.

This monograph contains a detailed examination of the available source material about the ʿĀliya or Upper Medina on the eve of Islam and at the time of the Prophet. The advantage of the new source material is evident throughout. We are now better equipped than ever before to conduct detailed studies on Medina (and the same is true for Mecca). This monograph, together with further research to be conducted on other areas of Medina, above all the Sāfila or Lower Medina, will provide us with some of the necessary background material for the study of the Prophet's biography.

It was found that the much quoted sources for the history of the Prophet, such as Ibn Hishām, Wāqidī, Ibn Saʿd and Ṭabarī, offer only a limited amount of evidence both on the topography, that is, the fortresses, groves and mosques, and on the inhabitants, those tribal groups living in the ʿĀliya. Above all, one has to turn to the famous history of Medina written by Samhūdī and to a variety of other sources, mainly geographical and genealogical, in order to discover the available evidence. Geographical evidence has a clear advantage over historical information in that it is not so susceptible to dispute. Thus, when we read that the Banū so-and-so had a fortress called such-and-such, we may assume that we are on fairly firm ground. To a somewhat lesser extent, this is also true of the genealogical evidence which accurately reflects the structure and main divisions of Medinan tribal society in the early period of Islam. Inevitable obscurities which sometimes emerge concerning the genealogy of individuals or clans do not effect the general picture for which we have comprehensive evidence.

Two historical questions regarding the Prophet's biography (both of course relating to the 'Āliya) are discussed in this monograph. First, the delayed conversion to Islam of a large tribal group, the Aws Allāh, inhabiting the 'Āliya. It was ascertained that the report of their delayed conversion is certainly historical. I believe that this finding supports the attitude of those who assume that the general outline or basic framework of the Prophet's history as recorded in the sources is trustworthy.[1] As for the details, research has not yet advanced far beyond the starting point.

Second, the far more complicated Ḍirār incident. It was demonstrated that the sources offer a large amount of evidence on the men and the sites involved in the incident, but do not explain the Prophet's real motives for acting against the mosque and its owners. It would be unrealistic to expect that all the ambiguities surrounding this incident will be removed, but at least we can achieve some order in the available evidence.

The formative period of early Islamic historiography was the first Islamic century and it should not be studied outside its social context, that is, Islamic society during that century. Historical apologetics (see below, Appendices) are a prominent feature of this social context and they demonstrate that the descendants of certain Companions were embarrassed by their fathers' and grandfathers' role during the time of the Prophet and tried to influence the way in which these ancestors went down in history.

The critical study of the Prophet Muḥammad's biography, and of early Islamic historiography in general, is a relatively young field of research. The difficulties are immense, but now that important new information is becoming available in ever increas-

[1] Cf. R. Paret, "Die Lücke in der Überlieferung über den Urislam", in *Westöstliche Abhandlungen: Rudolf Tschudi zum siebzigsten Geburtstag überreicht von Freunden und Schülern*, ed. F. Meier, Wiesbaden 1954, 147–53, at 151–52; W.M. Watt, "The reliability of Ibn-Isḥāq's sources", in T. Fahd (ed.), *La vie du prophète Mahomet*, Actes du Colloque de Strasbourg (octobre 1980), Paris 1983, 31–43, at 34–35.

ing quantities the prospects for genuine progress look favourable indeed.

APPENDIX A

MUJAMMIʿ B. JĀRIYA AND THE ḌIRĀR MOSQUE

Some Medinans had no cause to be proud of their role in the Prophet's time. We have reason to suspect that several of them were given a chance to "correct" their behaviour, and others to "explain" their actions in terms favourable to themselves. These historical apologetics refer to the motives or deeds of individuals and are of course unreliable as a source of historical information. But they form an important category in Islamic historiography and give the *sīra* a specific social context.

While the family was presumably the dominant factor in the correction of tarnished images, other elements also may have been at work, e.g., local or even sectarian rivalries. Thus, it was the Kūfans who reported that Mujammiʿ "collected" (i.e., memorized) the Qur'ān at the time of the Prophet, except one or two Suras.[1] According to the Kūfan Shaʿbī (who also transmits the former report), Mujammiʿ memorized the whole Qur'ān except two or three Suras. Ibn Masʿūd learnt from the Prophet himself more than ninety (or more than seventy) Suras and the rest he learnt from Muajmmiʿ.[2] This high esteem for Mujammiʿ's command of the Qur'ān may not have been shared by the Baṣrans or the Syrians, for example.[3]

---

[1] Ibn Saʿd, VI, 52; Dhahabī, *Nubalā'*, II, 339. Also see R. Paret's review of A. Guillaume, *The Life of Muhammad*, in *Der Islam*, 32 (1957), 334–42, at 336:–2, where he refers to Guillaume 244:2, "who had collected most of the Quran", *qad jamaʿa mina l-qur'ān aktharahu*: "Gemeint ist, daß er das meiste vom Koran auswendig konnte".

[2] Ibn Saʿd, II, 339 (ninety); Dhahabī, *Nubalā'*, II, 340 (seventy). Muqātil reports (above, 89) that Mujammiʿ b. Jāriya became a good Muslim and ʿUmar b. al-Khaṭṭāb sent him to teach Qur'ān in Kūfa; he taught Ibn Masʿūd and dictated the Qur'ān to him (*laqqanahu l-qur'āna*).

[3] For possible sectarian interests, cf. the fact that Zayd b. Jāriya's grandson, Muʿāwiya b. Isḥāq, was killed fighting with Zayd b. ʿAlī and was crucified with him at the Kunāsa (of Kūfa); Ibn al-Kalbī, *Jamhara*, 624; Abū l-Faraj al-Iṣfahānī, *Maqātil al-ṭālibiyyīna*, ed. Aḥmad Ṣaqr, Cairo 1368/1949, Index;

Mujammi' b. Jāriya, who was the *imām* of the Ḍirār Mosque, later became the *imām* of the Qubā' Mosque (what irony!).[4] In the following generation, we find yet another *imām* belonging to the same family: 'Abd al-Raḥmān b. Yazīd b. Jāriya, a nephew of Mujammi' who transmitted Ḥadīth from his uncle and was the *imām* "of his people" (i.e., the 'Amr b. 'Awf). 'Abd al-Raḥmān also officiated as the *qāḍī* of 'Umar b. 'Abd al-'Azīz (i.e., when the latter was the governor of Medina in the late eighties and early nineties of the first century A.H.).[5]

The family's fingerprints can presumably be seen on the claim (found in Muqātil) that the Prophet himself appointed Mujammi' as the *imām* of the Ḍirār Mosque (above, 88). They can also be noticed in Balādhurī's list of *munāfiqūn* from among the Aws which includes Jāriya b. 'Āmir and his sons Yazīd, Zayd and Mujammi'. Having remarked that they were among the builders of the Ḍirār Mosque, Balādhurī says that Mujammi' read the Qur'ān and led them in prayer in this mosque; some said, he adds, that Mujammi' was not a *munāfiq*, while others said that he was and that later his Islam became sound.[6] Elsewhere, his mention as one of the *munāfiqūn* is accompanied by this remark: "It was said that Mujammi' was not really a *munāfiq*. He was

---

Ibn Ḥabīb, *Muḥabbar*, 483.

[4] Mujammi' (who is sometimes called Mujammi' b. Yazīd b. Jāriya) died at the time of Mu'āwiya; see his biography in *Tahdh.*, X, 47 (under "Mujammi' b. Jāriya"), 48 (under "Mujammi' b. Yazīd b. Jāriya"); for a biography of Mujammi' b. Ya'qūb b. Mujammi' b. Yazīd b. Jāriya (d. 160/777), see Ibn Sa'd, *Qism mutammim*, 468 and the sources mentioned there. See in Dhahabī, *Maghāzī*, 34 the following family-*isnād*: Mujammi' b. Yaq'ūb < his father < Mujammi' b. Jāriya (printed: Ḥāritha).

[5] Abū Zur'a, *Ta'rīkh*, ed. Shukr Allāh al-Qūjānī, Damascus 1400/1980, I, 563 says of 'Abd al-Raḥmān that he was an early transmitter (*qadīm*), that he prayed behind Abū Bakr, 'Umar and 'Uthmān and that he was the *imām* of his people. Since 'Abd al-Raḥmān died in 98 A.H. (Khalīfa, *Ṭabaqāt*, 82), the statement that he prayed behind Abū Bakr (and 'Umar and 'Uthmān) seems to be exaggerated; indeed, it is based on 'Abd al-Raḥmān's own testimony (Abū Zur'a, 564; quoted in *TMD* MS, XVI, 264:23, s.v. Mujammi' b. Yaḥyā b. Yazīd b. Jāriya).

[6] Balādh., *Ansāb*, I, 276. Ibn Ḥazm, *Jawāmi'*, 75 emphasizes that Mujammi' b. Jāriya and another member of the 'Amr b. 'Awf (al-Julās b. Suwayd) later repented.

listed as one because his clan made him the *imām* of the Ḍirār Mosque".[7] In other words, this was not a voluntary action on his part.

Two unique reports give Mujammi' the chance to justify his behaviour in public. His constructive self-criticism (he refers to his own juvenile recklessness) paves his way back to respectability. In the first report we are told that Mujammi' replaced the former *imām* of the Mosque of Qubā', Sa'd b. 'Ubayd al-Qāri', who was killed at Qādisiyya. The 'Amr b. 'Awf contended for this post among themselves and referred the matter to Caliph 'Umar's arbitration. Finally, however, they unanimously agreed to nominate Mujammi'. He was blamed and despised[8] for having been the *imām* of the Ḍirār Mosque. 'Umar only gave his consent after he heard Mujammi''s arguments.

> Mujammi': "I was young and fast [strong] in speech (*wa-kānati l-qālatu lī sarī'a*). Today, however, I have realized what I am in and have understood the matters".

'Umar inquired about him and heard there was no fault in him and that he had memorized all of the Qur'ān except for a few Suras (*wa-la-qad jama'a l-qur'ān wa-mā baqiya 'alayhi illā suwar yasīra*).[9]

The apologetic ingenuity reaches its peak in creating a fine literary scene with 'Umar b. al-Khaṭṭāb as its protagonist. The grim 'Umar publicly "forgave" Mujammi' and "rehabilitated" him. The occasion was Mujammi''s candidacy for the office of *imām* in the Mosque of Qubā'. The 'Amr b. 'Awf, who built the Mosque of Qubā', asked 'Umar during his caliphate, to permit

[7] Dhahabī, *Maghāzī*, 21.

[8] *Yughmaṣu* [printed: *yughmaḍu*] *'alayhi*; cf., concerning Abū Lubāba, above, 118: *wa-kāna ghayra maghmūṣin 'alayhi fī l-nifāq*.

[9] Ibn Sa'd, IV, 372–73, quoting Wāqidī. Ibn Sa'd's concluding remark, *wa-lā na'lamu* (printed: *y.'.l.m.*) *masjidan yutanāfasu fī imāmihi mithla masjid B. 'Amr b. 'Awf*, presumably means that there was much controversy about the identity of the *imāms* of that mosque. Al-Zubayr b. Bakkār, *Akhbār al-Madīna* (quoted in *Iṣāba*, III, 68), reports on Sa'd's replacement by Mujammi' quoting 'Utba b. 'Uwaym b. Sā'ida; on 'Uwaym see above, 63.

Mujammiʿ to become the *imām* of their mosque. The following conversation followed:

> ʿUmar [frowning, as the name sounded familiar]: "Is he not the *imām* of the Ḍirār Mosque"?
> Mujammiʿ [who, as we suddenly find out, was present at the meeting, interjects without invitation; his incoherent speech reveals a state of great excitement; he will explain everything]: "Do not be rash with me. By God, I prayed in it not knowing what they concealed in their hearts. Had I known, I would not have prayed in it with them. I was then a young lad, a reader of the Qur'ān, and they were old men concealing their disbelief (*qad ghashshaw nifāqahum*), who were not reading any of the Qur'ān. So I prayed [i.e., I was their *imām*] not approving of anything they did except their [seeming] approach to God and I did not know what was in their hearts".

ʿUmar, the report goes on, forgave and believed him, ordering him to pray (viz., function as the *imām*) in the Mosque of Qubā'.[10] No *isnād* is given, but one may safely guess that it is the creation of Mujammiʿ's descendants. There was no point in denying that he had a role in the Ḍirār incident; yet some of the damage done to the family's reputation could be amended.

[10] Diyārbakrī, *Khamīs*, II, 131:5. See also Ibn Hishām, II, 169–70 (Ibn Isḥāq concludes by saying: "And they claimed that ʿUmar had let him pray as the *imām* of his people"; Ibn Isḥāq seems to have suspected this claim). On Mujammiʿ see also Ṭabarānī, *Kabīr*, XIX, 443f. Cf. ʿUmar's dismissal of a governor or tax-collector, having found out that he had been a *munāfiq*; *Usd al-ghāba*, I, 391:3.

APPENDIX B

THE IMAGE PROBLEM OF ABŪ QAYS B. AL-ASLAT

Considering the role given to Abū Qays in withholding the conversion to Islam of the Aws Allāh until a while after the Battle of the Ditch (5 A.H.), it is surprising to find in some reports that he died in the first or second year after the Hijra.[1] The conflicting dates again point in the direction of apologetics which played an important role in the formation of the *sīra*. This was, so to speak, a case of "premature literary death" and it was a component of an apologetic story, certainly created by Abū Qays' descendants or fellow tribesmen in order to present him in a relatively favourable light. The claim that Abū Qays was one of the pre-Islamic *ḥanīf*s was, I suspect, yet another component of the same story (see Appendix C).

Differences over chronology are common in Islamic historiography and are usually difficult to account for. In this case the discrepancy must be explained. If Abū Qays did indeed die a few years before the Battle of the Ditch, he could not have prevented the Aws Allāh from adopting Islam until the battle had ended.

I submit that Abū Qays was still alive after the Battle of the Ditch and that his alleged earlier death was invented by a friendly informant with the aim of negating the report about his hostile role in preventing the conversion to Islam of the Aws

---

[1] He died in Dhū l-Ḥijja, ten months after the Hijra; Ibn Sa'd, IV, 385; Balādh., *Ansāb*, I, 274; *Iṣāba*, VII, 335. He died at the end of Ramaḍān, 2 A.H.; Ibn Ḥibbān, *Thiqāt*, Hyderabad 1393/1973, I, p. 208. Cf. Watt, *Medina*, 165: "When he died, less than a year after the Hijrah", etc.; 178: "Abū Qays is said to have thought of becoming a Muslim, but to have died before he put his thought into effect; such thoughts without actions, however, make one suspect an attempt to save the face of the clan, for the one solid fact which is not denied is that Abū Qays did *not* become a Muslim". Actually, this "solid fact" *is* denied, see below, 157n (some claimed that Abū Qays embraced Islam on his deathbed). Rubin, "Ḥanīfiyya", 89f did not reconcile the two contradictory dates given for his death.

Allāh. This is suggested by the context in which the earlier date is found: it is part of a report which is favourable to Abū Qays and presents him as someone who *nearly* embraced Islam: had it not been for his premature death (and some scornful comments made by another arch-enemy of the Prophet, Ibn Ubayy, see below), he would have become a Muslim. In other words, the alleged earlier death belongs to the realm of apologetics. The apologetics were associated with the opposition to the Prophet and point to some distress among certain Anṣār over the role of their ancestors during the Prophet's lifetime.

This "rewriting of history" had only a limited effect in the long run because in the diversified Islamic tradition no single version is granted exclusivity; in other words, we often have the benefit of comparing these family claims with other material, originating with various informants. The story of Abū Qays' early death demonstrates that the *sīra* was not an academic project created in a void; "image-correcting" reports such as the one discussed here belong to the earliest stratum of Islamic historiography since at a later period they were no longer relevant.

APPENDIX C

ABŪ QAYS NEARLY EMBRACES ISLAM

The resourcefulness of the apologetic tribal tradition is beautifully demonstrated by the fabricated scene claiming to describe the exact circumstances in which Abū Qays was discouraged from embracing Islam. The blame is suddenly diverted, and we find out that the real villain was not Abū Qays, who was willing to convert, but no other than Ibn Ubayy.[1]

The scene with Ibn Ubayy is preceded by a short report not at all unfriendly towards Abū Qays: he was compared, we are told, to Qays b. al-Khaṭīm in his valour and poetic talent. Mughalṭay adds: "He used to apply himself to acts of devotion and claimed to have been a follower of the *ḥanīfiyya* (*wa-kāna ... yata'allahu wa-yaddaʿī l-ḥanīfiyya*); he also urged Quraysh and his own tribe, the Aws, to follow Muḥammad.[2]

Then comes the scene with Ibn Ubayy. The introductory remarks can be traced back to ʿAbdallāh b. Muḥammad b. ʿUmāra b. al-Qaddāḥ (d. around 200/815).[3] Ibn al-Qaddāḥ says that the meeting with Ibn Ubayy took place after Abū Qays had met the Prophet and heard his words.[4]

Ibn Isḥāq reports that Abū Qays and his brother, Waḥwaḥ, went (one version has: "fled") to Mecca with Quraysh (possibly after the Battle of the Ditch), and embraced Islam when Mecca

[1] Rubin, "Ḥanīfiyya", 90 accepts the scene as historical: "The circumstances which hindered Abū Qays from embracing Islam are elucidated in a report recorded by Mughalṭay". (Besides Mughalṭay, Rubin refers to the Ibn Saʿd, IV, 385; Balādh., *Ansāb*, I, 274; and *Iṣāba*, VII, 334.)

[2] Mughalṭay, *al-Zahr al-bāsim*, 32a–b (*kāna yuʿdalu bi-Qays b. al-Khaṭīm fī l-shajāʿa wa-l-shiʿr wa-kāna yaḥuḍḍu qawmahu ʿalā l-islām wa-yaqūlu: stabiqū ilā hādhā l-rajul*). On Abū Qays' *ḥanīfiyya* see below.

[3] His book *Nasab al-anṣār* was one of Ibn Saʿd's main sources for Anṣārī history. On Ibn al-Qaddāḥ see *GAS*, I, 268, 300.

[4] *Iṣāba*, VII, 334.

was conquered. Al-Zubayr b. Bakkār supported this claim (or at least quoted it).[5]

Abū 'Ubayd al-Qāsim b. Sallām's claim (no doubt basing himself on the descendants of Abū Qays) that Abū Qays and his son, 'Uqba, were Companions of the Prophet is in the same vain.[6] Hence, Ibn al-Qaddāḥ and Abū 'Ubayd preserve a dubious Anṣārī "image-correcting" tradition which coexists alongside the historical tradition without explicitly clashing with it.

The apologetic trend is again at its best in the following report (a combined one composed by Wāqidī), in the middle of which there is a dialogue between Abū Qays and Ibn Ubayy.[7] We are concerned here with what this combined report has to say about Abū Qays after the Hijra:

> When the Messenger of God came to Medina, it was said to him [= Abū Qays]: "O Abū Qays, this is your friend whom you used to describe". He said: "Certainly, he was sent with the truth". And he came to the Prophet and said: "What are you calling to"? The Messenger of God said: "To the testimony that

---

[5] *Istīʿāb*, II, 734; IV, 1734. Ibn 'Abd al-Barr disputes the claim that Abū Qays became a Muslim: *wa-fīmā dhakara al-Zubayr wa-'bn Isḥāq naẓar*. The text in *Istīʿāb*, II, 734, which has *lam yuslim*, must be garbled. Partial confirmation that it is garbled can be had from a comparison with another text. Al-Zubayr b. Bakkār's text includes the statement that Abū Qays' name was in fact al-Ḥārith, or, as some said, 'Abdallāh. The Ḥārith/'Abdallāh passage shows that this is in fact the report of Ibn al-Qaddāḥ which was quoted by al-Zubayr b. Bakkār's uncle, Muṣ'ab b. 'Abdallāh (*TMD* MS, VIII, 392:8), and probably by al-Zubayr as well. Now Ibn al-Qaddāḥ's report includes the claim that Abū Qays embraced Islam on his deathbed; see *op. cit.*, 392:22. A fragment of Ibn al-Qaddāḥ's report is found in *Iṣāba*, VII, 334:5.

[6] *Iṣāba*, VII, 334. Ibn Ḥajar quotes an entry on 'Uqba b. Abī Qays from a compilation by Abū 'Ubayd, probably the latter's *Kitāb al-nasab*; for a quotation from this book see *Iṣāba*, VI, 418.

[7] The fullest account is in Ibn Sa'd, IV, 385; *TMD* MS, VIII, 393–94; see also Balādh., *Ansāb*, I, 274; Tab., II, 406 [I, 1270]; *Usd al-ghāba*, V, 278 f (who quotes the *Istīʿāb* and the Companion dictionary of Abū Mūsā al-Madīnī [d. 581/1185]; on him see *GAL S*, I, 604); *Iṣāba*, VII, 335. The report in the *Iṣāba* is quoted by Ibn Ḥajar from the *Istīʿāb*, but he must have used a manuscript different to the ones on which the printed edition of the *Istīʿāb* was based (about which see the editor's introduction and vol. IV, 1985).

there is no god but God and that I am the Messenger of God". And he mentioned the laws of Islam. Abū Qays said to him: "How good and lovely this is! I shall look into my affairs and then return to you". And he nearly embraced Islam (*wa-kāda yuslimu*). [But] Ibn Ubayy met him [and the following dialogue took place]:
Ibn Ubayy: "Where [do you come] from?"
Abū Qays: "From Muḥammad. He proposed to me things that are so good! He is the one we used to know and the one the doctors of the Jews used to inform us about".[8]
Ibn Ubayy: "By God, you are tired of [literally: you hated] fighting the Khazraj".[9]
Abū Qays, angrily (*fa-ghaḍiba*): "By God, I shall not embrace Islam for one year".[10]
Then he went home and did not return to the Messenger of God until he [= Abū Qays] died before a year passed, in Dhū l-Ḥijja, ten months after the Hijra.

There is an appendix to this combined report from one of the four sources (or *isnāds*) used in its preparation, namely Ibn Abī Ḥabība < Dāwud b. al-Ḥuṣayn,[11] *ʿan ashyākhihim*: "They said, 'As he was dying he was heard uttering the testimony that there is no god but God'". The fact that this addition is located at the end of the combined report does not mean that the matter was insignificant; on the contrary, the question of Abū Qays' conversion to Islam was crucial. But Wāqidī could not incorporate it into the combined report because it was not supported by his other sources (who were more restrained and did not go that far).[12]

[8] The text in the *Iṣāba* is garbled at this point. This is a statement made by Abū Qays, not Ibn Ubayy's question.

[9] Jumaḥī, I, 227 has this variant: *khifta wa-'llāhi suyūfa l-Khazraj*, "By God, you are afraid of the swords of the Khazraj".

[10] Cf. *Khizāna*, VI, 88 < al-Marzubānī: *kāna qad ghaḍiba min ʿAbdillāh b. Ubayy fa-ḥalafa lā yuslimu shahran fa-māta qabla dhālika.*

[11] On Dāwud b. al-Ḥuṣayn al-Umawī (a *mawlā* of the Umayya, d. 135/752) see *GAS*, I, 285.

[12] Wāqidī here uses the usual formula: *fa-kullun qad ḥaddathanī min ḥadīth*

One may venture a guess that the elders ("*ashyākh*") quoted by Dāwud b. al-Ḥuṣayn who gave such a favourable account of Abū Qays' last minutes belonged to Abū Qays' clan, the Wā'il, or to another subdivision of the Aws Allāh.

The key words in the dialogue quoted above are Ibn Ubayy's: "By God, you are tired of [literally: you hated] fighting the Khazraj" (*karihta ḥarba l-Khazraj*). In other words, Abū Qays' intended conversion to Islam equals pacifying the old enemy, the Khazraj (among whom the Prophet enjoyed overwhelming support). But there is another possible interpretation of Ibn Ubayy's utterance: Ibn Ubayy, a Khazrajī, accuses Abū Qays of preferring to form an alliance with Muḥammad against the Khazraj, rather than continuing his war against them (on his own). This admittedly less probable interpretation is in fact supported by another report, quite similar to the one just quoted (see below). Remarkably, the latter interpretation presents Medina of that time as consisting of three major blocks: the Aws, the Khazraj, and the Muslims under the Prophet.

The dialogue quoted above is apologetic. It claims that Abū Qays was disposed to embrace Islam and would have done so had it not been for Ibn Ubayy's remark and Abū Qays' death less than two months before the latest date set for his conversion to Islam. The alleged date, like the rest of this report, is useless as far as historical fact is concerned, but is illuminating on the ways of Anṣārī historical apologetics.[13]

The same pattern is followed in another report which similarly refers to Abū Qays' war against the Khazraj. Again, there is a dialogue with Ibn Ubayy contained in a longer report by Ibn al-Qaddāḥ (probably made of earlier, independent texts), which is most favourable to Abū Qays and, to some extent, the Aws Allāh in general. The background is Abū Qays' call to the Aws Allāh

---

Abī Qays b. al-Aslat bi-ṭā'ifa fa-jama'tu mā ḥaddathūnī min dhālika; Ibn Sa'd, IV, 383; *TMD* MS, VIII, 393:6. The former source (385:-3) has another addition to the combined report coming from one of its sources: Mūsā b. 'Ubayda al-Rabadhī < Muḥammad b. Ka'b al-Quraẓī (concerning *nikāḥ al-maqt*).

[13] Cf. Gil, "The creed of Abū 'Āmir", 12: "Abū Qays ... died nine months after the *hiǧra*".

(which should obviously be dated after the Hijra) to embrace Islam: "He stood up [to preach] among the Aws Allāh and said: 'Hasten to this man, because I have never seen a good thing without its beginnings being its best part, and I have never seen a bad thing without its beginnings being the least evil'". It is implied here that Abū Qays intended to become a Muslim himself. This became known to Ibn Ubayy, who met him, and the following dialogue took place:

> Ibn Ubayy: "You have taken every possible route in your war against us: once you seek to be allied with Quraysh, and once you follow Muḥammad"! (*la-qad ludhta min ḥarbinā kulla malādhin, marra taṭlubu l-ḥilfa ilā Quraysh wa-marra bi-'ttibāʿ Muḥammad*).
> Abū Qays, angrily (*fa-ghaḍiba*): "Verily, I shall be the last person to follow him" (*lā jarama, wa-'llāhi lā ttabaʿtuhu illā ākhira l-nās*).[14]

[14] Ibn al-Qaddāḥ, quoted in *TMD* MS, VIII, 392:19; *TMD, Tahdh.*, VI, 456. Also Mughalṭay, *al-Zahr al-bāsim*, 32b (... *l-ḥilfa fī Quraysh* ...); *Iṣāba*, VII, 334. The last-mentioned source wrongly has *min ḥizbinā* instead of *min ḥarbinā* (see below). A comparison between the *Iṣāba* and the *TMD* leads to the suspicion that Ibn Ḥajar fragments Ibn al-Qaddāḥ's report (1. lines 5–8; 2. line 4 from below to the end). Unlike Ibn 'Asākir, Ibn Ḥajar seems to have cared little for the integrity of his source: he felt free to fragment it and place the fragments as he pleased. U. Rubin, who relies on the above-mentioned garbled text, with *ḥizb* instead of *ḥarb*, translates: "You have abandoned our party" which makes little sense and does not combine well with the mention of an attempted alliance. The apocryphal conversation is supposed to have taken place in the first year after the Hijra and Ibn Ubayy obviously refers to a pre-Islamic event. The *TMD* speaks of an attempted alliance with Quraysh: *marra taṭlubu l-ḥilfa ilā Quraysh*, while the *Iṣāba*, presumably less accurately, speaks of a concluded alliance: *tāratan tuḥālifu Qurayshan*. Rubin ("Ḥanīfiyya", 90) sums up the report with a straightforward historical conclusion: "This report indicates that Abū Qays was wavering between attraction to Muḥammad and loyalty to Quraysh". But the more one becomes aware of the apologetical orientation of these materials, the less one is likely to use them as historical evidence.

There are reports on a pre-Islamic attempt by the Nabīt, a subdivision of the Aws, to make an alliance with Quraysh against the Khazraj; cf. M.J. Kister, "On strangers and allies in Mecca", in *JSAI* 13 (1990), 113–154, at 142–43; Lecker, "The emigration of 'Utba b. Abī Waqqāṣ from Mecca to Medina" (forthcoming), n. 3.

The pre-Islamic enmity between the Aws and Khazraj is in the background of this dialogue. Its aim is to provide Abū Qays with an alibi: indeed, he did not hasten to embrace Islam, but it was not his fault. He was prepared to do so and even enthusiastically preached to the Aws Allāh that they should do the same. But then came the cruel remark by Ibn Ubayy hinting that Abū Qays' motives for embracing Islam were less than honourable, i.e., that Abū Qays wanted to embrace Islam (and be allied with the Prophet) in order to fight against the Khazraj. His anger aroused, Abū Qays said that he would be the last person to follow Muḥammad. The mention of anger is vital: had Abū Qays been balanced and calm, he would not have reacted so rashly. But, since a man of honour is supposed to stand by his word (even when uttered in anger), he could not immediately accomplish his plan to become a Muslim. The case for Abū Qays is built up in a short dialogue. His good intentions did not materialize only because of a fateful accidental exchange between the two leaders. Ibn Ubayy is also the culprit in the other report where Abū Qays promised the Prophet to "look into his affairs and then return to him" (above, 158).

Other sections of Ibn al-Qaddāḥ's report, including the alleged *ḥanīfī* inclinations of Abū Qays, further indicate its apologetical intention; there can be little doubt that it originated with clan members or even the descendants of Abū Qays.

Ibn al-Qaddāḥ continues: "They alleged (*fa-zaʿamū*) that when Abū Qays was on his deathbed, the Prophet sent him this message: 'If you say the words *lā ilāha illā llāh*, through them I shall intercede for you on the Day of Resurrection' and he was heard uttering it".[15]

We finally arrive at the *ḥanīfiyya* of Abū Qays. Ibn al-Qaddāḥ says: "He is the one who stood up [to preach] among the Aws Allāh, inciting them to embrace Islam (*wa-huwa lladhī waqafa*

[15] *TMD* MS, VIII, 392:22; *TMD, Tahdh.*, VI, 456; cf. *Iṣāba*, VII, 334. A similar apologetic claim comes from the clan (or family) of Suwayd b. al-Ṣāmit of the ʿAmr b. ʿAwf, who allegedly forfeited the chance to become the first Muslim in Medina when he failed to embrace Islam. Suwayd was killed by the Khazraj before the Battle of Buʿāth, *wa-zaʿama qawm Suwayd b. al-Ṣāmit annahu māta musliman*; Ibn Qudāma, *Istibṣār*, 328:4.

bi-Awsi llāhi yaḥuḍḍuhum ʿalā l-islām). Before the arrival of the Prophet, he applied himself to acts of devotion and claimed to have been a *ḥanīf* (*wa-qad kāna ... yataʾallahu wa-yaddaʿī l-ḥanīfiyya*),[16] and incited Quraysh to follow the Prophet".[17]

Now, was Abū Qays really a *ḥanīf*?[18] I sumbit that he was not. The *ḥanīfiyya* theme is part of a major effort to rehabilitate Abū Qays who, as the charismatic leader of the Aws Allāh, kept his fellow tribesmen from converting to Islam for years after the Hijra. Unlike the *ḥanīfiyya* of Abū ʿĀmir al-Rāhib (which seems to have been genuine), Abū Qays' *ḥanīfiyya* did not clash with that of the Prophet. On the contrary, it allegedly prepared him to accept Muḥammad as a true prophet.

[16] *Iṣāba: ... wa-yudʿā l-ḥanīf*; cf. Ibn Saʿd, IV, 384: *wa-kāna yuʿrafu bi-Yathrib yuqālu lahu l-ḥanīf*). Cf. Gil, "The creed of Abū ʿĀmir", 12.

[17] Ibn al-Qaddāḥ supports this with two verses from a long *qaṣīda* with which Abū Qays addressed Quraysh.

[18] Fück accepted this as historical: "That he was a *ḥanīf* is shown by verses in Ibn Hishām even if they are probably not genuine, for no Muslim could have had an interest in characterizing this opponent of the Prophet as one of the *ḥanīf*s"; see Fück, "The originality of the Arabian Prophet", in M. Swartz (trans. and ed.), *Studies on Islam* 98, n. 11. Fück was following Wellhausen, *Skizzen* IV, 16, n. 2, who, having quoted the afore-mentioned verses by Abū Qays, remarked: "Sind die Verse unecht, so reichen sie doch hin zu beweisen, daß Abu Qais für einen Hanif galt". (Wellhausen added, however: "Die hanifische Religion könnte allerdings hier die heidnische Religion bedeuten".) Rubin argues that those described as *ḥanīf*s included "some bitter opponents of Muḥammad" and, "as already noted by Fück, no Muslim could have had any interest in characterizing these opponents of the Prophet as *ḥunafāʾ*"; Rubin, "Ḥanīfiyya", 85 f; A. Rippin, "Rḥmnn and the Ḥanīfs", in Wael B. Hallaq and Donald P. Little (eds.), *Islamic Studies Presented to Charles J. Adams*, Leiden 1991, 153–68, at 162. A similar point was made many years ago by Ch.J. Lyall. In his correct criticism of D.S. Margoliouth's theory linking *muslim* with Musaylima and *ḥanīf* with the Ḥanīfa tribe, Lyall ("The words *Ḥanīf* and *Muslim*", in *JRAS* 1903, 771–84) argued (at 774) that "Islamic tradition would hardly have been likely to invent texts ascribing doctrines agreeing with Islam to an enemy of Muḥammad's" (i.e., in this case, Umayya b. Abī l-Ṣalt).

Buhl, *Leben*, 69–70 (also 99, n. 275) suspected, correctly I believe, the authenticity of the *ḥanīfī* verses ascribed to Abū Qays and his listing among the *ḥanīf*s based on the verses. (The verse concerning the pilgrimage comes, Buhl thinks, from a follower of Muḥammad "der Abrahams Religion mit der Wallfahrt als Mittelpunkt verherrlicht".)

The crucial question is, of course, whether or not he embraced Islam, and at this point even the most devoted apologists faced obvious difficulties. Abū Qays "nearly embraced Islam", or died prematurely, or, as the most extreme version claims, was heard pronouncing the *shahāda* on his deathbed. This was certainly not too late because the Prophet had promised to intercede for him on the Day of Resurrection.

In this context, the *ḥanīfiyya* claim is merely one component of an "image-correcting" effort by a later generation, possibly modelled on the genuine *ḥanīfiyya* of Abū ʿĀmir. This becomes even clearer in a combined report compiled by Wāqidī from several sources and quoted by Ibn Saʿd.[19]

In this combined report, the *ḥanīfiyya* theme is further elaborated. It begins by telling us that "no one of the Aws and Khazraj was more involved in describing the *ḥanīfiyya*, or more insistent in looking for it, than Abū Qays b. al-Aslat". He asked the Jews of Yathrib about religious matters and they called on him to become Jewish; he then went to Syria and asked the monks and the (Christian) doctors, who called on him to join their religion. Then a monk told him that the *ḥanīfiyya*, the *dīn* of Abraham, is where he came from; so Abū Qays returned to the Ḥijāz after having declared that this was indeed his belief and that he would cling to it to his death (*anā ʿalā dīn Ibrāhīm wa-anā adīnu bihi ḥattā amūta ʿalayhi*). During an *ʿumra* he met (the *ḥanīf*) Zayd b. ʿAmr b. Nufayl who told him about his own search for the true religion in Syria, Mesopotamia and Yathrib, which ended with the same result, viz., the conclusion that the true religion was that of Abraham. Here follows Abū Qays' comment (which is probably polemical and directed against the better known *ḥanīf*,

[19] Ibn ʿAsākir quotes it from the *Taʾrīkh Baghdād*. It is essential to use the complete version of the report which reveals its composite nature. ʿAbd al-Qādir Badrān's *Tahdhīb* of Ibn ʿAsākir creates the wrong impression that the report is from Ibn Saʿd < Muḥammad b. ʿAmr b. Ḥazm. In fact, Muḥammad figures at the end of one of the four sources (or *isnāds*) used by Wāqidī in the preparation of this combined report. One fragment of the report, i.e., the conversation between Abū Qays and Ibn Ubayy (*karihta ḥarba l-Khazraj*) has already been discussed above, 159; Ibn Saʿd, IV, 383 f; *TMD* MS, VIII, 392–93; *TMD, Tahdh.*, VI, 457; cf. *Iṣāba*, VII, 335.

Abū 'Āmir al-Rāhib), that nobody adhered to the *dīn* of Abraham except him and Zayd b. 'Amr.

The claim that Abū Qays was a *ḥanīf* merits no more trust than the claims that he died shortly after the Hijra and that he embraced Islam. Abū Qays' clan members or descendants created apologetic (tendentious and biased) reports on his role at the time of the Prophet.

BIBLIOGRAPHY

Abū Dāwūd, Sulaymān b. al-Ash'ath. *Marāsīl*, Cairo 1310/1892.

Aghānī — Abū l-Faraj al-Iṣfahānī. *Kitāb al-aghānī*, Būlāq 1285/1868.

Aḥmad — Aḥmad b. Ḥanbal. *Musnad*, Cairo 1313/1895. [Reprint Beirut.]

Bakrī — Abū 'Ubayd al-Bakrī. *Mu'jam mā sta'jama*, ed. Muṣṭafā al-Saqqā, Cairo 1364/1945–1371/1951.

Balādh., *Ansāb* — Aḥmad b. Yaḥyā b. Jābir al-Balādhurī. *Ansāb al-ashrāf*, I, ed. Muḥammad Ḥamīdullāh, Cairo 1959; IVa, ed. M. Schloessinger, revised and annotated by M.J. Kister, Jerusalem 1971; VIb, ed. Khalil 'Athamina, Jerusalem 1993.

Balādh., *Futūḥ* (Ṭabbā') — al-Balādhurī. *Futūḥ al-buldān*, ed. 'Abdallāh Anīs al-Ṭabbā' and 'Umar Anīs al-Ṭabbā', Beirut 1407/1987.

al-Bayhaqī, Aḥmad b. al-Ḥusayn al-Bayhaqī. *Dalā'il al-nubuwwa*, ed. 'Abd al-Mu'ṭī Qal'ajī, Beirut 1405/1985.

Biḥār al-anwār — Muḥammad Bāqir al-Majlisī. *Biḥār al-anwār*, Beirut 1403/1983. 110 vols.

BSOAS — *Bulletin of the School of Oriental and African Studies.*

Buhl, F. *Das Leben Muhammeds*[2], trans. H. Schaeder, Leipzig 1930. [Reprint Heidelberg 1955.]

Caskel, W. u. G. Strenziok. *Ǧamharat an-Nasab: Das genealogische Werk des Hišām ibn Muḥammad al-Kalbī*, Leiden 1966.

Crone, P. *Slaves on Horses: The Evolution of the Islamic Polity*, Cambridge 1980.

Dhahabī, *Maghāzī* — Muḥammad ibn 'Uthmān al-Dhahabī. *Ta'rīkh al-islām wa-ṭabaqāt al-mashāhīr wa-l-a'lām: al-Maghāzī*, ed. Muḥammad Maḥmūd Ḥamdān, Cairo-Beirut 1405/1985.

— *Nubalā'* — *Siyar a'lām al-nubalā'*, ed. Shu'ayb al-Arnāwūṭ *et al.*, Beirut 1401/1981–1409/1988.

al-Diyārbakrī, Ḥusayn b. Muḥammad. *Ta'rīkh al-Khamīs fī aḥwāl anfas nafīs*, Cairo 1283/1866.

Fatḥ al-bārī — Ibn Ḥajar al-'Asqalānī. *Fatḥ al-bārī sharḥ ṣaḥīḥ al-Bukhārī*, Būlāq 1301/1884.

Fraenkel, S. "Das Schutzrecht der Araber", in C. Bezold (ed.), *Orientalische Studien Theodor Nöldeke zum siebzigsten Geburtstag gewidmet von Freunden und Schülern*, Gieszen 1906, 293–301.

GAL — C. Brockelmann. *Geschichte der arabischen Litteratur*, Leiden 1943–1949.

GAL S — *GAL*, *Supplementbände.*

GAS — F. Sezgin. *Geschichte des arabischen Schrifttums*, Leiden 1967 f.

Gil, M. "The creed of Abū 'Āmir", in *Israel Oriental Studies* 12 (1992), 9–57.

— "The Medinan opposition to the Prophet", in *JSAI* 10 (1987), 65–96. [*Jāhiliyya and Islamic Studies in Honour of M.J. Kister Septuagenarian.*]

— "The origin of the Jews of Yathrib", in *JSAI* 4 (1984), 203–24.

Goldziher, I. *Muslim Studies*, ed. S.M. Stern, trans. C.R. Barber and S.M. Stern, London 1967–71 (= *Muhammedanische Studien*, Halle 1889–90).

Ḥamīdullāh, Muḥammad. *Majmūʿat al-wathāʾiq al-siyāsiyya li-l-ʿahd al-nabawī wa-l-khilāfa al-rāshida*[5], Beirut 1405/1985.

Ḥassān b. Thābit. *Dīwān*, ed. W. ʿArafat, London 1971.

Horovitz, J. "Judaeo-Arabic relations in pre-Islamic times", in *Islamic Culture* 3 (1929), 161–99.

Ibn al-Athīr, ʿAlī b. Muḥammad. *al-Lubāb fī tahdhīb al-ansāb*, Beirut n. d.

Ibn Durayd, Muḥammad b. al-Ḥasan. *al-Ishtiqāq*, ed. ʿAbd al-Salām Hārūn, Cairo 1378/1958.

Ibn Ḥabīb, Muḥammad. *al-Muḥabbar*, ed. I. Lichtenstaedter, Hyderabad 1361/1942.

Ibn Ḥazm al-Andalusī. *Jamharat ansāb al-ʿarab*, ed. ʿAbd al-Salām Hārūn, Cairo 1382/1962.

— *Jawāmiʿ al-sīra al-nabawiyya*, Cairo: Maktabat al-Turāth al-Islāmī, n. d.

Ibn Hishām, ʿAbd al-Malik. *al-Sīra al-nabawiyya*, ed. al-Saqqā, al-Abyārī and Shalabī, Beirut 1391/1971.

Ibn al-Kalbī, Hishām b. Muḥammad. *Jamharat al-nasab*, ed. Nājī Ḥasan, Beirut 1407/1986.

— *Nasab Maʿadd wa-l-yaman al-kabīr*, ed. Nājī Ḥasan, Beirut 1408/1988.

Ibn Mākūlā, ʿAlī b. Hibat Allāh. *al-Ikmāl*, ed. ʿAbd al-Raḥmān b. Yaḥyā al-Yamānī, Hyderabad 1381/1962; vol. 7, ed. Nāyif al-ʿAbbās, Cairo n. d.

Ibn al-Najjār, Muḥammad b. Maḥmūd. *al-Durra al-thamīna fī taʾrīkh al-Madīna*, printed as an appendix to al-Fāsī's *Shifāʾ al-gharām bi-akhbār al-balad al-ḥarām*, Cairo 1956, II, 318 f.

Ibn Qudāma, Muwaffaq al-Dīn ʿAbdallāh al-Maqdisī. *al-Istibṣār fī nasab al-ṣaḥāba min al-anṣār*, ed. ʿAlī Nuwayhiḍ, Beirut 1392/1972.

Ibn Qutayba, ʿAbdallāh b. Muslim. *al-Maʿārif*, ed. Tharwat ʿUkāsha, Cairo 1969.

Ibn Rusta — *al-Aʿlāq al-nafīsa*, ed. M.J. de Goeje, Leiden 1892.

Ibn Saʿd, Muḥammad. *al-Ṭabaqāt al-kubrā*, Beirut 1380/1960–1388/1968.

— *Qism mutammim — al-Ṭabaqāt al-kubrā, al-qism al-mutammim li-tābiʿī ahl al-Madīna wa-man baʿdahum*, ed. Ziyād Muḥammad Manṣūr, Medina 1408/1987.

Ibn Shabba, ʿUmar. *Taʾrīkh al-Madīna al-munawwara*, ed. Fahīm Muhammad Shaltūt [Mecca 1399/1979].

Iṣāba — Ibn Ḥajar, Aḥmad b. ʿAlī al-ʿAsqalānī. *al-Iṣāba fī tamyīz al-ṣaḥāba*, ed. ʿAlī Muḥammad al-Bijāwī, Cairo 1392/1972.

Istīʿāb — Ibn ʿAbd al-Barr, Yūsuf b. ʿAbdallāh al-Namarī. *al-Istīʿāb fī maʿrifat al-aṣḥāb*, ed. ʿAlī Muḥammad al-Bijāwī, Cairo n. d.

al-Jāsir, Ḥamad. "Mu'allafāt fī ta'rīkh al-Madīna", no. 1, in *al-'Arab* 4, ii (1969), 97–100; no. 2, in *al-'Arab* 4, iii (1969), 262–67; no. 3, in *al-'Arab* 4, iv (1970), 327–35; no. 4, in *al-'Arab* 4, v (1970), 385–88, 465–68.

JESHO — *Journal of the Economic and Social History of the Orient.*

JNES — *Journal of Near Eastern Studies.*

JRAS — *Journal of the Royal Asiatic Society of Great Britain and Ireland.*

JSAI — *Jerusalem Studies in Arabic and Islam.*

al-Jumaḥī, Muḥammad b. Sallām. *Ṭabaqāt fuḥūl al-shu'arā'*, ed. Maḥmūd Muḥammad Shākir, Cairo 1394/1974.

Kaḥḥāla, 'Umar Riḍā. *Jughrāfiyyat shibh jazīrat al-'arab*[2], Mecca 1384/1964.

Khalīfa b. Khayyāṭ. *Ta'rīkh*, ed. Suhayl Zakkār, Damascus 1968.

— *al-Ṭabaqāt*, ed. Akram Ḍiyā' al-'Umarī, Riyāḍ 1402/1982. [Reprint of the 1387/1967 edition.]

Khizāna — 'Abd al-Qādir b. 'Umar al-Baghdādī. *Khizānat al-adab*, ed. 'Abd al-Salām Hārūn, Cairo 1387/1967–1406/1986.

Khulāṣat al-wafā — 'Alī b. Aḥmad al-Samhūdī. *Khulāṣat al-wafā bi-akhbār dār al-muṣṭafā*, Medina 1392/1972.

Kister, M.J. "The battle of the Ḥarra", in M. Rosen-Ayalon (ed.), *Studies in Memory of Gaston Wiet*, Jerusalem 1977, 33–49.

— "'Do not assimilate yourselves ...: *Lā tashabbahū*'", in *JSAI* 12 (1989), 321–53, with Appendix by Menahem Kister, 354–71. [Haim Blanc Memorial Volume.]

— "The massacre of the Banū Qurayẓa: a re-examination of a tradition", in *JSAI*, 8 (1986), 61–96. Reprinted in *idem*, *Society and Religion from Djāhiliyya to Islam*, Aldershot: Variorum, 1990, no. VIII.

Kister, M.J. and Menahem. "On the Jews of Arabia — some notes", in *Tarbiẕ* 48 (1979), 231–47. [in Hebrew.]

Lane, E.W. *Arabic-English Lexicon*, London 1863–93.

Lecker, M. *The Banū Sulaym: A Contribution to the Study of Early Islam*, Jerusalem 1989. [The Max Schloessinger Memorial Series, Monographs IV.]

— "Ḥudhayfa b. al-Yamān and 'Ammār b. Yāsir, Jewish converts to Islam", in *Quaderni di Studi Arabi* (forthcoming).

— "Idol worship in pre-Islamic Medina (Yathrib)", in *Le Muséon* 106 (1993), 331–46.

— "A note on early marriage links between Qurashīs and Jewish women", in *JSAI* 10 (1987), 17–39.

— "Muḥammad at Medina: a geographical approach", in *JSAI* 6 (1985), 29–62.

— "On the Markets of Medina (Yathrib) in pre-Islamic and early Islamic times", in *JSAI* 8 (1986), 133–47.

— "Wāqidī's account on the status of the Jews of Medina: a study of a combined report", in *JNES* 54 (1995), 1–18 (forthcoming).

Lewis, B. *The Jews of Islam*, Princeton 1984.

Lisān al-'arab — Ibn Manẓūr, Jamāl al-Dīn. *Lisān al-'arab*, Beirut 1968.

Madanī, ʻUbayd. "Uṭūm al-Madīna al-munawwara", in *Journal of the College of Arts at the King Saud University*, 3 (1973–74), 213–26.

Maghānim — Majd al-Dīn Muḥammad b. Yaʻqūb al-Fīrūzābādī. *al-Maghānim al-muṭāba fī maʻālim Ṭāba*, ed. Ḥamad al-Jāsir, Riyāḍ 1389/1969.

Makki, M.S. *Medina, Saudi Arabia: A Geographical Analysis of the City and Region*, Amersham 1982.

Masālik al-abṣār — Ibn Faḍl Allāh al-ʻUmarī. *Masālik al-abṣār fī mamālik al-amṣār*, ed. Aḥmad Zakī Bāshā, I, Cairo 1342/1924.

al-Masʻūdī, ʻAlī b. al-Ḥusayn. *al-Tanbīh wa-l-ishrāf*, ed. M.J. de Goeje, Leiden 1894.

al-Mizzī, Abū l-Ḥajjāj Yūsuf. *Tahdhīb al-kamāl fī asmā' al-rijāl*, ed. Bashshār ʻAwwād Maʻrūf, Beirut 1405/1985–1413/1992.

Mughalṭay, Abū ʻAbdallāh b. Qilij. *al-Zahr al-bāsim fī sīrati Abī l-qāsim*, MS Leiden Or. 370.

Muqātil b. Sulaymān. *Tafsīr*, MS Saray, Ahmet III 74.

Naṣr b. ʻAbd al-Raḥmān al-Fazārī al-Iskandarānī. *al-Amkina wa-l-miyāh wa-l-jibāl wa-l-āthār*, MS Br. Lib. Add. 23,603.

Nöldeke, Th. "Die Tradition über das Leben Muhammeds", in *Der Islam* 5 (1914), 160–70.

Philby, J.B. *A Pilgrim in Arabia*, London 1946.

Qays b. al-Khaṭīm. *Dīwān*, ed. Nāṣir al-Dīn al-Asad, Beirut 1387/1967.

— ed. T. Kowalski, Leipzig 1914.

al-Qurṭubī, Muḥammad b. Aḥmad. *al-Jāmiʻ li-aḥkām al-qur'ān*[3], Cairo 1387/1967. [Reprint.]

Rahman, H. "The conflicts between the Prophet and the opposition in Madina", in *Der Islam* 62 (1985), 260–97.

al-Rāzī, Muḥammad b. ʻUmar. *al-Tafsīr al-kabīr*, Cairo n. d. [Reprint Tehran.]

Rubin, U. "Ḥanīfiyya and Kaʻba: an inquiry into the Arabian pre-Islamic background of *dīn Ibrāhīm*", in *JSAI* 13 (1990), 85–112.

al-Samʻānī, ʻAbd al-Karīm b. Muḥammad. *al-Ansāb*, ed. ʻAbdallāh ʻUmar al-Bārūdī, Beirut 1408/1988.

Samh. — ʻAlī b. Aḥmad al-Samhūdī. *Wafā' al-wafā bi-akhbār dār al-muṣṭafā*, ed. Muḥammad Muḥyī al-Dīn ʻAbd al-Ḥamīd, Cairo 1374/1955. [Reprint Beirut.]

Serjeant, R.B. "Meccan trade and the rise of Islam: misconceptions and flawed polemics" (review article of P. Crone, *Meccan Trade and the Rise of Islam*, Princeton 1987), in *JAOS*, 110 (1990), 472–86.

al-Sijistānī, Abū Ḥātim. *al-Muʻammarūna*, ed. ʻAbd al-Munʻim ʻĀmir, Cairo 1961 (bound with *al-Waṣāyā* by the same author).

Sīra Shāmiyya — Muḥammad b. Yūsuf al-Ṣāliḥī al-Shāmī. *Subul al-hudā wa-l-rashād*, I, ed. Muṣṭafā ʻAbd al-Wāḥid, Cairo 1392/1972; III, ed. ʻAbd al-ʻAzīz ʻAbd al-Ḥaqq Ḥilmī, Cairo 1395/1975; IV, ed. Ibrāhīm al-Tarazī and ʻAbd al-Karīm al-ʻAzbāwī, Cairo 1399/1979; V, ed. Fahīm Muḥammad Shaltūt and Jawdat ʻAbd al-Raḥmān Hilāl, Cairo 1404/1983.

al-Suhaylī, 'Abd al-Raḥmān b. 'Abdallāh. *al-Rawḍ al-unuf*, ed. Ṭāhā 'Abd al-Rā'ūf Sa'd, Cairo 1391/1971.

al-Suyūṭī, Jalāl al-Dīn. *al-Durr al-manthūr fī l-tafsīr bi-l-ma'thūr*, Cairo 1314/1896.

— *al-Ḥujaj al-mubīna fī l-tafḍīl bayna Makka wa-l-Madīna*, ed. 'Abdallāh Muḥammad al-Darwīsh, Damascus-Beirut 1405/1985.

— *al-Khaṣā'iṣ al-kubrā*, ed. Muḥammad Khalīl Harrās, Cairo 1387/1967.

Tab. — Muḥammad b. Jarīr al-Ṭabarī. *Ta'rīkh al-rusul wa-l-mulūk*, ed. Muḥammad Abū l-Faḍl Ibrāhīm, Cairo 1380/1960–1387/1967. [References to the European edition (ed. M. de Goeje *et al.*, Leiden 1879–1901) are added between square brackets.]

al-Ṭabarānī, Sulaymān b. Aḥmad. *al-Mu'jam al-Kabīr*², ed. Ḥamdī 'Abd al-Majīd al-Salafī, Cairo 1400/1980 f.

al-Ṭabarī, Muḥammad b. Jarīr. *Jāmi' al-bayān fī tafsīr al-qur'ān*, Būlāq 1321/1903–1330/1912.

al-Ṭabrisī, al-Faḍl b. al-Ḥasan. *Majma' al-bayān fī tafsīr al-qur'ān*, Beirut 1374/1954–1377/1957.

Tahdh. — Ibn Ḥajar al-'Asqalānī. *Tahdhīb al-tahdhīb*, Hyderabad 1325/1907.

TMD — Ibn 'Asākir, 'Alī b. al-Ḥasan. *Ta'rīkh madīnat Dimashq.*

TMD ('Abdallāh b. Jābir - 'Abdallāh b. Zayd), ed. Sukayna al-Shihābī and Muṭā' al-Ṭarābīshī, Damascus 1402/1981.

TMD MS — Facsimile edition, 'Ammān: Dār al-Bashīr, n. d. 19 vols.

TMD, Tahdh. — *Tahdhīb ta'rīkh Ibn 'Asākir*, ed. 'Abd al-Qādir Efendi Badrān, Damascus 1399/1979.

'Umdat al-akhbār — Aḥmad b. 'Abd al-Ḥamīd al-'Abbāsī. *'Umdat al-akhbār fī madīnat al-mukhtār*, ed. Muḥammad al-Ṭayyib al-Anṣārī and As'ad Ṭarābzūnī, n. p., n. d.

Usd al-ghāba — Ibn al-Athīr, 'Alī b. Muḥammad. *Usd al-ghāba fī ma'rifat al-ṣaḥāba*, Cairo 1280/1863.

Versteegh, K. "Grammar and exegesis: the origins of Kufan grammar and the *Tafsīr Muqātil*", in *Der Islam*, 67 (1990), 206–42.

al-Wāḥidī, 'Alī b. Aḥmad. *Asbāb al-nuzūl*, Cairo 1387/1968.

Waq. — Muḥammad b. 'Umar al-Wāqidī. *Kitāb al-maghāzī*, ed. Marsden Jones, London 1966.

"Waṣf al-Madīna" — "Waṣf al-Madīna al-munawwara fī 1303/1885", in Ḥamad al-Jāsir, *Rasā'il fī ta'rīkh al-Madīna*, Riyāḍ 1392/1972.

Watt, W.M. *Muhammad at Medina*, Oxford 1956.

Wellhausen, J. *Skizzen und Vorarbeiten* IV = *Medina vor dem Islam*, Berlin 1889.

Wüstenfeld, F. *Geschichte der Stadt Medina. Im Auszuge aus dem Arabischen des Samhûdi*, Göttingen 1860.

Yaq. — Yāqūt al-Ḥamawī. *Mu'jam al-buldān*, Beirut 1957.

al-Zurqānī, Muḥammad b. 'Abd al-Bāqī. *Sharḥ 'alā l-mawāhib al-laduniyya*, Cairo 1329/1911.

INDEX

Abān b. ʿUthmān, 98
ʿAbbād b. Ḥunayf, 101, 102, 119, 121, 122
al-ʿAbbās, 110
ʿAbd ʿAmr b. Qunayʿ, 106
ʿAbd al-Ashhal, B., 3, 20–22, 24, 35, 36, 39, 41
ʿAbd al-ʿAzīz b. ʿAbdallāh b. ʿUthmān, 119
ʿAbd al-Jabbār, 82
ʿAbd al-Malik, 12
ʿAbd al-Raḥmān b. ʿAbdallāh al-Balawī, 70
ʿAbd al-Raḥmān b. ʿAwf, 140
ʿAbd al-Raḥmān b. Saʿd b. Zurāra, 107
ʿAbd al-Raḥmān b. Yazīd b. Jāriya, 151
ʿAbd al-Raḥmān b. Zayd al-ʿAdawī, 97, 107
ʿAbd al-Razzāq, 76
ʿAbda b. Mughīth, 103
ʿAbdallāh b. al-ʿAbbās, *see* Ibn ʿAbbās
ʿAbdallāh b. Abī Aḥmad b. Jaḥsh al-Asadī, 105
ʿAbdallāh b. Abī Bakr b. Muḥammad b. ʿAmr b. Ḥazm, 20
ʿAbdallāh b. Abī Ḥabība b. al-Azʿar, 113, 114, 120
ʿAbdallāh b. Ḥanẓala b. Abī ʿĀmir, 109, 111
ʿAbdallāh b. Ḥunayf, 121
ʿAbdallāh b. Jaʿfar, 98
ʿAbdallāh b. Jaḥsh, 106
ʿAbdallāh b. Masʿūd, 89, 150
ʿAbdallāh b. al-Mubārak, 145
ʿAbdallāh b. Muḥammad b. ʿUmāra, *see* Ibn al-Qaddāḥ
ʿAbdallāh b. Nabtal, 114–116, 142
ʿAbdallāh b. Rawāḥa, 4
ʿAbdallāh b. Saʿd b. Khaythama, 29
ʿAbdallāh b. Salām, 53, 64
ʿAbdallāh b. Salima al-ʿAjlānī, 103, 136
ʿAbdallāh b. Ṣayfī b. Wabara, 70
ʿAbdallāh b. Ubayy, 29, 156, 158, 159, 161
ʿAbdallāh b. ʿUmar, *see* Ibn ʿUmar
ʿAbdallāh b. ʿUthmān, 98
ʿAbdallāh al-Qarrāẓ, 115
Abou el-Fadl, Khaled, 74
Abraham, 53, 162–164
Abū ʿAfak, 48, 52
Abū ʿĀmir al-Rāhib, 43, 54, 76–78, 81–86, 88, 92, 93, 97, 99, 106, 107, 109–111, 124, 125, 127, 131, 134, 144–146, 162–164
Abū ʿĀmir al-Yahūdī (*see also* Abū ʿĀmir al-Rāhib), 54, 88, 92
Abū ʿAmmār, 43, 44
Abū ʿAqīl, 68
Abū l-Baddāḥ b. ʿĀṣim b. ʿAdī, 109, 136, 138, 140
Abū Bakr, 6
Abū Bakr b. Muḥammad b. ʿAmr b. Ḥazm, 140
Abū al-Daḥdāḥ, 137
Abū al-Dhayyāl al-Yahūdī, 67
Abū Dujāna, 123
Abū Ḥabība b. al-Azʿar, 34, 101, 113, 120, 143
Abū l-Haytham b. al-Tayyihān, 60
Abū Ḥudhayfa b. ʿUtba b. Rabīʿa, 54
Abū Hurayra, 4
Abū Kabsha, 88
Abū Khaythama, 126

abū l-banāt, 105
Abū Lubāba, 55–57, 62, 117, 131, 137, 139, 141, 152
Abū Mālik 'Abdallāh b. Sām, 8
Abū Mulayl b. al-Az'ar, 113
Abū Mūsā al-Madīnī, 157
Abū Qays b. al-Aslat, 21, 24, 25, 33, 37, 38, 40, 44, 107, 137, 154–159, 161, 163, 164
Abū Qays b. Rifā'a, 42
Abū Ruhm b. 'Abd al-'Uzzā, 109
Abū Sabra b. Abī Ruhm, 109
Abū Sa'd b. Wahb, 48
Abū Sa'īd al-Khudrī, 79
Abū Salama al-Makhzūmī, 79
Abū Ṣayfī b. Abī 'Āmir al-Rāhib, 107
Abū Sufyān, 110, 145
Abū Sufyān b. al-Ḥārith, 104, 105
Abū 'Ubayd al-Qāsim b. Sallām, 157
Abū Umāma As'ad b. Sahl, 120, 124
Abū Wadī'a b. Khidhām, 105
al-'Adawī, compiler of *Nasab al-anṣār*, 26, 27
al-Aḍbaṭ b. Quray', 12
'Adhāra, B., 50
'Adhq, fortress, 69
'Adhq, well, 59, 68, 69
'Adī b. Ka'b, B., 10
al-adra', 114
agriculture, 1, 3, 60
Aḥjār al-Mirā', 104, 105
al-Ajashsh, fortress, 69, 70
al-'Ajlān, B., 59, 62, 103, 132, 135–137, 140, 144
'ajwa-dates, 3
'Alī b. Abī Ṭālib, 52, 123
Amalekites, 68
'Amīq bint al-Ḥārith, 107
'Āmir b. Abī 'Āmir al-Rāhib, 107
'Āmir b. Lu'ayy, B., 109
'Āmir b. Mujammi' b. al-'Aṭṭāf, 111
'Āmir b. al-Sakan, 141
'Ammār b. Yāsir, 91
'Amr b. 'Awf, B., 3, 4, 24, 28, 29, 34, 36, 37, 39, 41, 42, 48, 50, 51, 58, 74, 76, 78, 79, 83, 84, 88, 97, 101, 102, 104, 111, 117, 127, 128, 137, 152, 161
'Amr b. Bulayl b. Bilāl, 56
'Amr b. Jaḥḥāsh, 47, 48
'Amr b. al-Nu'mān al-Bayāḍī, 2
'Amr b. Qays, 94
'Amr b. Thābit b. Waqsh, 22
al-A'naq, fortress, 72, 134
Anas b. Qatāda, 117
apologetics, 22, 90, 92, 115, 117, 118, 128, 148, 150, 152, 154–157, 159–161, 163, 164
'Aqaba meeting, 29–31, 36, 60, 84, 135, 140
al-'Aqīq, 4, 6, 42, 58, 59, 96, 138
a'rāb, 109
al-'Arjī, 65
Arnab bint Asad b. 'Abd al-'Uzzā, 38
As'ad b. Zurāra, 20, 21, 79, 114, 120, 123, 124
al-'Aṣaba, 50, 55, 57–60, 62, 68, 71, 126, 127
'Āṣim b. 'Adī, 4, 92, 127, 131, 136–140, 142, 143
'Āṣim b. Thābit b. Abī l-Aqlaḥ, 53, 105, 112
'Āṣim, fortress in Qubā', 132, 133
'Āṣim, fortress in the Sāfila, 134
al-aslat, 108
Asmā' bint Abī Ṣayfī b. Abī 'Āmir b. Ṣayfī, 109
'Aṣmā' bint Marwān, 20, 38, 41, 52
'aṭā', 3
'Aṭā' b. Abī Rabāḥ, 76, 99
'Aṭiyya, B., 24, 33, 42–44
'Awālī, village, 1–3, 14, 18
'Awf b. al-Khazraj, B., 95, 124,

126, 127, 131
Aws Allāh, 16, 18–20, 23, 24, 30, 31, 84, 107, 120, 135, 137, 145, 148, 154, 159–162
Aws Manāt, *see* Aws Allāh
al-ʿAyn al-Zarqāʾ, 69
ʿAyr, 55
ʿAyyāsh b. Abī Rabīʿa, 59
al-ʿAyyāshī, 142
Ayyūb al-Sakhtiyānī, 78, 129
al-Azd, 103
ʿAzīz b. Mālik, B., 54, 105, 122
ʿAzza, fortress, 58

Badr, 4, 27, 36, 48, 52, 68, 81, 82, 84, 85, 120, 123, 135, 136, 138, 140, 144
Baḥraj, fortress, 105
Baḥzaj, 88, 101, 102, 105, 119, 121, 122
Bakr b. Wāʾil, B., 43, 106
Balī, 9, 45, 48, 50, 59, 62, 65, 66, 73, 82, 103, 132, 135, 136, 138
baqīʿ, 15
Baqīʿ al-Gharqad, 15
al-Bardaʿa, orchard, 72, 134
Bashīr b. al-Sāʾib, 55, 132
al-Bashshārī, 135
Baṣra, 78, 85, 106, 124
baṭn, 33, 46, 66, 67, 120
Bayāḍa, B., 2, 51
Baybars, 94
Bijād b. ʿUthmān, 101, 113
Bilāl b. Rabāḥ, 100
blood-wit, 55–57
Buʿāth, xiv, 2, 40, 114, 145, 161
Buʿbuʿ, fortress, 105
Buhl, Frants, 98, 125
Bukayr b. Jāriya, 112
Busse, Heribert, 54
Buṭḥān, 2, 9, 96
Buwayla, fortress, 15
Byzantines, 86, 145

Caskel, Werner, 86
Christians, 53, 64, 81, 163
clients, 46, 50, 52, 57, 59, 60, 62, 65, 68, 70–72, 101, 103, 108, 122, 124, 127, 132, 135, 137, 138, 144
clients of clients, 72
combined reports, 10, 24, 80, 85, 91, 95, 101, 157–159, 163
Companion status, 114
confederates, 46
Conrad, Lawrence, x
Cook, Michael, vii, 74
Creswell, K.A.C., 11

Ḍaʿ Dharʿ, fortress, 16
daʿwa, battle-cry, 30
al-Ḍaḥḥāk b. Khalīfa, 41, 144
al-Ḍaḥḥāk b. Muzāḥim, 82
al-Ḍaḥyān, fortress, 11, 56, 60, 61
dajjāl, 114
dakhala fī, 120
dār, 12, 16, 17, 23, 69, 99, 105, 106, 125, 126, 129, 130
David, 97
Dāwud al-Farrāʾ, 143
Dāwud b. al-Ḥuṣayn, 158, 159
Dharʿ, well, 16
dhawū ākāl, 43
Dhū Awān, 90–92
Dhū l-Jadr, 9
Dhū Qār, 143
ḍirār, 74, 83, 95, 98, 99
Dirham b. Zayd, 53
Ditch, Battle of, xvi, 19, 35, 36, 42–45, 49, 113, 154, 156
donkey, 80, 82–84, 93
Ḍubayʿa, B., 29, 34, 52–54, 101, 102, 104, 106, 112, 113, 120–122, 126, 127, 132, 136, 144
Dūmat al-Jandal, 86

al-fāḍiḥa, 116
Fāḍija, orchard, 14
family-*isnād*, 29, 48, 65, 114, 151
Fārs, 124
Fazāra, B., xv
fitan, 104

fortifications
in the ʿĀliya, 10, 14
of pre-Islamic Arabia, 11
fortress, *see uṭum*
Fück, Johann, 145, 162

Gabriel, Angel, 83, 90, 92, 105, 143
garlic, 3
Gaza, 17
Gehenna, 89–91
genealogies, xiv, 30, 32, 35, 42, 53, 60, 63, 65, 66, 102, 112, 113, 116, 120, 122, 126, 128, 136, 138, 156
Ghadaq, well, 69
Ghanm b. ʿAwf, B., 76–78, 102, 124, 126
al-Ghars, 16
Ghars, well, 16, 57, 59
Ghaṭafān, B., xvi, 43, 45
Ghishmīr b. Kharasha, 39
Ghurra, fortress, 57
Ghuṣayna, B., 59
Gil, Moshe, 43, 74, 84, 90–92, 94, 98, 102, 106, 111, 116, 117, 121, 122, 124–126, 130, 131, 133, 141, 159, 162
gold, 112
Goldziher, Ignaz, xiv

Ḥāʾ, well, 12
Ḥabīb b. ʿAmr, B., 58
Ḥabīb b. Ḥubāsha, 26, 27
Ḥabīb b. Zayd, 31
Ḥabība bint Abī ʿĀmir al-Rāhib, 107
Ḥabība bint Asʿad b. Zurāra, 120
al-Hajarī, 39
Ḥājib b. Zayd, 31
al-Ḥajjāj, 85, 129
al-Ḥakam b. Mīnā, 110
Ḥakīm b. ʿAbbād b. Ḥunayf, 119
ḥalīf, 25, 46, 50, 57, 60, 65, 68, 99, 103, 108, 132, 136, 138
ḥalqa wa-ḥuṣūn, of the Jews, 10
Ḥammād b. Zayd, 78
ḥammām, 105
Ḥamrāʾ al-Asad, 59
Ḥamza, 128
Ḥanadh, 60
Ḥanash, B., 34, 101, 119, 122, 124
ḥanīfiyya, 53, 88, 107, 145, 154, 156, 161–164
Ḥanẓala b. Abī ʿĀmir al-Rāhib, 88, 107, 110
Ḥarām, B., 72, 96
al-Ḥārith b. ʿAdī b. Kharasha, 27
al-Ḥārith b. ʿAwf, xvi
al-Ḥārith b. Ḥāṭib, 139
al-Ḥārith b. Hishām al-Makhzūmī, 118
al-Ḥārith b. Kaʿb, B., 12
al-Ḥārith b. al-Khazraj, B., 6, 79
Ḥāritha, B., 24, 36, 55, 114
Ḥarra, Battle of, 12, 111, 116, 119
ḥarra, lava-field, 8, 12, 59, 61, 62
Ḥarrat al-ʿAṣaba, 59
Ḥarrat B. Qurayẓa, 8
Ḥarrat Wāqim, 8
Hārūn al-Rashīd, 116
Hāshim b. ʿAbd Manāf, 56
Ḥassān b. Thābit, 38, 39, 41
Ḥāṭib, War of, xiv, 40
Hawāzin, B., 85
Hawdha b. Qays, 43–45
hijāʾ, 39
Hilāl b. Umayya, 128
Hind bint ʿUtba, 112
Hind bint Zayd b. Abī ʿĀmir al-Rāhib, 107
al-Ḥīra, 43
Hishām b. ʿAbd al-Malik, 47
Hishām b. ʿUrwa, 84
Ḥishna b. ʿUkārima, B., 63, 66
ḥiṣn, 11, 12, 29, 56, 104
Ḥubāb b. Zayd, 31
Hubal, idol, 88
al-Ḥublā, B., 42
al-Ḥudaybiyya, xi, xii, 108, 113
Ḥudayla, B., 11, 12
hudna, 108

al-Hujaym, fortress, 62
al-Hujaym, well, 62
Ḥumayḍa b. Ruqaym, 26
humour, 115, 142, 144
Ḥunayn, 85
Ḥusayn b. ʿAlī, 129
Ḥusayn b. al-Sā'ib b. Abī Lubāba, 132
Ḥuṣayn b. Wadaqa, 57
Ḥuyayy b. Akhṭab, 43

Ibn ʿAbbās, 76, 85, 86, 105, 107, 121
Ibn Abī Ḥabība, 158
Ibn al-Qaddāḥ, 156, 157, 159–161
Ibn ʿAsākir, ix
Ibn al-Ashʿath, 129
Ibn Bashkuwāl, 44
Ibn Jubayr, 135
Ibn Jurayj, 76, 81
Ibn al-Kalbī, ix
Ibn Lahīʿa, 30
Ibn al-Najjār, 98, 134
Ibn al-Qaddāḥ, 26, 27, 31, 33, 44
Ibn Shabba, x, xii
Ibn Shāhīn, 32
Ibn ʿUmar, 76, 79, 85, 86
Ibn Yāmīn, 48
Ibn Zabāla, xii, 6, 13, 51, 68, 132
Ibn Zayd, *see* ʿAbd al-Raḥmān b. Zayd al-ʿAdawī
Ibrāhīm b. Hishām, 46, 47
Ibrāhīm b. Yaḥyā b. Zayd b. Thābit, 114
idols, 41, 44, 52, 69, 88, 103
imām, 81, 88, 92, 93, 95, 111, 151–153
ʿiṣma, 77
istisqā', 93
ʿItbān b. Mālik, 95
ʿIyāḍ b. ʿAmr b. Bulayl, 56

al-Jaʿādir(a), 32–34, 46, 120, 125
Jābir b. ʿAbdallāh, 141
jabr, 105
Jaḥjabā, B., 52, 55, 58–60, 68, 70, 71, 103, 106, 107, 127, 136
Jamīla bint ʿAbdallāh b. Ubayy, 111, 128
Jamīla bint Abī ʿĀmir al-Rāhib, 29
Jāriya b. ʿĀmir, 88, 101, 111–113, 151
al-Jāsir, Ḥamad, xv, 70
al-Jathjātha, 59
Jaz' b. ʿAbbās, 103
Jerusalem, 79, 98, 143
Jews, xi, xii, 1, 2, 6, 9–11, 14, 16, 18–23, 25, 37–39, 41–46, 48, 50, 52–54, 57, 63, 64, 66–68, 71, 72, 84, 86, 88, 98, 104, 131–133, 135, 145, 158, 163
  Jewish faith and tribal leadership, 42, 44, 54, 88, 92
  Jewish proselytes, 38, 41–45, 48, 52, 54, 64, 66, 67, 88, 135
  synagogue, 41
Jifāf, 14
Judayy b. Murra b. Surāqa, 103
Judhām, B., 43
al-Julās b. Suwayd, 151
al-Jurf, 60

Kaʿb al-Aḥbār, 98
Kaʿb b. al-Ashraf, 48, 56
Kaʿb b. Mālik, 90, 118
Kaʿb b. ʿUjra, 66
al-Kaʿba, 53, 105, 143
Kabsha bint Asʿad b. Zurāra, 120
Kabsha/Kubaysha bint Maʿn b. ʿĀṣim 137
al-kāhinānī, 40
Kans Ḥuṣayn, fortress, 57
Khansā' bint Khidhām b. Khālid, 117
Khārija b. Zayd b. Thābit, 6, 79, 115
al-Khaṣī, fortress, 57, 58
al-Khaṣī, well, 58

Khaṭma, B., 4, 16, 21, 23–25, 29, 39, 41, 43, 44, 46, 47, 71, 111
Khawwāt b. Jubayr, 139
Khaybar, xi, xii, 43, 45, 140
Khayra bint Abī Umayya, 30
Khidhām b. Khālid, 88, 101, 105, 116, 117, 129, 130, 132, 143
Khubayb b. Yisāf, 6
Khuzā'a, B., 88
Khuzayma b. Thābit, 26, 27
al-Kibs, 67
Kināna b. Abī l-Ḥuqayq, 43, 45
Kinda, 8, 129
King, G.R.D., 11
kisar al-dhahab, 112
Kister, M.J., vii, xv, 10, 37, 63, 64, 79, 99, 114, 130, 135, 160
Kūfa, 78, 85, 89, 129, 150
Kulthūm b. al-Hidm, 93, 105
al-Kunāsa, 150

Lāwa, well, 69
Lawdhān, B., 114
leading families, 29, 38, 44, 111, 123, 126, 137
lists, in the *sīra*, 135, 137, 141, 151
Liyya, 80, 93
Lubnā bint 'Abdallāh b. Nabtal, 116

ma'mūra, a divinely-guided she-camel, 94
al-Mahdī, 51
Majda'a, B., 62
majlis, 68, 69
majlis al-mirā', 105
Majlis Banī l-Mawālī, 105
Majlis Ibn al-Mawlā, 105
Makhzūm, B., 47, 79, 118
māl Ibn Kharasha, 123
Mālik b. al-'Ajlān, 53, 127
Mālik b. al-Dukhshum, 127, 128, 140
Mālik b. al-Najjār, B., 4, 11, 94, 100
Ma'n b. 'Adī, 136, 140
Mandūs bint Ḥakīm, 119
manṣif, 90
Manwar, fortress, 15
al-Marāghī, Zayn al-Dīn, 133
al-Marāwiḥ, fortress, 105, 132
Ma'rib, 104
markets, of pre-Islamic Medina, 58
marriages, between Muslims and non-Muslims, 109
Mashrabat Umm Ibrāhīm, 8, 9
Masjid al-faḍīkh, 18
Masjid al-fatḥ, 72
Masjid al-tawba, 62
al-Maskaba, 57, 67
al-Maṭarī, Jamāl al-Dīn, 134
mawālī, 65
Maymūna bint 'Abdallāh, 46, 48
Mecca, 38, 43, 76, 81, 99, 105, 108, 112, 118, 145, 156
al-Mi'a, orchard, 69
mihrās, 16, 57
Mīnā, *mawlā* of Abū 'Āmir al-Rāhib, 110
minaret, 57
minbar, 110
mirbad, 72, 83, 93, 94
misāḥat al-arḍīna, 123
Moses, 99
mosque
    of the *jamā'a*, 100
    tribal, 98, 100
Motzki, Harald, 76
mu'ākhāt, 31, 36
Mu'attib b. Qushayr, 101, 102, 114
Mu'āwiya, 11, 12, 99
Mu'āwiya b. Isḥāq b. Zayd b. Jāriya, 150
Mu'āwiya, B., 24, 36, 51
al-Mughīra b. Ḥakīm al-Ṣan'ānī, 29
Muhājirūn, 3, 31, 36, 59, 62, 79, 86, 108, 109, 123
Muḥammad b. 'Abd al-Raḥmān al-'Ajlānī, 136

Muḥammad b. ʻAmr b. Ḥazm, 111
Muḥammad b. Ismāʻīl b. Mujammiʻ, 114
Muḥammad b. Kaʻb al-Quraẓī, 159
Mujāhid, 105
Mujammiʻ b. Jāriya, 88, 89, 92, 93, 101, 111, 121, 129, 150–152
Mujammiʻ b. Yaʻqūb b. Jāriya, 114
Mujammiʻ b. Yaʻqūb b. Mujammiʻ b. Yazīd b. Jāriya, 151
Mujammiʻ b. Yaḥyā b. Yazīd b. Jāriya, 111
Mujammiʻ b. Yazīd b. Jāriya, 114
Mukhallad b. al-Ṣāmit al-Sāʻidī, xiv
al-mukhallafūna, 90
Mulayka bint ʻAbdallāh b. Ubayy, 128
munāfiqūn, 37, 70, 77, 81, 86, 87, 89, 90, 94, 95, 97, 107, 111, 114–116, 118, 119, 122–124, 127, 128, 130, 134, 137, 141–145, 151
al-Mundhir b. Muḥammad b. ʻUqba, 56
Muqātil b. Ḥayyān, 108, 109
Muqātil b. Sulaymān, ix, xv, 54, 87, 91, 96, 102, 108, 131
Murayd, B. , *see* Murīd, B.
al-Muʻriḍ, fortress, 15
Murīd, B., 45, 46
Murra b. al-Ḥārith b. ʻAdī, 103
Murra b. al-Ḥubāb b. ʻAdī, 103
Murra b. Mālik b. al-Aws, B., 24, 25
Mūsā b. ʻUbayda al-Rabadhī, 159
Mūsā b. Jaʻfar, 77, 81, 86, 95
Mūsā b. ʻUqba, 30, 43, 106
Muṣʻab b. ʻUmayr, 19–21
Musaylima, 128, 140
Muslim b. Saʻīd b. al-Mawlā, 72
al-Mustaẓill, fortress, 57, 61
Muʼta, 86
al-Muʻtariḍ b. al-Ashwas, 72, 133
al-Muṭʻim b. ʻAdī, 91
muwādaʻa, 108
Muzayna, B., 117, 137

al-Nabīt, B., 3, 20, 24, 36, 37, 39, 41, 103, 160
Nabtal b. al-Ḥārith, 88, 101, 102, 114
Nabtal b. Qays, 114
Naḍīr, 2, 4, 8–10, 14–16, 25, 35, 37, 40, 41, 43–45, 47–50, 119, 123, 131, 133
Nāghiṣa, B., 72
Nāʻimat Ibrāhīm b. Hishām, 46, 47
al-Najjār, B., 70, 79, 80, 111, 118, 120, 126, 127
Najrān, 12
al-Naqīʻ, 138
naqīb, 29, 60, 84, 120, 123
al-Nawāʻim, 47
al-Nawwāḥāni, fortresses, 69
nikāḥ al-maqt, 137, 159
Nöldeke, Theodor, xv
al-Nuwayʻima, orchard, 47

Paradise, 22, 99
Paret, Rudi, 19, 148, 150
Philby, J.B., 1, 97
polemics, 59, 63, 79, 80, 163

al-Qāʻ, fortress, 69, 70
qadar, 105
qāḍī, 151
al-Qādisiyya, 152
al-Qāʼim, orchard, 68, 69
qaraẓ, 115
Qardam b. ʻAmr, 52
qarrāẓ, 115
qaṣaba, 17
qaṣr, 12, 47, 104
Qaṣr Banī Ḥudayla, 11
Qaṣr Ibn Māh, 62
Qaṣr Khall, 12
Qatāda, 97
Qawāqil(a), 125–127
Qaynuqāʻ, 6, 8–10, 42, 43, 119
Qays ʻAylān, B., 48
Qays b. al-Khaṭīm, 156

Qays b. Qahd, 118
Qays b. Rifā'a, 37, 41
Qayṣar, 85
qibla, 143
Qinnasrīn, 88
Qubā', 37, 39, 42, 50, 54, 56, 57, 59, 68, 71, 74, 85, 90, 95, 97, 100, 103, 104, 126, 127, 131, 139, 145
Qubā', well, 133
Qubār, well, 133
Quḍā'a, 50, 132, 135
al-Quff, village of Qaynuqā', 9
al-Qummī, 127
Quraysh, xi, 38, 43, 47, 52, 88, 98, 105, 143, 156, 160, 162
Qurayẓa, xiv, 2, 4, 8, 10, 14, 15, 25, 35–37, 40–42, 49, 54, 104, 117
Qurbān, 1–3, 14, 16
al-Quṣayṣ, B., 71

al-Raba'a, B., 66
al-Rabī' b. al-Rabī' b. Abī l-Ḥuqayq, 44
raḥba, 104
Raḥbat B. Zayd, 104, 106, 134
Rānūnā, 59, 62
Rātij, 32, 34, 35
Raydān, fortress, 17
al-Ribāṭ, well, 69
Rib'ī b. Abī Rib'ī, 103
Rib'ī b. Rāfi', *see* Rib'ī b. Abī Rib'ī
ridda, 31
Rifā'a b. 'Abd al-Mundhir, 29
Rifā'a b. Zanbar, 55–57
Rubin, Uri, vii, xv, 19, 38, 43, 53, 110, 154, 156, 160, 162
al-Ruwā' bint 'Umayr, 48

Saba', 104
sabab nuzūl, 76, 84, 85, 92, 116
Sa'd b. Ḥunayf, 119
Sa'd b. Khawla, 108
Sa'd b. Khaythama, 21, 29, 31, 80–84
Sa'd b. Mu'ādh, 21, 54, 86
Sa'd b. 'Ubayd al-Qāri', 152
Sa'd b. Zurāra, 107
ṣadaqa, charitable endowment, 9
sādin, 103
al-Ṣafāṣif, 58, 62
Ṣafna/Ṣafīna, 42
ṣāḥib al-ṣā', 70
Sahl b. Ḥunayf, 34, 119, 120, 123, 124
Sahl b. Rāfi', 70
Sahl b. Sa'd, 78
Sahla bint 'Āṣim b. 'Adī, 140
al-Sā'ib b. Abī Lubāba, 117, 132
Sa'īd b. Jubayr, 63, 76, 77, 84, 95, 124, 129, 141, 144
Sa'īd b. Murra, B., 31, 34, 36
Sa'īd b. al-Musayyab, 79, 107
Sā'ida, B., 78
al-Sa'īda, idol, 103
Salama b. Salāma b. Waqsh, 22
Salama b. Thābit b. Waqsh, 22
Salama b. Umayya, 72, 134
Sālim b. 'Awf, B., 124, 126
Sālim, *mawlā* Thubayta bint Ya'ār, 136
Salima, B., 35, 72, 96, 114
Sallām b. Abī l-Ḥuqayq, 43, 44
al-Salm, B., 25, 28, 36, 40, 50, 58, 83, 84, 91, 125, 126
Salmā bint 'Āmir, 107
al-Sam'ānī, 15
al-Samhūdī, xii, xv, 127, 133, 134, 147
al-Samna, orchard, 72, 134
Ṣan'ā', 12
al-Sarī b. 'Abd al-Raḥmān, 65
Sarif, 53
al-Sawād, 123
al-Ṣayāṣī, fortresses, 103, 134
Ṣayfī b. Abī 'Āmir al-Rāhib, 107–109
sayl, 95, 97
Sellheim, Rudolf, 135
Serjeant, R.B., 13, 125
al-Sha'bī, 150
Shaghb wa-Badā, 66

al-Shamūs bint Abī ʿĀmir al-Rāhib, 107
al-Shamūs bint al-Nuʿmān b. ʿĀmir b. Mujammiʿ, 143
Shaqīq b. Salama al-Asadī, 99
sharaf, 112
Shās b. Qays, 42
al-Shaykhāni, fortresses, 69
Shiʿb B. Ḥarām, 72
Shuʿbat ʿĀṣim, 138
Shumayla, well, 62
al-Shunayf, fortress, 102, 104
Shuraḥbīl b. Saʿd, 26
sidr (lote), tree, 142
Ṣiffīn, Battle of, 27
silent majority, 36, 71
Sirius, 88
al-Ṣīṣa, fortress, 104, 134
Stewart, Frank, vii
Suʿayda bint Bashīr/Bushayr, 108
Suʿayda bint Rifāʿa, 108
Subayʿa bint al-Ḥārith al-Aslamiyya, 108, 109
Ṣufiyy al-Sibāb, 105
Sulāfa bint Saʿd b. Shuhayd, 112, 113
Sulaym, B., xvi, 60
Sulaymān b. ʿAbd al-Malik, 12
Sumayr b. Zayd b. Mālik, 53
Sumayr, War of, 25, 53
al-Sunḥ, 6
Suwayd b. ʿAyyāsh, 141
Suwayd b. al-Ṣāmit, 58, 161

Tabūk, 74, 81, 86, 90, 91, 94, 110, 118, 126, 140, 142, 143
Ṭalḥa b. al-Barāʾ, 69, 70
Ṭalq b. ʿAmr b. Hammām, 129
Tawba b. al-Ḥusayn, 132, 133
Taymāʾ, 66
territorial basis, of the Prophet, 35, 146
Thaʿlaba b. ʿAmr b. ʿAwf, B., 111
Thaʿlaba b. Ghanm b. Mālik b. al-Najjār, B., 94
Thaʿlaba b. Ḥāṭib, 101, 142
Thābit b. Abī l-Aqlaḥ, 105, 132
Thābit b. Aqram, 141
Thābit b. al-Daḥdāḥ, 109, 123
Thābit b. Wadīʿa, 113, 129
Thubayta bint Yaʿār, 136
ṭīra, 133
Tubbaʿ, 61, 102
Turbat Ṣuʿayb, 6

ʿUbayd b. Zayd, B., 52, 54, 101, 102, 105, 113, 117, 129, 136
ʿUbaydallāh b. ʿAbbās, 98
ʿUbaydallāh b. al-Mughīra b. Muʿayqīb, 20
ʿUbaydallāh b. Mujammiʿ b. Jāriya, 116
Ubayy b. Kaʿb, 79
ʿUdayna, 62
Udovitch, Avrom, 74
Uḥayḥa b. al-Julāḥ, 56, 60, 102, 127
Uḥud, xiv, 26, 27, 32, 36, 82, 103, 105, 110–112, 117, 128, 136, 145
al-Ukaydir, 86
Umāma al-Murīdiyya, 48
Umāma bint Bijād b. ʿUthmān, 113
ʿUmar b. ʿAbd al-ʿAzīz, 85, 151
ʿUmar b. ʿAmr b. ʿUthmān b. ʿAffān, 65
ʿUmar b. al-Khaṭṭāb, 3, 29, 59, 72, 76, 89, 98, 99, 123, 150, 152, 153
Umayma bint Bishr, 123
ʿUmayr b. ʿAdī b. Kharasha, 26, 39
ʿUmayr b. Saʿd b. Shuhayd, 112
Umayya b. Zayd, B., 4, 20, 21, 23–25, 33, 34, 38, 39, 46, 47, 120
Umayya b. Zayd, B., of the ʿAmr b. ʿAwf, 29, 38, 46, 55, 57, 64, 101, 102, 106, 108, 112, 113, 117, 123, 130, 132, 136
Umm Ibrāhīm, Māriya, 8, 9

Umm Salama bint al-Nu'mān b. Abī Ḥabība, 114
Unayf, B., 59, 68, 72, 137
Unays b. Qatāda, 117
'Uqba b. Abī Qays b. al-Aslat, 157
'Urwa b. al-Zubayr, 30, 76, 80, 82–84, 95, 124
al-uṣayrim, 22
'Utba b. 'Uwaym b. Sā'ida, 152
'Uthmān b. 'Affān, 6, 12, 13, 116, 124
'Uthmān b. Ḥunayf, 119, 123
'uthmānī, 78
uṭum, 10, 12–14, 46, 51, 56, 57, 60, 61, 70, 102–104
uṭum al-Qawāqil, 126
'Uwaym b. Sā'ida, 57, 63, 64, 67
'Uwaymir b. Sā'ida, *see* 'Uwaym b. Sā'ida
'Uyayna b. Ḥiṣn, xv
al-'Uyūn, 3
al-'Uzzā, idol, 53

Wadī'a b. Khidhām, 101, 113, 116, 121, 131
Wadī'a b. Thābit, 88, 101, 130, 131, 143
Waḥshī, 91, 128, 141
Waḥwaḥ b. 'Āmir, 44
Waḥwaḥ b. al-Aslat, 33, 44, 156
Wā'il, B., 4, 21, 23–25, 33, 34, 39, 43, 44, 120, 159
al-Walīd b. 'Abd al-Malik, 59
al-Walīd b. 'Utba b. Rabī'a, 54
al-Wālij, 69
al-Wāqidī, 141
Wāqif, B., 4, 17, 21, 23–25, 28, 37, 39, 41, 107, 126, 128
Wāqim, fortress, 56–58, 61, 67, 132
Wāsiṭ, 85
Watt, W.M., xii, 18–20, 36, 38, 71, 86, 117, 118, 126, 127, 139, 148, 154
weapons, 10, 11, 103
Wellhausen, Julius, xiv, xv, 4, 12, 14, 19, 28, 29, 39, 42, 51, 61, 67, 130, 145, 162

Yaḥyā b. Mujammi' b. Jāriya, 116
Yamāma, Battle of, 31, 32, 128, 140
Yāmīn b. 'Umayr, 47, 48
Yathrib, 1
Yazīd b. 'Abd al-Malik, 99
Yazīd b. Jāriya, 101, 111, 151
Yazīd b. Zayd b. Ḥiṣn al-Khaṭmī, 39
Yūsha' al-Yahūdī, 23

Za'bal, 67
al-Zabīr b. Bāṭā al-Quraẓī, xiv
Ẓafar, B., 20, 24, 36, 103
Za'ūrā', B., 21, 23
Zayd b. 'Alī, 150
Zayd b. 'Amr b. Nufayl, 163, 164
Zayd b. Ḥāritha, 4
Zayd b. Jāriya, 88, 101, 111, 142, 150, 151
Zayd b. al-Khaṭṭāb, 29
Zayd b. Mālik, B., 101–103, 112, 113, 117, 129, 134–137, 144
Zayd b. Thābit, 3, 4, 114
zuhd, 145
al-Zuhrī, 4, 30, 66
Zuqāq al-Ḥārith, 47
Zurayq, B., 2, 9, 50, 57, 126

Corrigenda to the 1995 Edition[1]

p. 13 note 44: read: *wa-ʾbtanawu l-āṭāma.*

p. 23 note 11: read: rabīʿn l-awwali.

p. 123 line 3 from bottom: read: *al-araḍīna.*

p. 127 note 179: *wa-kāna Mālik b. al-ʿAjlān sayyidu l-Khazraj huwa ʾbn khālat Uḥayḥa b. al-Julāḥ*; Ibn Saʿd, *al-Ṭabaqāt al-kubrā*, III, 549.

p. 142 note, line 6: read: his clothes.

[1] I do not have access to the corrigenda on the margin of my own copy. I am grateful to Ms. Yaara Perlman for sharing her corrigenda with me.

www.ingramcontent.com/pod-product-compliance
Lightning Source LLC
Chambersburg PA
CBHW061447300426
44114CB00014B/1871
9781463206642